The Road Well Kept

Published by ECW PRESS
2120 Queen Street East, Suite 200, Toronto, Ontario, Canada M4E 1E2

NATIONAL LIBRARY OF CANADA CATALOGUING IN PUBLICATION DATA

Robertson, Heather, 1942–
The road well kept: Branksome Hall celebrates 100 years / Heather Robertson

ISBN 1-55022-544-8

1. Branksome Hall — History. I. Title.

LE4.T67R62 2002 371'.009713'541 C2002-902162-6

Cover photography: Michael Cooper Photographic
Typesetting: Wiesia Kolasinska, Gail Nina
Production: Mary Bowness
Printing: University of Toronto Press
All photos courtesy of Branksome Hall

This book is set in Garamond

The publication of *The Road Well Kept* has been generously supported by the Canada Council, the Ontario Arts Council, and the Government of Canada through the Book Publishing Industry Development Program. Canadä

DISTRIBUTION

CANADA: Stewart House, 195 Allstate Pkwy., Markham, ON L3R 4T8

PRINTED AND BOUND IN CANADA

ECW PRESS
ecwpress.com

The Road Well Kept

Branksome Hall Celebrates 100 Years

HEATHER ROBERTSON

Acknowledgements

As chair of Branksome Hall's centennial Book Committee, my heartfelt thanks go to so many who brought *The Road Well Kept* to life.

To our author, Heather Robertson, who agreed to take on the commission of writing this book to commemorate 100 years of Branksome Hall. We are delighted with the outcome and she deserves high accolades for working with so many "bosses," the fifteen members of the Centennial Book Committee.

To the committee members who spent hours and hours in fact-checking, proofing, selecting photographs, marketing and much more -- Auguste Bolté, Pat Strathy Davidson, Elizabeth Beattie Greenshields, Susan Kenny, Joyce Frankel Kofman, Nancy Adams MacDonnell, Linda McQuaig, Karen Murton, Kathryn Porteous, Medora Sale, Tom Stevens, Bill Stevenson, Monika Stevenson and Carol Wilton.

To Rachel Phillips Belash, Branksome's sixth principal, who put the process in motion.

To the volunteers in the Branksome Archives, especially Joy Waldie, Cindy Bundy Snell and Penny Lowndes Elliott who have been so helpful in unearthing information and photos for this book.

To all members of the Branksome community who sent in photos and stories, and who were interviewed by the author.

To Michael Cooper who was so patient and professional in shooting our cover photography.

To Rick McGrath for sharing his wealth of marketing expertise.

To Branksome administrators Karrie Weinstock, Nanci Smith and Ruth Ann Penny for their valuable input.

To Branksome's Director of Academic Studies, Rosemary Evans, and the Branksome history teachers who have embraced *The Road Well Kept* and have included it in the history curriculum.

To Michael Murton for his advice and support.

And, of course, to editor Tracey Millen and Jack David of ECW Press, our publisher. ECW has made our dream a reality.

Serving as Chair of this committee has been a great learning experience and an absolute pleasure. I hope you will have as much fun reading *The Road Well Kept*, as we have had in bringing it to you.

Joyce Walker McKeough
Chair, Branksome Hall Centennial Book Committee

Foreword

What a wonderful adventure! What an extraordinary way to pursue, down through the past century, the great social strides that make a new generation's hopes and relationships more open! The Branksome Hall story is far more exciting than I imagined it could be. Through my own daughters, I have caught glimpses of many schools in many countries — in Hong Kong, in India, in Kenya, Tanzania and Scotland, in Malaysia and Thailand — yet in an odd way I have also grown up with Branksome. There was a strange time when one of my daughters would attend Branksome and then, during vacations, go to school in Bangkok, where the scholastic season differs. It says a great deal about Branksome's flexibility that this curious arrangement was not only tolerated but also led to one of her Thai friends coming to the school, with more Thai girls to follow. I mention these things only because I want you to know that my enthusiasm for Heather Robertson's book is based on a certain amount of experience. The girls in her story have education on their side.

When it all began, nobody would have dared to say out loud that the goal was to empower femininity. The Victorian era had just ended. A few ladies, led by a certain Miss Scott, started their bold venture with obligatory obeisances to the male concept of fiscal responsibility and a general argument that a school for girls would wonderfully concentrate their minds and provide some relief from dreaming about boys. Not too much was said openly about saving the girls from being intimidated by the supposition of those days that males are much better at just about everything, but you will see from this story that the aim was always to challenge orthodoxy.

The founders of Branksome might be discreetly astonished by the advanced technology found in the classrooms today. Otherwise, I suspect they would be delighted to find that the school has prospered in good times and bad by sticking to its faith in the courage and good sense of girls who have never been exclusively the products of privilege or the beneficiaries of good fortune, other than the luck of being part of a living organism adapting to change in the middle of a major commercial community. The City of Toronto has crept up on Branksome, but the school has defended its unique forestland in much the same way that its principals have found ways to adjust to or even oppose any political or opportunistic encroachment that might destroy its special place on the map and in history.

By the summer of 2001, it did not seem unusual that Principal Karen Murton was at a global conference in Africa talking about the different ways in which girls and boys exercise leadership. Nor was it surprising that Branksome girls were helping Father Joe Maier in Thailand to deal with social problems that challenge basic freedoms. (The girls were working at the HDF mission for street youth and the Mercy Centre, an AIDS Hospice for children and adults.) These events were part of the school's evolution.

If you run together some of the images evoked by Heather Robertson, the school's history becomes theatre, a real-life drama reflecting the changes that have taken place since the start of the twentieth century.

Francean Campbell-Rich's parents were wealthy socialites when Francean was enrolled at the age of nine. The Great Depression hit her family hard. By 1930, her father had been arrested, tried and convicted of conspiracy to manipulate the stock market. Francean, through nobody's fault, felt she was an outcast and was bounced from one school to another. A compassionate principal heard of her plight and ushered her back to Branksome. "Every opportunity was there for me," Francean said later. "I felt no stigma."

The Battle of Britain raged over Sherborne in Dorset during the glorious summer of 1940. A German invasion seemed imminent. Twenty-seven girls were despatched to Canada and safety. Branksome found local families to take them in. More girls arrived. After much feverish activity, Sherborne heard that sixty more still had no place to go; nor did the exiles have a dime between them. Britain had run out of convertible currency and, with a terrifyingly small U.S. $12 million in reserve, was forced to suspend dollar purchases. The principal swiftly sent a decorous but reassuring telegram to Sherborne: "The cost of maintaining this establishment is being met by the directors and friends of the school and alumnae."

A visit by Princess Alice is a marvellous example of how far ahead of the times Branksome always managed to be. Newspapers ran photographs of her surrounded by Branksome prefects. What was more important, though, was expressed in a girl's letter: "Then a man came to lecture to us about the Jews. He helps get Jews out of countries where they are being persecuted." This was in a period when a Canadian government official, speaking of Jewish immigrants, said publicly "None is too many." Branksome was already telling its girls about Hitler's Final Solution.

Paul Robeson gave a concert when bigots regarded him as not only black but also subversive. The girls were bowled over by the magnificent voice of what we would now call an African American, although he never had any illusions about the names by which blacks were known in those days. A young African Canadian contralto from Nova Scotia, Portia White, was taken under Branksome's wing. Edith Read advertised the recital as a charitable benefit for war work. As Heather Robertson comments, "Who could refuse? Edith called her dressmaker, booked the chic Eaton auditorium and mobilized alumnae to sell tickets for Portia's Toronto debut." Portia was launched on tours throughout North America, and the *New York Times* reviewed her as "one of the finest contralto voices . . . since Marian Anderson."

There were small dramas going on all the time. The Branksome ladies seem to have regarded fighting city hall as a blood sport. Here we read about Miss Read looking like a fierce elf in her crimson doctor of laws gown, stopping traffic on Mount Pleasant Road after it had been bulldozed right through the school property. The city had failed to put up stop signs for the girls to safely cross the road. Miss Read said "Stop!" to the impatient motorists, and city hall had to surrender.

If the girls thought Branksome had done something silly, they said so, as when they were asked by Principal Allison Roach not to drink pop in uniform off school property. "With an attitude like this," wrote Swith Bell in the *Kilt Press,*

> the uniform begins to look like a sexist symbol of the Victorian era. It is hardly feminist of us to pretend that women do not *eat* or *drink.* This is the first step to making impressionable young girls ashamed of their bodies. Miss Roach uses pop as a sinful item — but what about *juice boxes?* What about *Evian water?* Let's go one step further. . . . Have we the right to pick our noses in uniform off school property?

Allison Roach had only wanted to stop the girls from littering neighbourhood lawns with pop cans. In the next issue of *Kilt Press,* Swith Bell denounced the Lord's Prayer, recited daily, "as an anti-feminist mantra." Miss Roach never lifted so much as an eyebrow. She had been a Branksome girl, and old schoolmates, like Joyce Frankel Kofman, thought she was made of the right stuff for the role of principal. Allison Roach had not sought it, but she had many years of experience in the public school system and was worldly-wise. She awarded Swith the Principal's Prize at her graduation.

Rachel Belash took over in 1993 and voiced those thoughts that once required a discreet silence from the school's tough-minded founders. Rachel had retired as head of Miss Porter's School in Connecticut. She had taught at Vassar, and she spoke with the authority of someone known far and wide for her scholarly writings. At Branksome, she said,

> Before they enrol in a single-sex school, girls seem unsure that anything worth calling 'fun' can take place without the opposite sex. Once acclimatized, they become aware of new possibilities, of a freedom to deal with their own changing self-image, to explore who they are and who they are becoming. . . . The case for girls' schools rests on the importance for young women of a place of their own.

There's a magical world to be found here. Yet all of it is true and vastly encouraging. At the start of the past century, there was plenty of doom and gloom, more than enough to discourage those brave souls who gambled on a brighter future. Now, after a succession of innovative ladies who battled against economic stress and survived intervals when girls' schools were frowned upon, we arrive at the beginning of a new century to discover yet another generation of pupils whose world also seems awry and filled with menace. The girls of 1903 were as staunch and true as those who today take racial and religious differences in stride, who can laugh at the silliness of the tired old world of adults, whose confidence and excitement and sense of mischief remind us that the young are infinitely capable of dealing with whatever lies ahead.

Karen Murton in Africa told her audience that none of the gender barriers are present in a girls-only school: the students learn that "women can aspire to distinguished leadership positions." That would have been a revolutionary message to speak out loud in the Dark Continent a hundred years ago. Yet it is consistent with the impulse to establish Branksome Hall among ladies brought up in a Victorian age who knew that girls should be free to discover their full potential without the distraction of competitive and condescending males. Growing up with a glinting set of moral and romantic ideals, the girls today benefit from the progressive growth of a school that has become a sanctuary. It emerges from this book like a fairy tale, with ornate gates and secret gardens, offering lessons like spires pointing skyward, promising answers.

— William Stevenson,
author of the bestselling book
A Man Called Intrepid and
father of two Branksome girls

Introduction

SCHOOLS ARE MYSTERIOUS PLACES. We spend most of our childhood and adolescence in schools, like it or not, and, although we form opinions about teachers and the subjects we study, we take going to school for granted. Once we have left, we lose interest in schools unless we have children there or choose to become active in an independent school's alumnae association. Schools are also secretive, and the media ignore them unless students are shot or assaulted. Our personal experience in school becomes instantly obsolete, yet, as adults, we are given almost no information about what children are learning, and how they are learning it, unless those children are our own. What makes a good school? How do we tell? Public schools are accountable to the taxpayers, but they leave it to professional educators to mould their children into productive citizens.

Families looking for more than the public schools offer turn to independent, or private, schools. The independent school is shrouded in mythology, most of it derived from scary or scandalous stories about English boarding schools, including Charlotte Brontë's classic novel *Jane Eyre*. The popular stereotype is that rich, spoiled snobs go to independent schools, and if an independent school is sheltered by trees and surrounded by acres of playing fields, it looks exclusive.

This is not Branksome Hall. A major traffic artery, Mount Pleasant Road, runs right through its thirteen-acre campus, and the campus is a few blocks around the corner from Toronto's famous intersection, Yonge and Bloor. A downtown, "subway school," Branksome Hall may be the most visible independent school in Canada, and its buildings, many of them Victorian mansions, look lived in. Branksome's openness to the world reflects its educational philosophy.

Like other girls' schools, Branksome has had to put up with the "rich bitch" stereotype, but it is really an upper-middle-class school, not that different in student population from public schools in affluent neighbourhoods. Many parents scrimp and save, or take extra jobs, to pay the fees — fees and expenses for day girls total about $18,000 a year — and a growing number of girls are assisted by scholarships and bursaries.

Branksome Hall *is* different because it is a girls' school. After thirty years of controversy, during which many Canadian independent boys' schools became co-educational, recent research in the United States and Great Britain has revealed that alumnae of girls' schools overwhelmingly believe that they received an excellent education, including leadership opportunities, preparation for university and the skills to achieve success in their chosen careers. British graduates even thought that attending a girls' school was an advantage in preparing them for their relationships with men. In Canada, polls conducted early in 2001 showed that a majority of parents supported a controversial decision by the Ontario government to give an income tax credit to parents who enrolled their children in independent schools. The most convincing evidence of success, perhaps, has been the growth and prosperity of Toronto's four venerable, and once highly competitive, girls' schools: Bishop Strachan School, Havergal College, St. Clement's School and Branksome Hall.

Many factors play a part in any school's achievements: family income and expectations, language skills, class size, discipline, quality of teaching and motivation. At a single-sex school, however, girls learn to play roles, whether in class projects, sports, politics or drama productions, that might otherwise go to boys. At a public high school, boys play football, girls watch. At Branksome, girls play hockey, field hockey and rugby, as well as other sports, against other teams of girls. Girls still watch —

somebody has to be a fan — but they are watching other girls compete. And they are not being watched by boys.

"In class, a girl will have no qualms about making a fool of herself," says mathematics teacher Tom Stevens. Stevens, who has taught at co-ed schools, notices a difference. "The girls at Branksome are freer, more energetic, less inhibited. They'll dance around, goof around. They may look like complete idiots, but they don't care." Stevens cautions, however, that girls can dominate a class as easily as boys.

Girls can also be kind and cruel, lonely as well as loved, conformist and rebellious, popular and unpopular. While Branksome, unlike some Toronto public schools, is free of weapons and sexual predators, it shares their ongoing concerns about drugs, drinking, cigarettes and the social tensions common to any community. At a girls' school, however, issues of body image, eating disorders and sexuality can be addressed more forthrightly than they might be in a co-ed school, and the girls are not taunted by boys in the schoolyard.

A school is a village where children outnumber adults about ten to one, and an independent school has to be a self-sufficient village. Independent schools receive no government money, nor do they want it. Every cent they spend they raise from fees, bequests or donations, and their annual budgets run into the millions.

The Branksome village numbers, altogether, about one thousand girls, women and men, with an international diaspora of 4,500 active alumnae and a changing circumference of parents, grandparents, spouses and financial supporters. In an age of big-box public schools, Branksome's close-knit community, especially its small classes, is a virtue. It is a secular school committed to ethical behaviour and academic excellence. Girls go to Branksome because they want to be well prepared for university and a successful career in a competitive world. Although it is an independent school, Branksome follows, and tries to surpass, the curriculum required by the Ontario Department of Education, and it is accountable to the department's inspectors.

Other independent schools do this too, and every school offers something unique and intangible, an identity, a personality, a culture that evolves over time. Identity is created by architecture, colour, cleanliness, smell, light and landscape, but personality is determined by the people who give the school life. A school's culture is never static. Attempts to nail it down, or cast it in concrete, could be fatal, yet everybody knows that it's *there.* Susan Duncanson Pigott, a 1968 Branksome graduate and former board member, sums up Branksome Hall this way: "There is a strong Presbyterian streak in the psyche of the school, puritanical but not prissy. It was a *virtue* not to spend money, show off, be wasteful. The attitude was 'We can *make do* with what we've got.' How often people talked about 'modesty'! It was unseemly to publicize your virtues."

Branksome Hall, unlike its early Methodist, Church of England and Roman Catholic rivals, has never been affiliated with a church. Its puritanical streak, critical, confident, giving no ground, comes from its first principal, Margaret Taylor Scott, an Ontario Presbyterian for whom founding her own school was truly an act of independence.

Chapter One

The girls crowding into the big brick house at 102 Bloor Street East are abuzz with anticipation. Monday, September 7, 1903, is their first day of school, and their nervous whispers have an edge of curiosity. Are the teachers strict? *Must* we do needlework? Will I have to memorize the *whole* Bible?

As the girls assemble in the conservatory for prayers, all eyes are fixed on the poker-straight, white-haired figure of Principal Margaret Taylor Scott. Standing, Bible in hand, with her back to the windows, Miss Scott smiles, but her forehead is puckered in an anxious frown. This is her first day too, the official opening of her new school, Branksome Hall: A Residential and Day School for Girls, and although the word *gamble* is not part of her Presbyterian vocabulary, she is risking both her family's investment and her own professional reputation.

Private girls' schools are a dime a dozen in Toronto. Anyone can start a school, and most of them last, at best, a few years. How will Branksome Hall be able to compete with the big, established girls' schools, Bishop Strachan and Havergal Ladies' College, which has just moved into a handsome building on Jarvis Street, or for that matter with St. Clement's, St. Monica's, St. Margaret's, Glen Mawr, Miss Meneilley's, Miss Williams' and the Toronto Presbyterian Ladies' College, where Miss Scott had recently spent a year as principal? And will Branksome Hall be able to offer as high a standard of education as Toronto's public high schools?

The public high schools, run as private fiefdoms by autocratic male principals, varied in quality according to their principals' tastes and temperaments, and like Branksome Hall, they charged fees. The nearest, Jarvis Collegiate, a ramshackle firetrap of a school a few blocks south of Bloor Street, was, like most of Toronto's public schools, dirty, antiquated and overcrowded. It was to rescue refined young women from such squalid surroundings that Miss Scott and her business partner, Florence Merrick, had founded their own school.

Branksome Hall, however, lacks the financial backing of a church foundation. The Church of England endows Bishop Strachan, Havergal and St. Clement's; Loretto Abbey and St. Joseph College are run by the Roman Catholic church; and the Methodists support the Hamilton Ladies' College and the Ontario Ladies' College to the east in Whitby. One of the first girls' schools in Ontario was the Wesleyan Methodist Female College in Margaret Scott's home town of Dundas.

As a member of the Free Kirk, young Margaret would never have been allowed to darken the door of the Wesleyan Female College — she attended public schools — but she would almost certainly have met the school's head, Mary Electa Adams. Miss Adams had studied classics and advanced mathematics at ladies' academies in Ontario and the United States, and she had taught at several girls' preparatory schools, including schools she and her sister Augusta ran themselves. The Female College's curriculum reflected the Adams sisters' accomplishments and ambitions for their students: mathematics, logic, rhetoric, classical languages, modern languages, philosophy, music and fine arts. Branksome Hall would not be this highbrow, but the Adams sisters' example may have persuaded Margaret she could provide for girls an intellectually challenging education in a Christian context.

The Scotts were Scots immigrants from the Lowland County of Roxburgh. Margaret's father, James, a carpenter and contractor, had built several handsome buildings in Dundas, including the Town Hall, yet while the family had become settled and prosperous, Margaret was encouraged to make her own way in the world. Presbyterians, believing that the devil makes work for idle hands, wanted their daughters to make themselves useful in the community, and as Margaret was growing up, teaching had become a Christian calling suitable for young unmarried women.

Egerton Ryerson, appointed Director of Education for Canada West in 1844, four years before Margaret's birth, had slowly established a system of universal public education at the elementary school level. Public education broke the stranglehold of the Anglican and Catholic churches, yet Ryerson's own religious belief, evangelical Methodism, put a strong Protestant stamp on public education in Canada West.

Schools sprang up in cities and villages and at rural crossroads, and every school needed at least one teacher. Teachers, until then, had typically been schoolmasters. Often they were remittance men from Great Britain, university graduates down on their luck or sadists who believed knowledge could be beaten into children with whips and canes. They were poorly paid, but school boards discovered that single women could be paid half a man's salary. Women, moreover, could be counted on to sing, sew, stay sober and treat children kindly. After Ryerson established the Toronto Normal School in 1847, teaching became a profession, and for a bright girl like Margaret, it was the opportunity of a lifetime. In 1866, when she was eighteen, she enrolled in the Normal School.

Margaret had attended a secondary, or grammar, school in Dundas, but only the year before, in 1865, had girls finally been admitted to Toronto's prestigious Home District Grammar School, and then strictly to study French. The principle of equality, however, had been established in the primary schools, although girls and boys were often segregated in separate classes, and graduates of ladies' colleges were agitating to be allowed to attend the University of Toronto.

In *The Development of Education in Canada,* Charles Phillips describes the Toronto Normal School as it was in Margaret Scott's era.

The headmaster spent five hours a day lecturing on the philosophy of grammar and parsing, on mathematical, physical and political geography, on the art of reading, on linear drawing, on lessons, on reasoning, [on] history and on trigonometry. His assistant spent four hours a day, in the afternoon and evening, lecturing on geometry, algebra, arithmetic, physics and agricultural chemistry. These were regular subjects scheduled for five days a week. There was also "repetition" on Saturdays from nine to twelve, and apparently in off hours time was found for music, the mode of teaching writing, writing from dictation, composition, orthography, derivations of words and the philosophy of education. Students also attended a model school for an hour a day for observation and practice teaching.

Margaret Scott prior to founding Branksome Hall.

Personal records show that Margaret studied bookkeeping, school drill and school law as well, and, almost as an afterthought, she was marked on her ability to teach.

Margaret thrived on hard work — she chose "Industry and Knowledge" as the motto for Branksome Hall — and her success at the Normal School, where she stood near the top of the class, shaped her ideas about the virtue of a rigorous education. She began teaching in Pickering, Ontario, in 1867, the year the Dominion of Canada emerged from Britain's motley group of North American colonies, and ten years later, after teaching at Strathroy and the Institute for the Blind in Brantford, she landed a plum job at the Ottawa Ladies' College.

The principal of this Presbyterian college was Reverend William Moore, soon followed by Reverend A.F. Kemp, but Miss Scott appears to have been the principal in practice. Ladies' colleges were customarily headed by men, or by married couples, while the actual work of running the school fell to a woman teacher capable of taking on administrative duties. Margaret later referred to herself as having been principal, and she was such a success in Ottawa that in 1884 she was invited to take over as headmistress of the girls' division of the Toronto Model School, the demonstration school affiliated with the Normal School where she had earned her certificate. The Model School set the standards for Ontario, and Miss Scott was paid a generous salary of $950 a year.

The Normal School's fiftieth jubilee report, published in 1897, gives a brief glimpse of Margaret in her role of headmistress. Praising Miss Scott and the boys' headmaster, Angus McIntosh, Chief Inspector Dr. Putman singled out "their poise, their naturalness of manner, the ease with which they controlled, their skill in questioning, the way they used their pupils' answers and the little use they made of text books." They were, he said, "shining examples of what elementary teachers could and should be."

In 1900, Margaret Scott abruptly resigned from the Model School. The school, it appears, decided to have only one principal, and Margaret, passed over for a man, would not likely have accepted a humiliating demotion to a position described as "first female teacher." Within a year, she became principal of the Toronto Presbyterian Ladies' College, and its vice-president, the scholarly pastor of St. Enoch's Church, Alexander MacMillan, would become one of Branksome Hall's greatest champions.

Margaret had visited girls' schools in England, Germany and the United States, and she was ready to combine the best of their examples in a school of her own. She was convinced, too, that education had to begin

Margaret Taylor Scott, 1903.

early. According to a Scott family story, Margaret, invited to admire a newborn niece, leaned over the cradle and solemnly observed, "The time to start training this child is *now.*"

Margaret's dream of her own school was supported by her sister, Elizabeth, a teacher in Dundas, and her youngest brother, William, Commissioner of Immigration in the Laurier government's Department of the Interior. Margaret also had two enthusiastic friends, Matilda Elliott, Principal of Toronto's Refuge for Girls, and her boarding house neighbour on Church Street, Florence Merrick.

Miss Merrick, like so many middle-aged, single women, was struggling to support herself. Christened Annie Florence, she had grown up in a splendid stone house on the Rideau River in eastern Ontario. Her United Empire Loyalist family of millers and merchants had founded the town of Merrickville, but the family fortune was ebbing by the time her father, Aaron, died in 1870. Florence was fifteen, and until she moved to Toronto in 1900, she had lived with her mother in Kingston. She had no training as a teacher, but her father had founded the public library in Merrickville, and unlike Margaret Scott, Florence Merrick had been schooled in household management and the feminine graces of polite society.

They made a perfect combination. When Branksome Hall was incorporated on June 19, 1903, Miss Scott, with $3,100 in shares, became president, and Miss Merrick, with an investment of $300, became secretary. Both, with Miss Elliott, were directors, and both were described as "principals." The rest of the school's $4,500 in capital came from Elizabeth and William Scott and a Toronto merchant, John Catto. Male approval was essential to any female enterprise, and endorsements were obtained from the premier and lieutenant-governor of Ontario, the principals of Queen's University, Knox College and Wycliffe College, the missionary secretary of the Methodist Church, the provincial minister of education and a variety of clergymen, school inspectors and Members of Parliament. The school's name, suggested by Alexander MacMillan, came from Sir Walter Scott's famous poem "The Lay of the Last Minstrel," which begins "The feast was over in Branksome Tower, / And the Layde had gone to her secret bower." It was an inspired choice. The name Branksome Hall implied a kinship between the school's founder, Margaret Scott, the famous poet, Sir Walter, and the aristocratic owner of the real Branxholme Castle, Scott of Buccleuch. The poem was instantly familiar to Canadians who, like MacMillan, had memorized

Branxholme Castle, 1935.

Scott's poetry, and it appealed to Toronto's self-made Scots and Irish Protestants who wanted no truck with English-style schools.

In Ontario, as elsewhere in Canada, descendants of immigrants who had arrived with only pennies in their pockets were amassing fortunes as railway contractors, lumber merchants, real estate speculators, meat packers, mining prospectors and manufacturers of farm machinery: the Massey Manufacturing Company in Toronto's west end was one of the biggest in the world. Henry Ford was preparing to build automobiles in Canada, and by 1908 the McLaughlin Carriage Company in nearby Oshawa would be making Buicks. Toronto, once a city of churches, was becoming a city of banks, department stores, insurance companies and railways, a centre of trade with a population of 200,000. To the north of Branksome Hall, the owners and executives of these enterprises were building mansions in suburban Rosedale. Often men of rough manners and little education, they could afford to send their daughters to a private school, and they wanted them to be industrious as well as accomplished. Miss Scott and Miss Merrick were respecting their patrons' work ethic when they opened for business on the Labour Day holiday.

With seventy pupils, ranging in age from six-year-old beginners to seniors preparing for university, they had their hands full. Branksome Hall was a non-denominational school (Miss Merrick was Church of England), and its curriculum reflected Margaret Scott's experience in the public system. Miss Scott, however, saw to it that "Scripture," taught by her, headed the list of required academic courses. As she stated in the next year's school calendar, "Being fully persuaded that *the Bible* is the foundation of all true moral as well as religious development, the Word of God will be fully studied."

Miss Scott's voice can also be heard in this expression of principle: "In all the life and work of the school, there will be kept in the foreground, as the most important feature of all, *the development of character*. All the teaching and discipline will be directed to this great end." Character would be developed by "thoroughness, accuracy and carefulness" in study, with the goal of "enabling pupils who have successfully completed the Branksome course to earn their own livelihood, should circumstances at any time so require."

This was an enlightened attitude, and it reflected the fact that paid work was becoming less of a taboo for women. The women who drudged in factories, sweatshops and domestic service were poor, and to be pitied, yet female idleness, a privilege of the rich, had fallen out of fashion. The invention of the telephone and typewriter had opened up "white blouse" jobs for women as switchboard operators and secretaries, and, as natural gas and electricity entered the home, housework became elevated to "domestic science."

"Since women are the home-makers," the Branksome calendar read, "and the home is the foundation of individual and national strength, a high ideal of their privileges and responsibilities will be inculcated. Domestic arts are encouraged as being essential to a girl's education, as well as to her future usefulness and dignity." The girls were taught basic nutrition as well as cookery, floor waxing, waiting on tables and "plumbing, etc." In addition, every resident pupil would be taught to sew and care for her own wardrobe.

"Miss Scott was a disciplinarian with an appreciation of a child's sensitivity," student Muriel Moores Ellis recalled years later. "Deportment she felt very important. She would appear at a classroom, study the students' postures and have us get up and sit down until she was satisfied we would do it gracefully. Each boarder's trunk, on arrival, was carefully gone through, and only the modest and suitable clothes were kept. The rest were returned home, as she did not approve of any show-off." Resident girls were also required to give Miss Scott a list, signed by their parents, of their correspondents and the friends they might visit. They were forbidden to use the telephone without special permission, and they could not have books or magazines other than class books and those belonging to the school library.

"The physical set-up of 1903 was makeshift," said another student,

Constance Macdonald Sitwell, "but the teaching, if one took advantage of it, was good, and the general air one of, what can I call it, gentility?" Grace Morris Craig, a boarder from Pembroke, Ontario, described the school: "It was in a handsome old house approached by a curved driveway through flowerbeds and shrubs. The house was wide and low, the most interesting feature being the two bay windows which gave light to the drawing room. The drawing room had an air of elegance with a white marble fireplace at each end and much rich Victorian furniture. Other rooms on the ground floor were a study, where we did our homework each evening, a conservatory with a tile floor, where we had our sewing lesson every Saturday morning and where we danced on Friday evenings, and a large dining room with a bay window looking towards the garden at the back."

Elsie Taylor Baird recalled, "We sat around one large table, Miss Scott at the head, Miss Merrick at the foot. Miss Merrick was our housemother, quiet, kind and self-effacing. The only time there was trouble in her department was when we decided we'd had too many curry fix-ups

Branksome's first home, 102 Bloor St. East, 1903.

and the next time we would all refuse it. The threat was enough, and we had much less curry."

Bedrooms for the thirty girls in residence were on the upper floors. "My first year we were four in a room," recalled Constance Macdonald Sitwell, "with Miss McCurdy, our Latin and math teacher, in the curtained-off end of the huge, third-storey room." Miss Scott and Miss Merrick also lived in the school, and the resident teachers doubled as chaperones.

"Every morning immediately after breakfast," said Grace Morris Craig, "the boarders were required to go 'on the walk' in a double line accompanied by a teacher. I had a 'crush' on Miss Mary Macdonald, our form teacher, and was happy when she took the walk so I had a chance to chat with her. We usually crossed into Rosedale by the Huntley Street bridge and returned to Bloor Street by the Glen Road bridge. Occasionally, as a great treat, we were taken along Bloor Street and caused some traffic congestion as we ambled across Yonge Street. Many of the girls liked this walk best because it gave us a chance to see a little of city life. We were always encouraged to spend time out of doors, mostly on the grass tennis courts which occupied most of our recreation area and were flooded in the winter to provide a skating rink."

Physical culture, as it was called, was a required subject at Branksome Hall. According to the school calendar, systematic physical training "is a remedy for defects such as round shoulders, flat chest, weak ankles, etc. It develops courage and self-possession, muscular and mental control." Lectures on "physiology and hygiene" were given by the school's consulting physician, Dr. Helen MacMurchy.

The academic curriculum emphasized languages, especially English and French, and in the senior years Latin and German were required. Italian and Greek were available as options. Mathematics was compulsory. Physics and chemistry were taught to matriculation students, but most girls took "nature study," described as "the observation of plant and animal life." In addition, Branksome Hall offered instruction in piano, organ, voice, violin, mandolin, banjo and guitar, as well as music theory, and the artistic could study drawing and design, oil and watercolour painting, clay modelling and ceramic painting. At a private school, girls were still expected to be "finished."

It was an expensive process. Branksome Hall charged $10 or $12 a term for Junior School, depending on the grade, $15 for matriculation, but languages and the arts, usually taught by independent professionals, were extra. French and German, for instance, cost $3 to $6, Italian $6. Music lessons could run from $8 to $40 or more, depending on the instructor's time, and piano practice was $2 for the first hour, $1 for each additional hour. Courses in drawing and painting were $15, art needlework $5 and dancing $5. The school charged more for some compulsory subjects — domestic science and advanced science were $6 each — and residence girls paid $60 for room and board, $5 for laundry and $1 in pew rent. Fees for a talented, energetic girl — arrangements could also be made for riding lessons — might run well over $100.

Toronto offered social and cultural opportunities too, particularly to boarders from rural and remote areas (four girls had arrived from Dawson City, Northwest Territories), and girls were allowed to leave the school for the afternoon and evening, properly chaperoned, on alternate Saturdays. They were taken to lectures, art shows and concerts at Massey Hall. Grace Morris Craig recalled, "In our 'party' dresses, we were taken to the concert hall by way of the Church streetcar, which at that time ran into Rosedale. I consider myself fortunate to have heard Caruso and to have seen Pavlova dance." There were trips to the Old Mill on the Humber River, canoeing parties and excursions to the local hangout, McConky's, on Yonge Street. One reason girls were sent to Branksome Hall was to meet eligible young men, and St. Andrew's College was conveniently located in North Rosedale.

"I remember best our Sundays," said Elsie Taylor Baird. "Prayers at the breakfast table, marching to church morning and evening two by two with a teacher front and rear. We sat on one side of the gallery, the St.

Margaret's girls on the other side and the St. Andrew's boys in the middle. Of course, we were supposed to keep our eyes on the minister, but the poor man had lost an ear. Just where *to* look was a problem."

In the afternoon, the girls wrote a summary of the sermon that was graded for content, spelling and penmanship, and Bible verses were assigned to be memorized. A "quiet hour" followed for prayer and meditation. "After supper, church again," Elsie recalled, "and after church as many girls as Miss Scott had time for were called in for a friendly private session. Sometimes not so friendly. I had many private sessions with Miss Scott, but when I won the gold thimble for memorizing Bible verses, all was forgiven."

Grace Morris Craig, winner of Branksome Hall's first gold medal for scholarship, dreaded "Miss Scott's evenings" on Sundays: "She sat in her charming sitting room, and one by one we went up to say our Bible verses. This was indeed an ordeal from the moment we entered her room, walked solemnly across to a low lady-chair, crossed our ankles, placed our hands, palms up, on our lap and began to recite. It was always a long passage from the Old Testament containing difficult words such as 'priests,' every consonant of which had to be sounded clearly. If this was successfully accomplished for a whole year, one was awarded a Margaret T. Scott Bible. I still prize mine because of the effort which went into the winning of it."

For the rest of her life, student Delphine Burr remembered Miss Scott saying, "Get down on your knees, girls, and thank God there are no men in Heaven!" God was certainly the Father of Margaret Scott's household. If a girl misbehaved, Miss Scott would kneel with her, and they would pray together for God's forgiveness. It was effective discipline, and if Miss Scott's religious views raised some girls' eyebrows, her common sense and dedication to their welfare won their respect. Elsie Taylor Baird described her as "strict but fair," and Grace Morris Craig admitted, "She did send out into the world a group who understood the meaning of 'being a lady.'" Grace, however, wanted to be an architect.

Branksome Hall's enrolment grew so quickly the drawing room had to be surrendered for classroom space. Most classes were taught in a converted stable and carriage house at the rear of the yard; the art room was on the top floor of the carriage house, over the gym. Louise MacLennan Whitehead described the school as it was in 1906: "Wooden chairs behind long board tables seating three abreast, Ainslie McMichael beside me, a regular 'cut-up,' facing Miss Ramsay, an Englishwoman dressed in formal garb with long silver chains hanging around her neck that tinkled as she walked. One morning she was annoyed at some antics Ainslie was indulging in and pounded her pencil right into the inkwell: the splash was dramatic — and messy."

Louise may have been a bit of a "cut-up" herself. "There was a walk up to the main house," she recalled, "and I remember Miss Scott, of whom we were in awe, stopping me to tell me I was not taking life seriously enough, my age at that time being all of ten years. We gathered for prayers in a long hall, probably the former carriage house. It was just a rough-walled room, with a small iron stove at one side, where we used to toast the stale soda biscuits that were presented to the boarders at recess. We nearly always burnt them. After prayers, we marched to our classrooms to the tune of 'Onward Christian Soldiers.'"

Military drill was one of the many accomplishments of the school's new mathematics teacher, Edith MacGregor Read. "She was a shy, serious person," Louise recalled, "but we all adored her. She taught us to play basketball, our first taste of sports. Later she took some of us to a political meeting in Massey Hall, and one Halloween night, when we had a masquerade party, she rented a hurdy-gurdy, dressed up to suit the part and played it for the dance music. She could teach any subject. One year our literature teacher was ill, and she took over to teach us 'The Lay of the Last Minstrel.'"

Edith MacGregor Read was twenty-five, but with her small, childlike body, chubby face and unruly blonde hair, she looked, and often acted, younger than many of her students. EDM, as the girls privately called her, had come to Branksome Hall in 1906 after teaching for a year at Netherwood School in New Brunswick. Edith had no training as a teacher, but she had an M.A. from Dalhousie University in Halifax, with honours in pure and applied mathematics, and B.A. degrees from both Dalhousie and Radcliffe College in Cambridge, Massachusetts.

Edith's academic achievements, however, were not as outstanding as they appeared on paper. The truth was, Edith had flunked out of Radcliffe College. Records for 1900–01 show that, in her first year of graduate studies, she received a D in one of three mathematics courses, C and C+ in the others. She got A- in physics but an E in German. She did not qualify to continue toward her M.A., and the college's academic board voted against awarding her a B.A. The following year, however, after the college had received a terse letter from Edith's father, Dr. Herbert Huntington Read, the board reversed its decision. The minutes of June 19, 1902, read

> Professor Hall moved and it was voted that Edith MacGregor Read be recommended by the Academic Board to the Council for the degree of Bachelor of Arts, as of the year 1901, this action to be now taken because of information received since June, 1901, to the effect that Miss Read was, while here, under some misunderstanding for which she was not wholly responsible, as to the conditions imposed on her in her candidacy for the degree.

The exact nature of Edith's "misunderstanding" remains a mystery, but her failure at Radcliffe effectively ended her hope of teaching at any women's college in the United States, and Canadian universities did not hire women to lecture in mathematics, physics or much else. Disappointment, however, did not blunt her optimism. In an employment form Edith submitted to Radcliffe's appointment bureau, she claimed to be able to teach, in addition to mathematics and physics, chemistry, English composition and literature, geography, history (ancient and modern), Latin, mechanics and physiology.

Self-confidence and boundless energy were EDM's great strengths, and Edith blew into Branksome Hall like Mary Poppins. EDM loved team

Edith MacGregor Read.

sports, and she soon had the BH teams decked out in long bloomers, with handsome school sweaters and, in winter, matching toques. Wearing bloomers was as controversial an innovation for girls as basketball, but with bicycling having become the rage, the long, full skirt was a hazard as well as a nuisance.

Vigilance was another of EDM's virtues as a teacher. "I shared a room with three other girls next door to Miss Read," Grace Morris Craig recalled, "which was a drawback at times as she always noticed when we tried to toast marshmallows over the gas jet." Edith also had a flair for organization that came in handy as the school grew to more than eighty girls and a staff of eleven, plus sixteen "visiting teachers."

It was the custom for schools to publish each pupil's standing in class at the end of the year, and although Miss Scott accepted an academic average of seventy percent as "honours," the Branksome Hall calendar for 1906–07 indicates that few girls attained this standard. Some were "recommended," but many appear to have spent more than one year in a grade, and others took only those courses they liked. Margaret Scott didn't want a school full of dimwits, but could she afford to lose girls who failed? The school awarded no prizes for scholarship, but Miss Scott appeased the girls by awarding school certificates and prizes for "neatest workbook in mathematics," "best plain sewing" and, of course, "scripture memorizing."

When Branksome Hall celebrated its fifth birthday in 1908, Margaret

Scott was sixty, an age when she might have been expected to retire. Florence Merrick, ill, apparently with cancer, had returned to Kingston to live with a sister, and she died there on November 8, 1908. According to her obituary in the *Kingston Weekly British Whig,*

> The long illness which was accompanied by great suffering ended at one o'clock on Saturday morning. Miss Merrick for some years had been the much-loved partner of Miss M. Scott, as one of the Head Mistresses of "Branksome Hall", a girls' school in Toronto. The girls who came under her care were deeply attached to her, for she was always bright, sympathetic and helpful in all matters.

Miss Merrick's place had been taken by a secretary, Jean Hume, but the next year Branksome Hall lost its home. The school had been renting the house at 102 Bloor Street East from the estate of a deceased senator, Sir Frank Smith, and in 1909 the province purchased the property to build a new Government House. Branksome Hall had to vacate quickly — the house was going to be demolished — and temporary quarters were found around the corner in a big, vacant house at 592 Sherbourne Street.

By September 1910, Branksome Hall had a new principal. In June, Miss Read had purchased the school from Miss Scott for $5,000: $1,500 in cash and the rest in instalments of $500 payable, with interest, over seven years. It was a bargain. In 1903, Branksome Hall had been capitalized at $40,000, although only $4,500 had been invested, and in its seven years of operation, it had acquired a staff, a fine reputation and no debt. Apart from its furniture, however, the school had no assets. Margaret Scott had enough money to support herself — she moved to a boarding house at 77 Huntley Street — and Miss Read had apparently persuaded her that Branksome Hall was nothing more than a name, goodwill, and a headache.

Branksome's second home, 592 Sherbourne Street, 1910-12.

Where did Edith get the money? In 1910, it was almost unheard of for women to buy anything — men paid their bills — and $1,500 was more than Edith, who had been teaching only five years, would likely have saved from her salary. For a teacher, however, she was well off and well connected. Her father, a prominent Halifax physician, was related to Henry Robert Emmerson, a former premier of New Brunswick, a Member of Parliament and a cabinet minister in the Laurier government from 1904 to 1907. Edith's great-grandfather, James MacGregor, had been the first Presbyterian missionary to arrive in Pictou County, Nova Scotia. One MacGregor uncle had become lieutenant-governor of Nova Scotia, and another, also James, had taught her physics at Dalhousie. For all her abruptness and tomboyish ways, Edith was accustomed to the society of the clever, prosperous and powerful, and when she wanted to buy Branksome Hall, she turned to a plump, genial Toronto banker, William Donald Ross.

W.D. Ross, general manager of the Metropolitan Bank, had been born in Nova Scotia, and before moving to Ontario, he had married Edith's cousin, Susan MacGregor. In 1909, Susan had died giving birth to twins, leaving William with two motherless daughters. William's sister Christine Barker, who had come from New York City to care for her grieving brother, had brought her daughter, Mary. Christine had studied law and was certified as a chartered accountant. For the Ross household, Branksome Hall was an attractive proposition, and while by Edith's Baptist standards William's personal behaviour risked damnation (Ross enjoyed cigars, wine and good Scotch, played poker and bet on horses), Edith could be tolerant of human frailty.

By the end of 1910, Branksome Hall, with a record enrolment of 135 pupils, had settled into 592 Sherbourne Street. Miss Scott, now Honorary Principal, still taught scripture, but this description of the school by the anonymous editor of the Christmas edition of *The Branksome Slogan* reflects the influence of its new principal:

> An aggressive, independent-looking building this. Square and upright, strong and determined, it seems to say, "I stand for the modern spirit of womanhood. Any girl entering here must learn that it is possible for her to be a lady, yet to look out for herself in this busy world. Industry and knowledge should make anyone independent. Be independent."
>
> Inside all was wondrously comfortable. The bright-faced principal explained, apologetically, that if the building and location should prove suitable much would be done in [the] way of improvement. To our eyes very little seemed lacking. The classrooms were bright and sunny, the dining room downstairs large and airy, and the bedrooms dainty and comfortable.

Edith Read was on her own, and she turned to the girls to help her. She appointed four seniors as prefects, formed a Beta Kappa society to organize dances, concerts and other social events and involved the alumnae in games, sports nights and basketball tournaments. She changed the school motto to "Industria et Scientia" — the girls came to dread memorizing Virgil's *Aeneid* as much as Bible verses — and encouraged the French teacher, Jeanne Compondu, to put on short French plays.

"A great deal of time was spent on French under the watchful eye of Mlle. Compondu," recalled Grace Morris Craig. "She presided at one of the tables in the dining room, and throughout my years at Branksome I always sat at the French table. Being part of 'The French Society,' as a few of us were called, had its advantages and disadvantages. Occasionally, we were invited to have tea in the drawing room with some of Mamselle's friends, but the strain of carrying on a conversation in elegant French was scarcely recompensed by the delicious cakes."

Edith Read could be proud of her school. While most Branksome Hall graduates "came out" as debutantes, toured the continent and married young, five were attending university (a former Branksome Hall teacher, Miss Fotheringham, was in third-year medicine), three were training as nurses and others were studying at Macdonald College in Guelph and Toronto's Royal Conservatory of Music. Muriel Robertson was teaching piano at Havergal Ladies' College, and Lillie Shannon led Branksome Hall's choral class. The move to Sherbourne Street had not damaged the school's reputation, but if Branksome Hall were to grow, it was imperative that the school own its own building.

When a Rosedale estate, Hollydene, came on the market in January 1912 for $48,000, Edith Read raised the $20,000 down payment in less than a month. Three mutual friends, W.D. Ross, S.J. Moore, President of the Baptist Convention of Ontario, and stockbroker F.H. Deacon, whose wife, Ethel, was Edith's cousin on her father's side, each loaned $2,500; the balance came from Edith, her father and two MacGregor relations in New Glasgow, Nova Scotia. Edith's $7,500 contribution, the largest, may have been an inheritance from Susan MacGregor Ross.

Hollydene (10 Elm Avenue), Branksome's third home, 1912.

Hollydene, located on the quiet northeast corner of Elm Avenue and Huntley Street, was a monumental red-brick house set in a large lot. A stable and two-storey carriage house were located at the back, and, to the west, a small stream, bordered by willows, trickled into the ravine. Hollydene's spacious lawns were perfect for tennis, games and garden parties, and the front of the property was safely enclosed by a wrought-iron fence. The new Rosedale Presbyterian Church around the corner would serve, when needed, as a chapel, and if boys were required, St. Andrew's College was only blocks away.

In spite of its size, however, the house was not ideally suited for a school. The halls were narrow, the rooms were cramped and the tall windows, while attractive, didn't let in enough light. The conservatory was too small, and the open veranda was useless in cold weather. The previous owner, railway contractor Hugh Ryan, had died in 1899, and the house, built in 1880, had become entangled in a squabble among his heirs. It needed renovation, especially since it was going to house fifty

The pupils' sitting room in #10 (above) was converted into a library (below).

boarders, including the principal, and accommodate one hundred day girls. To do this, Miss Read needed a bank loan.

Fortunately, Moore and Ross, both directors of the Bank of Nova Scotia, were intimate friends of its president. The loan would be secured by a mortgage on the property, and to negotiate this, Miss Read and her group of financial backers incorporated a holding company, the Rosevale Realty Company, in June 1912. Christine Barker became secretary-treasurer, Edith Read became president and with nearly five hundred of Rosevale Realty's eight hundred shares, valued at $100 each, Edith remained in charge.

Miss Read had bought 10 Elm Avenue, as Hollydene came to be called, through an intermediary. She had been fearful that the neighbours would disapprove of a school, but the neighbours, worried that Hollydene would deteriorate into a rooming house, welcomed the improvements. "The coach house was made into classrooms and a gymnasium," Lucy Booth Martyn writes in *Aristocratic Toronto,* "while the upstairs of the main house became the art room and other classrooms. The conservatory became a delightful kindergarten, and French classes were held in the closed-in verandah. An addition to the back of the house held classrooms and bedrooms."

Slogan editor Jean Morton, who visited the "New Branksome Hall" in October 1912, found the house, with its oversized porte-cochère, "awe-inspiring," but she was reassured by the familiar girlish cacophony of music students practising their scales. Jean was greeted by a maid, and a teacher, Miss Gardiner, took her through the new wing. "We then went upstairs to see the girls' rooms," she writes,

> and that's where you reach the heart of the whole house. Oh, those rooms with their little blue cots, and gay pennants and photos! Some of them were so neat and tidy, others so jolly and happy-go-lucky with things in riotous confusion. A mysterious excitement seemed to be in the atmosphere, for it was the night

of the annual Halloween masquerade, and all sorts of marvellous feminine concoctions peeped from unexpected corners.

A mood of "riotous confusion" was not what many Toronto parents desired in a private girls' school, and Branksome Hall stood in sharp contrast to the dour discipline of its larger rivals. As W.D. Ross's daughter, Jean Ross Skoggard, recalled, "A friend's mother removed her from Branksome Hall Junior School because she was 'having too much fun' and sent her to Havergal, which she hated. I'm afraid her personality was adversely affected consequently." Mary Barker, Christine's daughter, who also went to Branksome Hall, found Miss Read very understanding: "Being 'sent to Miss Read' was supposed to be a disgrace," she said, "but I never found it so. I was 'sent to Miss Read' frequently for being impertinent, being late, having my hands dirty. She never chewed me out. She'd send me to the drawing room, where I could curl up and read. Once, one of the teachers wrongly accused me of cheating. I lost my temper, and so did the teacher. We had a showdown. Miss Read explained, 'I know you didn't cheat, but I have to stand up for my staff.' Miss Read knew everybody in the school, and she knew who had drunks for fathers. She never told on girls to their parents."

EDM, after all, was young, and her teachers were mostly friends and relatives from Nova Scotia. EDM went to Halifax at every opportunity, and she returned from one vacation armed with a loud, brass ship's bell. Installed next to the staircase, the hated bell, rung by hand, clanged all day from the "rising bell" at 7:15 a.m., through the warning bell at 7:35 a.m., morning run bell, breakfast bell, class bells, recess, lunch and rest bells, games bell, study bell, dressing bell and dinner bell, to the "lights out" bell at 9:30 p.m. At night, the "fire bell" would often rouse girls out of their beds and send them shivering into the street.

For girls like Betty Hire, a student at Branksome Hall in 1916, gym was worse. "I could never connect with a moving ball," Betty said, "and you could bang into the posts in the gym beautifully if you didn't watch." Ainslie

McMichael, who had grown from a mischievous child into a slim, olive-skinned, dark-haired woman, taught basketball, and Mary Hamilton, Director of Physical Culture, was expert in the latest fad, Swedish gymnastics. Betty, who was studying piano, thought that music didn't cut much ice at Branksome Hall. "The pianos were out of tune, and they were not very good pianos," she said. "Miss Read was totally unmusical. She didn't know 'Rule Britannia' from 'God Save the King.'"

The infamous ship's bell.

Both songs became staples of Branksome Hall's morning prayers after Great Britain declared war on Germany on August 4, 1914. Ontario, like Nova Scotia, was passionately loyal to the Old Country, and militia regiments recruited volunteers for what would become, during the four terrible years of the Great War, a proud Canadian army. Fathers enlisted and went overseas, mothers sold Victory Bonds, knitted and rolled bandages for the Red Cross. Some officers' wives joined their husbands in England, and for many fragmented families, boarding a daughter at school was preferable to leaving her at home alone.

The immediate, visible impact of the war on the school was its new military-style uniform. To aid the war effort, women were exhorted to economise in every way, including dress material, and Miss Read responded by raising the hems on her girls' navy skirts to the knee. Blouses were replaced by a white cotton sailor's middy trimmed with navy blue braid, the school's crest embroidered in red on the right sleeve.

Buccleuch House victory salute, 1919.

The outfit was completed by black cotton stockings, black shoes and a smaller version of Mrs. Bloomer's ugly undergarment. Scarves were silk, navy for juniors, pale blue for seniors and red for prefects. Miss Read did not require hats, and white skirts were worn on formal occasions.

The girls adapted their uniforms to suit their figures by rolling up their middies and pinning them in at the waist or by surreptitiously hiking their skirts above the knee. The uniform was a little scratchy but comfortable, and it liberated the older girls from tight corsets and petticoats. The braver girls were bobbing their hair, to Miss Read's horror, but Edith appreciated their need for more freedom from adult supervision. In 1917, for $15,000, she bought the house next door, 14 Elm Avenue, as a senior-class residence, on the condition that the girls speak only French when inside the house. It was called French House.

Four years of war had an emotional and psychological impact on the school. Fathers and brothers were killed or wounded — Edith's younger brother, John, was badly injured — and the girls developed a sense of social responsibility far beyond knitting trench caps or raising money for disabled veterans.

"'Helplessness' is just another word for 'Hopelessness,'" senior student Lois Howard wrote in an angry editorial in the 1918 *Slogan.*

> If more people understood this, there would no longer be that class of misguided women constantly crying, "Oh, I feel so helpless! This awful war — will it never end?" Let us not join these futile exclaimers when there are so many services we can render our country in her time of need. One who is not accustomed to self-sacrifice should commence by a few small tasks daily. Gradually the art of helping others will become a firmly established principle in our lives, and the old, useless days will be entirely forgotten.

Lois Howard had some political opinions too:

> The more advanced and gifted women claim more than the care of the wounded and sick as their share. It is time to dispense with the idea that women can only perform certain clearly-defined duties. Just now it is an indisputable fact that the country needs every resource at its command, and if bigger and quicker results come from a wider recognition of women's rights in a nation's councils, then by all means let us win that recognition.

Women had already won the vote in Manitoba and Alberta, and Branksome girls had read the popular novels written by the suffragette who had fearlessly spearheaded those campaigns, Nellie McClung. Reluctantly, with much foot-dragging, the federal government was preparing to give women the right to vote and to be voted for. Branksome

Hall had already joined in the fray. "On Friday, January 25th, a most exciting election was held in the school," the 1918 *Slogan* reported.

> The parties opposed were the Micmacs, who were against having women in Parliament, and the Mugwumps, who believe that women should be in Parliament. Speeches at recess and hot arguments at all hours were the order of the day. An election was held, the voting being done at different polling booths, as in the Dominion elections. The Micmacs got in counting the individual votes, but taking the election results en masse in the different forms there was a tie, so the Mugwumps feel that there is still hope the Micmacs may see the light, and the Micmacs rejoice that they have saved the country and swamped the Mugwumps.

Edith Read certainly considered herself to be equal, if not superior, to any man, and she encouraged her girls to be assertive and self-reliant. Branksome girls played a man's game, ice hockey, and while they often got trounced by St. Margaret's or Moulton College, they did a man's work too. "Owing to frequent heavy snowfalls, the girls found it difficult to keep the ice in very good condition," the *Slogan* reported, "and many arranged matches never materialized on this account, but at least we can say that the Branksome girls (a few of them!) were the only ones who made, flooded and shovelled their own rink, thus saving man labour."

One Branksome student, Eleanor Stanhope, died in the influenza epidemic that swept the country as the war ended in November 1918, and others, like Betty Hire, were forced to drop out because of illness. The armistice wasn't signed until November 11, but Branksome Hall celebrated with a formal dance for senior boarders on November 1. "Dancing took place in the gymnasium," reported the *Slogan,*

> and supper was served in French House, both being decorated for the occasion. The guests included the prefects of St.

Branksome students playing ice hockey, 1920s.

> Andrew's and Upper Canada Colleges, and some of those who came to town for the McGill-Varsity rugby match. Twelve o'clock came all too soon, and brought to an end one of the most popular parties Branksome has ever had.

The school's attitude toward men had changed since Miss Scott's day, and Margaret, now in her seventies, had become a ghostly presence. She moved to Vancouver to live with a brother, and she died there on June 30, 1921. Margaret seems to have retired from Branksome Hall without recognition or reward, but after her death, Miss Read named her newest purchase, 125 Huntley Street, Scott House, and the alumnae raised enough money to fund the Margaret T. Scott Memorial Prizes for memorizing scripture. The school also adopted Miss Scott's favourite mission, a refuge for widows and children in India run by a Christian

Scott House, just south of Rosedale Presbyterian Church, 1921.

convert, Pandita Ramabai, and the girls raised $178 in their first Ramabai Week campaign.

Some of the $35,000 to buy Scott House, formerly the residence of writer Marshall Saunders, author of *Beautiful Joe,* had come from Branksome Hall students and alumnae. In the spring of 1921, Miss Read was selling them $100 shares in the school, not only, she said, "to assure the future of the school, but [also] to create an added interest helpful to the school and to themselves." Havergal Ladies' College had plans to build in the country, and in 1915 Bishop Strachan School had relocated to a suburban property north of the city near Upper Canada College. EDM had been hoping to raise $250,000 to build a new gym and swimming pool for Branksome Hall, but possibly because the women had little money of their own to invest, the campaign fell far short. Miss Read needed another big bank loan, but would she have to surrender control of Branksome Hall to get it?

Chapter Two

By June 1923, Branksome Hall's twentieth anniversary, Miss Read had come up with a satisfactory solution. Warning her guests at the school's birthday banquet that, as long as Branksome remained under private ownership it was in danger of closing down, she announced that Branksome Hall would become a non-profit corporation. All revenues would be reinvested in the school, beginning with the building of a new gym, swimming pool and classroom wing.

"Everyone felt that we were celebrating not only the anniversary of the founding of the school, but also the inauguration of a new era in our history," the *Slogan* reported.

> The school will endure, for the spirit behind it is not one of commercialism but altruism. The school is not a chattel but a trust; it is not a venture to be kept in existence as long as it is profitable, but an institution which, each succeeding year, will exert a wholesome effect upon a widening circle of human lives, and to which an ever-increasing number of Canadian women will owe allegiance and devotion.

Branksome Hall was going to be a corporation with a high moral purpose. Its new mission statement made it clear that it did not intend to become a school for snobs and elitists, nor would it be exclusively Christian. Edith Read was an evangelical Christian — she admired the missionary work of The People's Church — but her educational philosophy was broad enough to accommodate Jews, agnostics and humanists. While Branksome Hall had always attracted its share of boarders from wealthy, socially prominent families (including Lord Beaverbrook's niece, Margaret Aitken, from New Brunswick, and two early boarders, Eleanor Bluck and Virginia Outerbridge, from Bermuda), most of its students came from the surrounding Rosedale neighbourhood. Branksome Hall was a community school, and the biggest threat to its existence came from the nearby public schools.

Branksome, like other girls' schools, had succeeded because it taught religion, art, music, physical culture, home economics and other subjects the parsimonious, conservative Toronto Board of Education had dismissed as expensive frills. Now, finding itself forced to educate immigrant children from a variety of cultural backgrounds, the board realized it had an obligation to educate children of various abilities. It also had plenty of taxpayers' money to build immense modern schools with every frill imaginable.

By 1923, plans were afoot to build a showpiece collegiate on Jarvis Street south of Wellesley. With an auditorium, art room, cafeteria, library, swimming pool and gymnasium with a running track, Jarvis Collegiate threatened to make Branksome Hall, with its stable, carriage house and old Victorian houses, obsolete.

In order to expand and modernize her school, Miss Read once more called on her old friends, W.D. Ross, F.H. Deacon and S.J. Moore. With their support, Branksome Hall was incorporated on April 14, 1924. Ross, Deacon and Moore were joined on the five-person board of directors by John A. Tory. Tory, a Nova Scotian, was a director and manager of Sun Life Assurance and the school's hockey coach. The president, of course, was Edith MacGregor Read.

The first item of corporate business was to convert the shares in the old Rosevale Realty Company into $100, twenty-year bonds secured by a second mortgage on Branksome Hall's property. Edith Read had managed to sell only 780 of the 2,500 shares to thirty-eight people, and she had bought six hundred of the shares herself. With $60,000 in Branksome Hall bonds — the next largest investors had $2,500 each — Miss Read retained a dominant interest in the school, although, if the school defaulted, her bonds, which paid six percent annual interest, would be worthless. In addition, she negotiated the sale to the corporation of her "interest and goodwill," including school furniture, for another $10,000 in Branksome Hall bonds. Branksome Hall was very much Edith Read's personal corporation. The by-laws required no public notice or advertisement of members' meetings, nor was it necessary to send the members any report, statement or balance sheet.

At subsequent meetings that spring, the board issued bonds worth a total of $200,000. It paid off the old mortgage on 10 Elm Avenue and arranged to borrow $100,000 from the Mutual Life Assurance Company. The loan was guaranteed by a first mortgage on school property and a $50,000 insurance policy on Miss Read's life. Edith was indispensable. Not only was she principal of the school, but also she had created a second position for herself as managing director of the Branksome Hall Corporation. The minutes of the July 25, 1924, meeting describe the terms of her contract:

> Whereas the said Edith M. Read has devoted a great deal of her time and attention to the affairs of Branksome Hall Corporation in addition to discharging the duties of the principal of Branksome Hall School,
>
> And whereas the said Edith M. Read has been identified with Branksome Hall School for many years and it is expedient and in the best interests of the conduct of the said school that to assure the continued support of the public and the good will of the alumnae that the said Edith M. Read continue actively in charge of the said school and its activities,

Now therefore this agreement witnesseth that Branksome Hall hereby appoints the said Edith M. Read as Managing-Director of Branksome Hall during the remainder of her lifetime or so long as she desires to retain such office, such appointment to date from the first day of September, 1924.

As Managing-Director, the said Edith M. Read shall have sole and absolute and full power and authority to manage and direct the business and affairs of the Corporation and of Branksome Hall School, including the authority to establish, change, amend, direct and superintend the curriculum of studies, to employ and discharge all teachers, employees, agents and servants of the Corporation and to assume and carry out all duties and responsibilities formerly discharged by the said Edith M. Read as the sole proprietress of Branksome Hall School.

The said Edith M. Read may resign as Managing-Director of Branksome Hall upon three months' notice in writing. She may be removed from the office of Managing-Director upon becoming unfit or incapable, and by the passing of a resolution by the board of directors of Branksome Hall, PROVIDED that such a resolution be confirmed by a special general meeting of the members of Branksome Hall and carried unanimously by seventy-five per cent in number of the members of Branksome Hall.

Should the said Edith M. Read resign as Managing-Director, she shall have the right to nominate her successor to the office and Branksome Hall shall appoint such nominee as Managing-Director.

The said Edith M. Read covenants and agrees that she will faithfully, honestly and diligently serve Branksome Hall and

> she will devote her entire time, labour, skill and attention to such employment.
>
> The said Edith M. Read shall be paid the sum of $2,000 per annum payable in ten equal monthly installments of $200 the first of such payments to be due and payable on the first day of October, 1924.

In case Miss Read, as Branksome Hall's president, chief bondholder and chair of the board, appeared to have a conflict of interest over her appointment as the company's managing director, the minutes add that "Miss Read, the chairman, fully disclosed her interest and refrained from voting with respect to said agreement."

While a benevolent dictatorship certainly suited Miss Read, it may not, in the long run, have been in the best interests of the school. Through charm, persuasion and family ties, Edith had gathered around her boardroom table some of the best business brains in the country, people familiar with charitable trusts and foundations, but the idea of establishing an endowment fund to guarantee the school's future financial security was not on the agenda. Her management style was based on frugality, and she believed she could make do, as well as pay off the loan, from student fees. Branksome Hall, however, charged less than Havergal and Bishop Strachan. Branksome's fees were only $100 a year for a junior day pupil, $200 for a senior and $700 for a boarder, and Edith was reluctant to raise fees for fear of losing students to the public schools.

Money was so scarce that, when construction of the red-brick gymnasium began in the summer of 1924, the swimming pool, intended for the ground floor, had to be postponed. The stream to the west of 10 Elm Avenue was filled in, and the gym was built adjacent to Huntley Street. Designed by architect Herbert Horner in the popular "collegiate gothic" style, it blended in well with the school's other buildings, and the institutional-looking classroom wing was out of sight from the street.

The new gymnasium, 1924.

The gym doubled as an auditorium, and Horner's design included a musicians' gallery, a concave cedar ceiling and a small, recessed stage. The carriage house, the stable and a covered wooden passageway connecting them to 10 Elm Avenue were demolished.

EDM may have had a tin ear, but she loved a show. She hired an orchestra and invited five hundred guests to the formal opening of the school's new additions on November 14, 1924. "It was in the new Gymnasium, specially decorated for the occasion, that the chief interest of the entertainment centred," reported the *Slogan.*

> At the North end of the hall, the stage was set for the much-anticipated feature of the evening — the presentation by a

group of present and former members of the History of Art classes of a series of Tableau Vivants, representing a number of well-known pictorial works from the old masters. The large gilt frame, in which the pictures were arranged, was placed at the back of the platform, contrasting admirably with the rich blue of the stage hangings and producing a charming colour effect, which was much enhanced by the new system of stage lighting. Those taking part acquitted themselves with credit, calling forth many expressions of appreciation for the beauty and success of the production. At the close of the programme, supper was served in the new dining room, concluding one of the happiest occasions in the history of the School.

Miss Read knew how to show off her students as well as her stage, and the success of the opening gala was followed on May 15, 1925, by the school's first gymnastics display. "The Maypole by the primary class was one of the nicest features of the evening," the *Slogan* reported. The

Maypole physical culture.

display featured folk dancing, exercises with wands and Indian clubs and rhythmic Swedish gymnastics. It closed with a Grand March, at the end of which everyone sang "God Save the King."

EDM's theatricals were superb public relations. Parents enjoyed seeing their children perform, and the performances gave the alumnae a chance to return to the school. "Branksome has always had reason to feel proud of her school spirit," student Jessie Wright wrote in the 1925 *Slogan,* "and this year it has been more evident than ever. We find that we now have both past and present girls united into a strong body."

A Branksome Hall alumnae association had been formed in 1908 by Margaret Scott. Miss Scott saw it as an intellectual endeavour, rather like a book club or a literary society, and the first issues of the *Slogan,* which began as an alumnae publication, were full of poems, essays and travel stories. The *Slogan,* however, was taken over by the students, and apart from sending their daughters to the school, the alumnae had found little reason, other than nostalgia, to visit Branksome Hall.

Now they had something to brag about, and while EDM scolded them, to no avail, that a swimming pool would not be built until they bought more Branksome Hall bonds, she encouraged an emotional attachment to the school. "Bricks and mortar are all very well, but it's the *spirit* of the school that counts," Miss Read told her pupils, defining the four cornerstones of the school's spirit as truth, honesty, justice and purity.

The Branksome school flag.

Spirit, however, was invisible, and to celebrate Branksome Hall's twenty-fifth anniversary in 1928, Miss Read needed something more tangible. With the help of the prefects, she designed a school flag, two white crosses on a red background, with the school's circular crest, black on green, in the centre. "The cross of St. George is the Cross of Sacrifice," student Babs Goulding explained in the *Slogan,* "and the diagonal cross is the Cross of Service. Sacrifice and Service express in a condensed form the great purpose of Christ's life, and these are the two doors through which one must pass to attain happiness and spiritual growth."

Four flags were made up in plain colours representing the school's virtues — red for truth, green for honesty, black for justice and white for purity — with the school's crest in gold in the centre of each flag. "The colours of these four flags," said Babs Goulding,

> render it possible to weave in the Prefect's motto — "Live pure, speak true, right wrong" — a charge given by King Arthur to his knights. It is henceforth the duty of every one of us at Branksome so to live as to uphold the worthy ideals portrayed so well on our flag until the time comes when we shall entrust the torch to our successors. Therefore, "Serve God, keep well the road" in accordance with the ancient motto of Branxholme Castle:
>
> "In varld is nocht nature has vroucht yat sal lest ay. Thairfore serve God, keip veil ye rod, thy fame sal nocht dekay."

The previous year, Miss Read had visited Branxholme Castle in the Scottish border country, and this inscription, carved on the lintel over the main door, had made a deep impression on her imagination. She translated it this way: "In the world there is nothing nature has wrought that shall last forever. Therefore, serve God, keep well the road, thy fame shall not decay." In the sixteenth century, however, when this motto had been carved, "rod" meant "rood" or cross. Strictly speaking, it translated as "follow the cross," but Edith can be forgiven for her twentieth-century interpretation as "stick to the straight and narrow." The motto appealed to both her romanticism and her sense of Christian duty. "Have we not been so intent that the road should be more smooth and more wide that we have forgotten that it is the destination that is the real quest of life," she asked, "and that it is only those who keep the road who finally arrive at the desired destination, the destination of achievement, of the fullest development of one's character?"

The school's new motto, not yet official, was joined by a new school song, "Up and On," a poem written by John Oxenham in 1915 and set to music by Edmund Jones.

Lives are in the making here,
Hearts are in the waking here,
Mighty undertaking here,
    Up, and On!
We are arming for the fight,
Pressing on with all our might,
Pluming wings for higher flight,
    Up, and On!

Up then! Truest fame
Lies in High Endeavour.
Play the game! Keep the flame
Burning brightly ever!
Up then! Play the game!
    Up, and On!

Foes in plenty we shall meet,
Hearts courageous scorn defeat,
So we press with eager feet
    Up, and On!
Ever onward to the fight,
Ever upward to the light,
Ever true to God and right,
    Up, and On!

Up then! Truest fame
Lies in High Endeavour.
Play the game! Keep the flame
Burning brightly ever!
Up then! Play the game!
Up, and On!

GOD SAVE THE KING

The dedication of the flag ceremony in the gym in the autumn of 1928 brought everything together in an impressive ritual. "The Prefects, who were given the honour of placing the flags in their respective places, marched slowly into the gymnasium," the *Slogan* reported.

> The School Flag, carried by the Head Girl, led the procession, followed closely by the Union Jack and the Canadian Ensign. Directly behind these were the four other flags each representing a school colour symbolizing the four pillars of Branksome Hall, Truth, Honesty, Justice and Purity.
>
> When the flag bearers had taken their positions in a semi-circle on the platform, Miss Read and several members of the staff, wearing their hoods and gowns, took their places within the semi-circle of flags.
>
> The ceremony was opened with a short address by Miss Read, who explained the meaning of Our Flag, and at that very opportune time appointed four new Prefects, after which we sang the School Song. A slow march was then played and the four flags, which represent the pillars of the school, were carried to the four corners of the gymnasium respectively. Margaret Withers, our Head Girl, repeated a passage from the Bible taken by Philippians, IV:8:

> "Finally brethren, whatsoever things are true, whatsoever things are honest, whatsoever things are just, whatsoever things are pure, if there be any virtue, and if there be any praise, think on these things."

> As the words truth, honesty, justice and purity were repeated, the flags representing these were placed in their permanent positions. The ceremony was then ended by the singing of God Save the King.

The 1928 flag ceremony was so successful that to this day the Installation of the Prefects remains, with some changes, a highlight of the school year. The flags added colour and pageantry to Branksome Hall's public events, including the gym display, which moved to Varsity Arena in the spring of 1929. Gym teachers Donna Smellie and Mary Barker had spent the previous summer studying fundamental gymnastics in Denmark, and the more athletic Danish program replaced the Swedish

Prefects carrying flags, 1929.

exercises. The girls were still expected to exercise in full uniform, and while the school gym had rings, ropes and other apparatus, dancing and drills took precedence. Mary Barker taught basic swimming and lifesaving skills in the pool, which had been installed in 1926. "Branksome Hall was the first girls' school to have a pool," Mary recalled. "There was no competitive swimming. I didn't emphasize competition."

The school's population had grown to more than 250 students. Prefects and the head girl sported smart red blazers with white piping, and the head girl was distinguished by her tartan middy scarf. In 1930, Miss Read enhanced Branksome Hall's Scottish identity by dividing the students into eight "clans" with appropriate tartan banners. Boarders were assigned to clans McAlpine, MacGregor, Campbell and Douglas, day girls to Mcleod, MacLean, Ross and Stewart. The clans were a brilliant adaptation of the British boarding school "house" system, adopted by Havergal College two years before. Belonging to a clan gave the girls a sense of community, and clan rivalry encouraged participation in sports and other student activities.

"The clans were pure fiction!" laughed Betty Hire, who, as Mrs. Partridge, had returned to Branksome Hall to teach piano. "The girls had the school colours *implanted* in them. Miss Read was a wow at marketing. She had no self-consciousness. She didn't mind what she did if she was furthering her ends."

EDM wasn't shy about promoting herself either. Wearing a pince-nez, pearls and an expensive silk dress, her hair fashionably bobbed and waved, she sat for her portrait photograph, and soon the first of many pictures of Branksome Hall's principal joined the portraits of King George V and Queen Mary on the school's walls.

"Miss Read was fearsome looking," recalled Donald Deacon, "sharp as could be, and she had a super sense of humour. You could get into good discussions with her. She had no fear of anybody. Dad admired her as a businessperson; I thought she was fantastic."

Edith enjoyed the company of men, and when, in 1918, the Deacons

Basketball team, 1921.

Senior girls practise for Gym Demonstration.

Clan chieftains, 1937-38: Joan Franks, Margaret Parks, Phyllis Holden, Joan Mitchell, Dorothy Hoyle, Eleanor Reed, Mary Glendinning, Leona Comstock.

had moved to Glenhurst, a six-acre estate west of the school, she had become a part of their big, sociable household. Branksome Hall's sports days were held on the Deacons' spacious lawn, and some of Edith's inspiration may have come from Donald's grandfather, John Scott Deacon, a school inspector known for his ability to motivate children to learn. Edith still lived in a bed-sitting room at 10 Elm Avenue, but while she seems to have had no interest in marriage — "Married women lie around all day" was a characteristic comment — she enjoyed parties. She recruited Deacon boys and their friends as blind dates for her school dances, and when W.D. Ross was appointed Lieutenant-Governor of Ontario in 1927 — a social and political coup for Branksome Hall — Edith was a frequent guest at Government House.

Miss Read treated the men on her board of directors much as she did her pupils. She would announce what she was going to do, and they would reply "Yes, Miss Read." John A. Tory liked to joke, "If Miss Read were in business, I'd be her office boy." He was closer to the truth than he may have realized. Edith M. Read *was* in business, and she may have been the only woman in Canada to be president, chairman and chief executive officer of a corporation in which she was also the principal investor.

"Miss Read was one of the first feminists," said Betty Hire Partridge. "She could twist any man around her finger. They were wax in her hands." Miss Read didn't approve of married women teachers. "I only got on because my husband came from Nova Scotia," Betty laughed. EDM had a very practical reason for preferring single women teachers from Nova Scotia: they lived in the school. Classes at Branksome Hall ended at 1:15 p.m. The day girls went home, and after lunch, the teachers organized games for the boarders. They supervised the girls' study periods both afternoon and evening, ate with them daily in the dining room, a teacher sitting at the head of each table, and acted as both chaperones and housemothers. For a twenty-four-hour-a-day job, the teachers received, in addition to their modest salaries, free room and board.

The teachers were expected to patrol the halls after "lights out," but, not surprisingly, they fell asleep. Quiet as the mice that scurried through the dark halls, girls crept along the roofs to each other's rooms or lowered themselves out the windows on ropes made of bedsheets. While they were gone, other girls would hide disgusting things under their sheets — touching a dead bird with her feet made one girl hysterical — or leave notes warning "The Black Hand Was Here." The boarders, crowded five and six to a room, all hoarded contraband food in their grub boxes; if there was a birthday or something else to celebrate, the stale, sticky mess was transformed into a midnight feast. Jean Ross Skoggard, who went into boarding to get away from home, was more imaginative: "Our house on Crescent Road was only about a block away," she said, "and on our morning walk I'd run by the house and yell to the cook an order for éclairs to be delivered to the school in the afternoon. The chauffeur would drive over and leave a big, mysterious box for me with Miss McMichael. Midnight feasts were a lot of fun."

Edith Read's nephew, Tom Read, who later visited Branksome Hall on weekends when he was a student at St. Andrew's College, remembered the food fights in the school dining room on nights when Aunt Edith was entertaining the teachers in her private dining room. "They were the most outrageously badly behaved girls I've ever encountered," Tom said.

Inexperienced, ineffectual teachers fled the classroom in tears, terrorized by the girls' merciless teasing, and even ageing, deaf Violet Robinson, who had taught art history since Miss Scott's day, would find thumbtacks on the seat of her chair. "We felt sorry for Miss Robinson," Jean Ross Skoggard explained. "She wore so many woollies we thought she wouldn't feel the tacks." Jean liked Dorothy Phillips, her mathematics teacher, and Ruth Craig, who taught Latin. "You could always get Miss Craig to laugh," she said. Young English teacher Jennie MacNeill discovered that the girls did not share her enthusiasm for memorizing poetry, and she learned to entertain them by telling stories, albeit censored, about the Romantic poets' scandalous private lives.

At least Miss MacNeill wasn't apocalyptic, like the scripture teacher, Katherine "Armageddon" Armstrong. "Miss Armstrong had been a missionary in Burma," recalled Ruth Hamilton Upjohn, who graduated in 1929. "She was a fundamentalist. She'd hold up the Bible and say 'This is the Word!' She'd talk about the end of the world. A lot of parents were furious with her because she got the children so frightened." Miss Armstrong, however, had an admirer in Joan Morrow Rivington. "She influenced me very greatly," Joan said. "I had always been serious about religion. I could ask Miss Armstrong whatever I wanted, and she would reassure me." There were, however, sceptics. One morning Miss Armstrong found a note taped to her door: "Go back to Burma!" It was signed "God."

On Sunday evenings, Miss Read gathered the boarders in her drawing

Dorothy Phillips, Dorothy Campbell, 1935.

Ruth Craig, 1939.

room, the Blue Room, or, after 1929, in the new Common Room, to pray, sing hymns and listen to an uplifting talk by a missionary recently returned from Asia or Africa. "I *hated* Sunday nights!" said Gwynneth "Ginty" Sinclair Powell. "We always sang 'Abide with Me.' It was so gloomy, and we were all homesick."

The girls' parents, too, were willing to lay down the law. "We did what we were *told,"* said Ruth Hamilton Upjohn. "We didn't have our hair done. There was no lipstick or powder. I remember Mary Robertson had red nails. I was *fascinated* by this. We were simple little kids, when you think of it." Infractions — usually late homework — were punished by making the delinquent come in to write out lines of scripture on Saturday morning.

"I was terrified of Miss Read," said Eleanor Hamilton, who came to

Branksome Hall from a Rosedale public school in 1927. "She was a wiry little person, and when she'd come up to us in the schoolyard, we'd all freeze." At night, a light in Miss Read's window meant that Edith had seen, or heard, something suspicious, and she would soon be prowling the corridors in her pale blue kimono, flashlight in hand. Who knew which bedroom closets she flung open for inspection during the day? Her mere presence acted as a deterrent to unacceptable conduct, and she never berated or humiliated a pupil, or a teacher, in public. Parents whose daughters behaved like gangsters were quietly asked to withdraw their children from the school, and troublemakers could be refused the next year. It was a blessing, although a financial worry, that rebellious girls were free to go elsewhere.

EDM was respected for her tolerance. An alcoholic science teacher who dozed off, her head on her desk, after handing out class assignments, was not dismissed in disgrace, and if her students guessed the reason for her behaviour, nothing was said. Rather than punishing mischievous girls, Miss Read won them over by awarding annual prizes for integrity, perseverance, comradeship, courtesy and loyal co-operation. When Ginty's friends tried to involve her in pranks, Ginty thought "I can't break the rules, I've won the integrity prize!"

Miss Read's rewards were more practical too. Clan teams competed for cakes, and at the 11 a.m. recess, the girls could buy a sweet, sticky bun for five cents. The Chelsea buns were hoarded and traded for other treats, and boarders, whose buns were free, used them to entice day girls to smuggle in forbidden candy and chewing gum from Hooper's drugstore at the corner of Sherbourne and Bloor. "At recess, we danced to jazz piano in the gym," recalled Ruth Hamilton Upjohn. "You'd see the whole gym full of girls dancing. Miss Read was *always* at the basketball games. She wanted you to win. She *loved it* when we won at basketball or hockey." Ruth was captain of the team that won Branksome Hall's first Toronto girls' school basketball championship in 1929.

To girls like Ginty Sinclair, Miss Read was a friend. "When I was seven years old and in Grade One," Ginty recalled, "we had a French teacher who wore a black hat with a big hat pin and black buttoned boots. She had a very shrill voice, and I was petrified of her. One day when she had singled me out for some minor mistake, I ran out of the classroom and locked myself in a bathroom cubicle. She sent one of the pupils to get me, then came herself, but I would not come out. The next thing I knew, Miss Read was in front of the door saying 'Gwynneth, come out immediately!' I came! She asked me why I was hiding in the cubicle, and when I told her I was frightened of the teacher, she spoke to her. She never wore the hat, hat pin or boots again and modulated her voice from then on, especially to me! The nice thing about Miss Read, she always gave you the benefit of the doubt."

Ginty's mother had died when Ginty was two, not long after her younger sister, Muriel, was born. The girls, who lived down the street, walked to and from school together until their father remarried when Ginty was twelve. "Our stepmother decided we had to go into boarding," Ginty said. "We cried and made such a big fuss when we went home for weekends; we were only allowed to go home for holidays."

Boarding school, unhappily, was a handy place for parents to dump unwanted children. "There were a lot of children from divorced parents, children whose mothers had died," Ginty said. Miss Read didn't pry — "She didn't believe in psychology," Ginty noted — but she was sensitive to the girls' private miseries. When one American boarder's parents were killed in an accident, Miss Read arranged for the girl's four-year-old sister to come to live with her at the school.

Ginty was astonished when, in her graduating year, 1933, Miss Read asked her to be head girl. Ginty had taken part in her share of hijinks — "And I was one of the *good* ones," she said — and she thought she couldn't live up to the standard of conduct set by the girls who had gone before. Miss Read, however, saw that Ginty's sense of humour had made Ginty popular with the girls, and she knew everything that was going on. "I like different types," Miss Read told her.

"She and I worked together very well," Ginty said. "When some innovation was about to take place, she would ask 'What do the girls think?' The worst misdemeanour in those days was to tell off-colour jokes. Miss Read said, 'Gwynneth, we must take a definite stand against these jokes.' She thought it would be more effective if I, as Head Girl, stood on the platform beside her at prayers to bring the message home. While she was emphasizing to the girls about taking a definite stand, I noticed a standing lamp on the stage behind her. I reached back and pulled it forward just as she said the words *definite stand.* The whole school burst out laughing. Miss Read didn't know what they were laughing at, but the girls remembered the 'definite stand,' and hopefully the jokes were fewer as a consequence."

First day of school for Ginty Sinclair Powell '33 and Muriel Sinclair Osburn '34.

Miss Read was sympathetic to girls who didn't have the money to attend Branksome. Joan Morrow Rivington's physician father died suddenly in 1935, Joan's second year in the Senior School, leaving his young widow and three daughters in desperate financial straits. "It was her policy, as part of her Christian belief, to give scholarships to children in need," Joan said. Daughters of missionaries and clergymen attended free, and during the Depression, when many Rosedale families struggled to keep up appearances, Edith Read found the means to pay for their daughters' education. To this day, no one knows where the scholarship money came from. "It wasn't Miss Read's style to announce it or let the girls know," said Francean Campbell-Rich. Francean learned of her own financial support on her graduation day in 1938, when her aunt suggested she might thank Miss Read for the bursary she'd received for the past three years. Francean had no idea what a bursary was, and when she mentioned it, Miss Read made no comment at all.

"During the Depression, there was Old Money and No Money," Francean quipped. She knew both. When she was enrolled in Branksome at age nine in 1929, her parents, Austin and Alicia Campbell, were, she said, "socialites in the swim of Toronto." Austin, a junior partner with the brokerage firm D.S. Paterson, had invested his father's fortune in the stock market. When the market crashed in October, he was ruined. "I didn't understand what was going on," said Francean. "I didn't know we were rich. Daddy would give me five cents to buy a bun. That was it. I remember being driven to school by George the chauffeur a few days after the crash and mother saying coolly, 'George, I'm sorry, we have to let you go.' Everything began to collapse. Overnight, it was all gone."

In the spring of 1930, Austin Campbell was arrested. One of nine stockbrokers tried and convicted of conspiracy to manipulate the stock market, he was sentenced to two years in prison. Francean remembers her mother taking her to visit her father in Collins Bay penitentiary and the fierce quarrels that led to their separation and divorce after Austin's release.

Having a convict for a father was bad enough, but the taboo against divorce was so strong that in December 1936 King Edward VIII of England was compelled to renounce his throne for "the woman I love," the twice-divorced American Wallis Warfield Simpson. Miss Read was not censorious. After bouncing from school to school for five years, Francean, now living with her father, his mother and his sister, was welcomed back to Branksome. "I was not hurt," she said. "I didn't suffer any stigma, my father being in jail. It didn't reach me. I wasn't aware of the stigma of not having money. It was 'genteel poverty,' I guess you could call it. Every opportunity was there for me. Nobody stood in our way.

Under Miss Read, we could do anything, and she would help us do it."

Miss Read was busy buying real estate. W.D. Ross joked how Edith would glowingly describe to the Branksome board a piece of property she had her eye on. If anyone raised doubts, she'd announce, "Gentlemen, I've already bought it!"

In 1935, EDM bought a fifty-acre farm fronting on Yonge Street, about three miles north of the village of Richmond Hill at the Jefferson Road. Clansdale Heights, as she called it, adjoined the Toronto Ski Club, and the club agreed to open its cross-country trails on the Summit Golf Course to Branksome students. St. Andrew's College had already moved its campus to Aurora, only five miles farther north, and Miss Read may have bought her property, twenty miles from Toronto, as a possible future location for her school. In the meantime, "the farm," with its century-old board-and-batten farmhouse, served as an autumn picnic site and winter recreational opportunity for Branksome Hall boarders, prefects and senior day girls.

A busload of about forty girls left the school first thing Saturday morning and returned in the afternoon. Outings to "Ready Acres," as the girls dubbed it, were a lot of fun, but many of the girls had never skied before, and some of the trails, especially "Banana Peel Corner," were treacherous. The school nurse, Althea Faulkner, a stately figure with snow-white hair, patrolled the trails on skis in case of accidents.

"Nobody taught you how to ski," recalled Helen Franks Strathy, who still nurses an ankle hurt at Ready Acres. "There were injuries, but Miss Read admired girls who had initiative, who got into mischief. She wanted people to enjoy life." Edith herself had plenty of initiative, and by the time she was sixty, blithely indifferent to the risk of bruises, sprains and broken bones, she could ski farther and faster than most of her students. The sight of their redoubtable principal sprawled flat on her back in the snow was disconcerting to the girls, especially when the bus driver, helping an indignant Miss Read to her feet, called out, "Hop up, buttercup!"

Clansdale Heights, 1935–64.

Having fun at the farm.

The farm was one of the few places where EDM could let down her hair and have fun. She presented a much more formidable persona during school hours. Francean Campbell-Rich remembers Miss Read as "a tiny woman with grey hair that might have been a wig. A lot of people wore wigs in those days. Her expression was always one of surprise, as 'Oh, my goodness, I never heard of such a thing!' Of course, she'd seen everything. Her eyebrows were always up in her hair, and her chin pulled in tight, not military, but stern."

Miss Read.

Francean found her "distant" from the girls. "I never saw her in the school day except on the boardwalks. She never dropped into classes. You rarely saw her in the halls. She had an apartment upstairs, and that was her home. Nor were we ever invited up there. I don't know anyone who was."

By 1936, Edith thought she needed a home of her own. For $15,000, Branksome Hall Corporation had bought 16 Elm Avenue from the estate of Ella E.C. Smith, and in exchange for $6,000, Edith negotiated with the board a lifetime lease on the property. It was an arrangement destined, like her terms of employment, to cause the school grief, and it embroiled Miss Read in the first of many bitter altercations with the City of Toronto.

As a school, Branksome Hall was exempt from property taxes, and as far as Miss Read was concerned, this exemption applied to the principal's residence. But as far as the City of Toronto was concerned, 16 Elm Avenue was a private home, and in June 1937, the city sued the school for unpaid taxes. Miss Read countered by retaining a bed-sitting room for herself on the second floor and using the rest of the building for school purposes. The dining room, which seated twenty-four, became a lunch room for Senior School and resident teachers, the cook had a room near Edith's suite on the second floor and the maids and kitchen staff were housed on the top floor. The main-floor sitting rooms were available for student activities. Branksome Hall appealed the city's assessment to the Ontario Court of Revision, initiating a legal wrangle that would drag on for eight years.

Miss Read hated paying taxes of any kind — she was chronically in arrears on her income tax — and she was endlessly creative in finding ways to save money, attract students and get the most out of her staff. One June morning EDM accosted music teacher Betty Hire Partridge in the hall and barked, "Do you know shorthand and typing?" Betty said she had a smattering of business training. "Good," said Miss Read, "you'll be teaching the business and commercial class in the fall." "I spent an *intensive* summer at the Shaw Business College," Betty sighed. "I shudder to think what my students were exposed to. I was barely two chapters ahead in the textbook." EDM believed that anyone could do anything, and in Betty's case, she was right. Betty emphasized, "Miss Read never hesitated to take in girls with physical handicaps." Betty taught a student with petit mal, a mild form of epilepsy, and a girl with cerebral palsy: "She could read shorthand, but she could not write it. She typed with one finger, holding her hand with her other arm. She was slow but accurate, and she eventually got a job with the Ministry of Labour at Queen's Park."

Jane McPherson Kastner is one grateful graduate of the business and commercial program. "I wasn't doing well in school," Jane said. "My marks weren't good, and my parents expected me to get one hundred percent. I remember Miss Read saying, 'If one door doesn't open, you knock on another.'" Jane graduated first in her class, receiving as her prize the collected works of Shakespeare. "Miss Read was small but mighty," Jane said. "She ran a tight ship. That's why the girls were here."

Branksome revived its domestic science department, where senior students learned cooking, canning, household management, fine sewing and dressmaking. Home economics, as the course was usually called, reflected Branksome's traditions as well as the new reality that, if a girl's ambition was to be a homemaker, she could expect to manage without servants. It was a haven for girls in danger of failing or dropping out of school and for parents who wanted their daughters to be prepared for marriage. At Branksome, domestic science was an alternative to similar courses offered at community colleges such as Macdonald Hall in Guelph, but since it was not an accredited part of the provincial high school curriculum, it became known as the "arts" or "special" class. It produced wives and mothers who were gourmet cooks, in addition to professional caterers, fashion designers and interior decorators.

Miss Read was a stickler for social graces. Students stood to attention as a teacher entered the classroom. The class monitor called out "Miss Sime, girls," and the girls, jumping up, chorused "Good morning, Miss Sime!" They stood when asking or answering a question and when the teacher left the room. All the girls were taught to write, and reply to, formal invitations and, at dances, to introduce their blind dates, boys they had met only moments before, with the correct formula: "Miss Read, may I present . . . umm . . . ummmm. Ummm . . . may I present Miss Read."

Charles Tisdall recalled being among a busload of St. Andrew's College boys recruited as dates for a Branksome spring formal: "Dressed correctly in tuxedos and clutching wrist corsages purchased at a florist in Aurora, my fellow Andreans and I descended on the school. We streamed into the main building to be greeted by an attractive young person. In my innocence, I blurted, 'Are you my date?' The official greeter was the school's games mistress. She took each boy down the long hall to the festooned gymnasium, where I was introduced to my partner, Barbara Thomas, a student from New York. The music started, and before embarking on the dance floor, I asked my date if she had ever danced before. 'Of course, we all know how to dance, and you should too!' she said. 'Why did you come here if you didn't know how to dance?' But I didn't. Barbara attempted to show me what was expected of me. Somehow we 'floated' around the dance floor and, I think, enjoyed the evening. I was sixteen, and it was my introduction to boy-girl relationships."

Branksome girls were taught to speak up, and if they whispered or mumbled a message at prayers, they had to repeat it until it was clearly audible. EDM always spoke in a precise, emphatic manner, and she enforced her own rather idiosyncratic rules of pronunciation. "We were taught to say 'to*mah*to,'" recalled Joan Franks Macdonald. "Squirrel was 'squeerill,' and girls sounded like 'giddles.' Newfoundland was pronounced 'New-found-land,' and Toronto was always 'To-ron-*to*.'"

While Miss Read respected Margaret Scott's foresight in preparing her pupils to be both ladies and career women, she quietly ignored the delicate subject of "physiology and hygiene." Branksome Hall had a small infirmary, presided over by Miss Faulkner, and a consulting physician, Dr. Robert Macmillan, but the girls received no instruction in human anatomy or reproduction. The word *menstruation* was never spoken, and birth control, still officially illegal, was a subject unmarried women were not supposed to know about. "Innocents all, we looked to the Wise Ones to lead the way in What Every Girl Should Know," laughed Francean Campbell-Rich. "One such leader was Lori, who never lacked an audience for her messages. Enthroned on a leather-covered 'horse' in the gym, surrounded by her serfs, Lori demanded, 'How many of you know what the "curse" is?' Lori's lecture enlightened us, sort of, and eyes were opened, sort of."

From time to time, girls eloped, quit school to marry or disappeared, as they did at other high schools. Helen Franks Strathy was baffled when a friend left school suddenly for no apparent reason. "Years later," Helen said, "I learned that she was pregnant, and Miss Read sent her a gift for the baby."

A model of tact and discretion, EDM came up with inspired ways to deal with misbehaviour. Tired of girls hanging out on the fire escapes, she declared a "fire escape climbing day" and made them run up and down the fire escapes until they were exhausted. Soon after some boarders were caught pilfering cutlery and dishes from a local restaurant, protesting that they had only been taking "souvenirs," they complained to their teachers that jewellery and other cherished objects were being stolen from their dressers. The teachers returned their valuables, saying, "Oh, we were not stealing, we were just taking souvenirs." The girls got the point, and no one was punished.

The problems at Radcliffe may have made Edith especially sympathetic to girls having difficulties, but she was adamant that a girl blessed with a good brain should use it. Like Miss Scott, Miss Read made it her business to find out what her girls intended to do with their lives. "She was very angry with me," said Eleanor Hamilton. "I knew I was going into child care, but Miss Read wanted me to be a lawyer or a doctor. We had an argument. 'You're *foolish,'* she said. 'You're *very foolish!'"* Eleanor ignored her and became a pioneer in kindergarten education.

Unemployment and economic collapse had taught women that it could be risky to depend on a man, and by the end of the 1930s, women were challenging the status quo. Branksome alumna Eileen Magill had become the first woman in Canada to obtain a pilot's licence. In 1932, American aviator Amelia Earhart had flown solo across the Atlantic Ocean, equalling Charles Lindburgh's feat of 1927, and Earhart was trying to fly around the world in 1937 when her aircraft disappeared in the South Pacific. Earhart's short, tousled hair and pilot's uniform of pants, sheepskin jacket and helmet created a craze among fashionable women for comfortable man-tailored slacks, shirts and army-style shorts. For Branksome sports teams, EDM designed a one-piece green cotton uniform with a detachable skirt.

Everyone was reading "My Day," the chatty column in the *Ladies' Home Journal* written by Eleanor Roosevelt, First Lady of the United States. Eleanor, estranged from her husband, President Franklin D. Roosevelt, had built a career for herself as a lecturer, journalist and political activist famous for her liberal, even socialist, opinions. She was regularly voted the most admired woman in the United States, and close behind, in Canada, was Agnes Macphail, the first woman elected to Parliament. Agnes mocked men who spouted the old platitude that a woman's place was in the home. "A woman's place," Macphail retorted, "is any place she wants to be."

For adolescent girls, deciding where, and who, they want to be is always a perilous struggle, but EDM, creating Branksome Hall in her own muscular Christian image, paid scant attention to the painful power politics of her small, tight-knit, female community. "Girls could be very cruel if they knew they had the upper hand," said Joan Franks Macdonald. "Girls would be picked on, shunned. I was the butt of that. I'd be with two of my friends, and one would say 'Let's run away from Joan.' They'd take off, and I'd be left." As a prefect boarding in her final year, Joan was expected to supervise her table in the dining hall. "I dreaded it," she said. "The girls would start playing with their spoons, there'd be a terrible clattering. I'd get upset, and then they knew they had me. I couldn't keep order."

Since the girls all belonged to the same social class, pecking orders were based on scholastic achievement, personality, appearance and athletic ability. Junior girls developed "crushes" on seniors, much as they now worship pop music icons, and popular girls, often to their annoyance, were followed by a swarm of younger acolytes. Apart from dinner duty and handing out black marks for uniform infractions — no lipstick, no jewellery — prefects had few responsibilities, and the sports captain had more influence than the head girl, whose role was largely ceremonial. The clan chieftains, distinguished by their tams with tartan bands, ran the school's extra-curricular activities with the ferocity of a Highland blood feud.

"You were *supposed* to go into everything," Joan Franks Macdonald said, "and I liked games, even though I had two left feet." Teams were chosen according to the girls' abilities, and even the uncoordinated were expected to participate in clan sports. "You could always learn something about the game," Joan said, "and you *do* make the physical effort. It was a way younger and older girls could get to know each other."

Basketball team, 1940.
Back row: Margaret Buller, Winnie Clarke, Elizabeth Dickie.
Front row: Rosemary Baker, Margaret Smith, Alixe Hogg.

All the girls took part equally in school activities and had close friends throughout the school, but Branksome Hall followed the public school practice of streaming students into classes according to their examination results, encouraging intellectual snobs among the A students to look down on the rest, although girls in the B form, special and commercial courses had talents that examination marks did not measure. Each class elected a president, but there was no student council and no newspaper or debating society where the girls could freely express their ideas and opinions. Miss Read, an avid newspaper reader, spoke to the school about world events, but it would have been improper for her, a fierce Liberal herself, to introduce political discussions. Political beliefs, like religion and money, were considered private, and any controversy could ignite a chain reaction of student withdrawals. The closest Branksome came to politics during the 1930s were visits by the wives of two Canadian governors general, Lady Bessborough and Lady Tweedsmuir.

At home, however, many of the girls heard worried talk of fascism and communism, dictatorships in Spain, Italy and Germany, the invasion of Austria and Czechoslovakia by the German army and the persecution of Jews by the Nazis in Germany and German-occupied countries. One of these girls was a Jewish student, Joyce Frankel. Joyce's parents were actively involved in helping Jewish refugees, but Canada's immigration policy was summed up in these cynical words: "None is too many." When Joyce arrived at Branksome in Grade Five in 1937, an ignorant girl accused her of "killing Christ." Joyce set her straight, and they became fast friends. Patricia Morrow Morley recalled that having Jewish classmates opened many girls' eyes to their own prejudices and liberalized their attitudes.

Prime Minister Mackenzie King, however, admired German dictator Adolf Hitler and supported the British policy of appeasement. Europe seemed far away, and for Branksome families who annually vacationed there, "the continent" was a magical land of castles and deluxe hotels, operas, concerts, galleries, country homes and five-star restaurants. In Rosedale, Branksome girls in formal gowns danced to live orchestras in private ballrooms, idled away their summers at camps or at cottages in Muskoka and, in their graduating year, squabbled to get into Branksome Hall's annual Christmas pageant.

The nativity pageant or, more accurately, tableau was the climax of the school's Christmas Carol Service. Since 1922, the service had grown from a simple sing-along into a spectacular chorale at St. Andrew's Presbyterian Church. A massed choir of three hundred girls, having practised for weeks, sang the old, favourite carols in a church packed with parents, teachers and alumnae. As they began the last carol, girls dressed as shepherds, magi, Joseph and Mary, carrying a doll-like Jesus, materialized as if by magic in the gallery over the altar. Behind them stood angels in white robes, their towering, gauze-covered wings illuminated by a blue floodlight. "My sister Helen was always an angel in the Christmas pageant," Joan Franks Macdonald recalled. *"I never was an angel!* You had to be blonde to be an angel. I wasn't a blonde, so I wasn't an angel." Helen matter-of-factly replied, "I was an angel because I was nearly six feet tall, with long blonde hair, and I had no voice."

In their own way, Branksome students were learning the power of stereotypes, and their eyes were opening to the world. "During the Lenten season we collected $50 for the Jewish refugees in Germany," the Opheleo society reported in 1939. The Opheleo society — *opheleo* is Greek for "I serve" — had been formed in 1931 to incorporate all the school's charitable causes. "Because of the house girls eating plainer food," Gladys Baalim reported, "we saved $40 which was added to the collections of Ramabai Week. We were able to send $200 in all to the Ramabai mission for the support of the child widows of India."

The Ramabai mission provided a refuge for women escaping *suttee,* the practice of forcing widows to immolate themselves on their husbands' funeral pyres. By starving themselves to save a dollar, the girls were learning a shocking lesson about how women were treated in a different culture. In addition to Ramabai, they helped to support an Indian orphan, a teacher and a hospital, and they distributed Christmas hampers to Toronto's poor.

"At present, mankind is living in fear, dictators are ruling with a stern and harsh hand," *Slogan* editor Joy MacKinnon wrote in the spring of 1939.

> People are persecuted for their religion; the right of free speech is no longer universal. Old democracies have fallen and many 'isms' are swaying the world. Although affairs are at a dangerous crisis and threats of war terrify and sadden many hearts, now as in the past we must faithfully continue to believe that in the end the "earth shall be filled with the glory of the Lord as the waters cover the sea."

Chapter Three

Germany's blitzkrieg invasion of Poland on September 1, 1939, followed by Great Britain's declaration of war on Germany on September 3, caught Canada unprepared. Prime Minister Mackenzie King was still personally committed to "peace at any price," and Canada, like Great Britain, had turned a deaf ear to Nazi threats and propaganda. The United States chose not to become embroiled in what most Americans saw as a European conflict. As soon as Winston Churchill, determined to defy Hitler, had become British prime minister, an overwhelming majority of Canadians had supported Great Britain, but Canada did not declare war against Germany until September 10.

During the summer of 1939, Edith Read's thoughts were on battles closer to home. Some City of Toronto councillors were threatening to tax all the private schools, and Edith began to consider building a new Junior School outside city limits. It may have been during a trip up Yonge Street to visit the school farm that she spied an attractive nineteen-acre property for sale in the Hogg's Hollow area of the municipality of North York. The land, with trees, shrubs and a shallow stream that fed into the Don River, was only a few miles from downtown Toronto and could be easily reached by streetcar. It looked like an ideal location, and Edith bought the property in May for $1,000 an acre. She paid $5,000 cash and took a mortgage for the remaining $14,000 at four percent interest.

Miss Read had bought the property without consulting her board of directors, and at their next meeting on June 2, she casually offered to sell

Hogg's Hollow property, 1939–48.

it to the school for the price she had paid for it. The minutes of this meeting state that, "After some discussion, the Board refused to accept this proposed gift."

What a shock! The instigator of the revolt was probably the newest member of the board, J.S. McLean, the owner and president of Canada Packers. A self-made businessman accustomed to making his own decisions, McLean would not have appreciated Miss Read's high-handed conduct, and it no doubt appeared to the board that Edith intended to saddle the school with nearly $1,000 a year in mortgage payments for a piece of swampy ground in the middle of nowhere.

Miss Read's passion for speculating in real estate would come back to haunt Branksome Hall, but Edith, with her uncanny sense of timing, had come up with a more popular innovation: a new school uniform. The

The New School Uniform

●

THE school uniform now consists of a kilted skirt of the Royal Stewart hunting tartan, a beige cotton blouse, tartan tie, long beige lisle hose, dark bloomers and a navy school blazer

These articles are sold only at the school and may be procured when the pupils enter in September. There is also a summer uniform of green cotton which, however, is not obligatory.

PRICE LIST

Skirt	$4.50
Blouse	2.00
Hose	.75
Bloomers	.50
Tie	.50
Summer Uniform	4.00
Blazer	6.00

The picture on the opposite page shows one of the prefects wearing the school uniform. She is playing the bag-pipes as teaching the bag-pipes was introduced this year.

Lib Dickie models the new school uniform, 1939.

middy, born in the First World War, had become dated, and the sailor image didn't mesh with the school's emerging Scottish identity. The inspiration may have come from one of Edith's many visits to Scotland, the sight of a little girl wearing a kilt or a suggestion from her dressmaker, but by 1939 she had designed a new uniform for Branksome students: a dark green Hunting Stewart kilt topped by a beige cotton shirt and Stewart tie. Prefects were outfitted with red Royal Stewart kilts, matching ties and red blazers. On ceremonial occasions, the clan chieftains and head girl wore tartan sashes, known as plaids, draped over their left shoulders. Hems were precisely three inches above the knee.

Kilts in the royal colours were a source of tremendous pride to Branksome students (and of envy to others) in the patriotic autumn of 1939. Any British subject was entitled to wear Hunting Stewart, but the red Royal Stewart kilts signalled the school's connection with the owner of Branxholme Castle, the Duke of Buccleuch, a descendant of the Duke of Monmouth, an illegitimate son of England's King Charles II.

The kilt, a masculine garment with a bloody military history, was a provocative choice for a sheltered girls' school in Toronto but appropriate for a country at war. In Canada, however, war meant doing without, among many things, woollens from Scotland. "The material was crummy," recalled Mary Craig Tasker. "The pleats were shallow and lost their shape." The kilt was little more than a wrap-around skirt, the shirt a one-piece cotton romper that fastened with two buttons at the crotch. "They were dreadful things," shuddered Diana Beck Bolté. "They were starched, and they shrank. We undid the buttons." Junior girls could wear green knee socks, but senior girls were expected to wear beige lisle stockings. They were ugly, and it may have been the school's secretary, Ainslie McMichael, infuriated by the sight of girls constantly hitching up their sagging stockings, who persuaded Miss Read to allow all the girls to wear knee socks. The socks, of course, also sagged, and the girls rolled them down to make bobby socks.

Edith Read and Ainslie McMichael, 1920s.

By 1940, Ainslie McMichael had become as much a Branksome Hall institution as Miss Read herself. They had both arrived at Branksome more than thirty years before, Ainslie as student, Edith as teacher, and they shared a deep bond of loyalty and affection. Edith's appearance had changed very little over the years, but Ainslie, now in her forties, had grown into a huge, intimidating figure with a lantern jaw, immense bosom and loud, gruff manner. Together, they looked like the comic strip characters Mutt and Jeff, and the girls, who guessed that Miss McMichael was more bark than bite, nicknamed her "Chamberlain" after the bear in the Jack Benny radio comedy.

Seated to Miss Read's right in the school office, a cat in her lap, Ainslie McMichael ran Branksome Hall like a sergeant-major, bellowing a constant stream of orders and admonitions to girls as they passed in the hall. The most terrifying thing about being "sent to Miss Read" was Miss McMichael, and Ainslie was unsparing in her criticism of the girls' dress, manners and pronunciation. Woe betide the student who fidgeted, or failed to say "please," or asked *"Can* I use the telephone?" Ainslie stood guard over the school's only telephone, stored the boarders' valuables and handed out black marks for rudeness, tardiness and running in the halls. She knew every student by name, and she knew their mothers and grandmothers too. As Miss Read's Gorgon at the gate, Miss McMichael knew everything that was going on in the school, and it was likely Ainslie who tipped Edith off about girls who were having personal problems or troubles at home. Even Ainslie's handwriting was larger than life. As one father quipped, "She's the only woman I know who shouts when she writes."

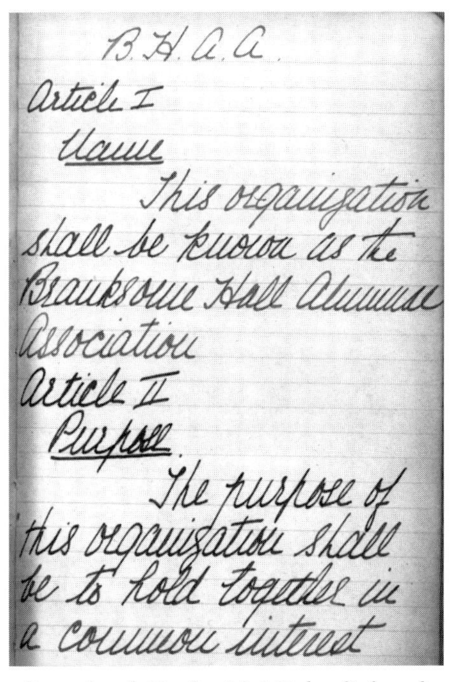
B.H.A.A.
Article I
Name
This organization shall be known as the Branksome Hall Alumnae Association
Article II
Purpose.
The purpose of this organization shall be to hold together in a common interest

Sample of Ainslie McMichael's handwriting in the Alumnae Constitution.

The "phoney war" was a period of eerie calm in Canada. Men and boys enlisted in the armed forces and went away to boot camp, but apart from raising money and knitting socks for the Red Cross, Branksome girls seemed to have little to do except sing "For Those in Peril on the Sea" at prayers. Even when the German army, virtually unopposed, invaded Denmark, Belgium and Holland in the spring of 1940, Canadians assumed that Britain and France would stop the German advance. French defences, however, collapsed, and the German occupation of France forced the British army to evacuate in disarray at the port of Dunkerque on the English Channel. France surrendered to Germany on June 22, 1940.

The fall of France was to have a swift, astonishing impact on Branksome Hall. Bridget Gregson Lawson, then a fourteen-year-old student at Sherborne School for Girls in Dorset, England, noted how it came about. "I was at home on compassionate leave because my father had been at Dunkerque," Bridget recalled. "One morning at the breakfast table, he read out a letter from Sherborne School saying that it was thinking of establishing a branch in Canada in the quiet, cathedral town of Kingston, Ontario. My father said my sister and I should go. He feared a German invasion. We thought it was great — cowboys, Indians — that's all we knew about Canada. I had been at boarding school since I was seven, so it didn't seem a huge thing to do, plus 'the war will be over by Christmas' attitude was very prevalent, in spite of the fact we might be invaded."

Fears of a German invasion were scoffed at, but they were realistic. Sherborne School was less than one hundred miles across the English Channel from the German-occupied port of Cherbourg, and the prospect that its students might be raped, tortured and murdered by German troops was horrifying for both teachers and parents. The school's plan was to send girls to Canada in stages — about 280 volunteered — beginning immediately with a group of twenty-seven.

The exodus was masterminded by Sherborne School's headmistress, H.V. Stuart, with the help of Viscount Bennett of Mickleham, Calgary

These English evacuees have just arrived to attend Branksome Hall, 1940.

and Hopewell (formerly Canadian prime minister R.B. Bennett), who made arrangements through the Canadian Red Cross, and Major Ney, Executive Secretary of the National Council for Education in Canada. Miss Stuart put the girls in the care of a twenty-seven-year-old Sherborne teacher, Diana Reader Harris, a gym mistress, Betty Lee-Evans, and house matron Jean Ross Sanderson.

The Sherborne girls sailed for Montreal on the *Duchess of Atholl* at the end of June. "It was a horrible crossing," Bridget recalled. "We were down on E deck in the bowels of the ship. A lot of people were seasick — and homesick." The *Duchess of Atholl* was packed with hundreds of frightened children being sent to relatives and guardians in Canada. Many were travelling without adult companions, including eight-year-old Patricia Cave, in sole charge of her six-year-old brother and his six-year-old friend. These children, as well as other shipboard orphans, attached themselves to Sherborne School.

At sea, the Sherborne girls learned that they would be going to Toronto, not Kingston, and their likely destination would be another

Anglican girls' school, Bishop Strachan. "We didn't know until we got off the train at Union Station that we'd be going to Branksome," said Bridget. "There was Miss Read, her secretary, a very tall lady, and all these wonderful-looking Canadian alumnae she'd rallied around. The alums were young, about eighteen or nineteen, and they looked so glamorous to us."

In fact, Miss Read, Miss McMichael and the Branksome alumnae were meeting not only the Sherborne girls but also girls and boys from other British boarding schools who were arriving in Toronto with no place to live. In their eagerness to help the war effort, influential Canadians were arranging to evacuate children from Great Britain before they had found proper accommodations for them in Canada. There had been no welcoming committee for the Sherborne girls in Kingston, and in Toronto, all schools, including Branksome Hall, were closed for the summer. Only days before, Edith Read had been settling in at her ocean-front cottage at Boutilier's Point, Nova Scotia.

The Department of External Affairs, through Vincent Massey, High Commissioner to Great Britain, was monitoring the British evacuation via coded cable messages between London and Ottawa. By good fortune, Edith's brother John Erskine Read, formerly Dean of Law at Dalhousie University, was legal advisor to O.D. Skelton, Deputy Minister of External Affairs. John alerted Edith, and she returned immediately to Toronto to reopen her school as a clearing house for the British evacuees. Before the *Duchess of Atholl* was in the mid-Atlantic, Miss Read was ready to receive her war guests.

Branksome, like other private schools, was already boarding English students who had been stranded on vacation in Canada when war broke out. The girls at Branksome were from Harrogate, and 14 Elm Avenue, once French House, had been renamed Harrogate in their honour. Miss Read was on cordial terms with the other girls' schools — she had been elected president of the Canadian Headmistresses' Association in 1934 — and Branksome, BSS and Havergal worked in concert with the boys' schools, churches, charities, Rotary International and the University of Toronto to make sure all the children were properly housed. Space was found at summer camps — Bridget went to Camp Tanamakoon — and students' parents invited the English children to their cottages.

"We've had a remarkable response," Miss Read told the *Toronto Telegram.* "Everybody has been so kind. The telephone rings incessantly with offers of homes." The *Telegram* reporter, who met the children at Union Station, commented that "The arrival of the first 'guests of Canada' was an inspiration here to everyone, and a feeling of gratitude arose for the chance to lend a hand in this way to the Motherland."

Twelve hundred children were expected to arrive in Toronto within two weeks, and Miss Read intended to have them all placed in private homes within forty-eight hours of arrival. Sherborne School, however, posed a problem. Miss Stuart, who was organizing a second group of fifty evacuees in England, insisted that her Sherborne branch in Canada remain an autonomous boarding school.

"We thought we'd be 150 and independent of Branksome in teaching," Diana Reader Harris recalled later. "Miss Stuart thought she'd be able to go on paying in money. But we were informed by the Toronto banks that the money we had was the only money we would have. There was a moment when we knew that the next day we could no longer exchange pounds, frightened that even the money we'd got was going to be taken away. By early July, we were dependent on Branksome."

The British government's decision to freeze the export of sterling stranded the Sherborne exiles in Canada without a cent. Miss Stuart, a formidable classics scholar and a personality best described as "indomitable," was undeterred. "Miss Stuart was angry at the idea that we'd be in different homes in the city and be day girls," Diana Reader Harris recalled. "We could not phone but sent cables and long letters. By July 23, plans were still fluctuating."

"There are still about 60 girls at Branksome Hall who have no place to go," the *Telegram* reported in mid-July.

> The cost of maintaining this establishment is being met by the directors and friends of the school and by the alumnae. "We've had to make rapid changes," Miss Read said laughingly. "It was suddenly necessary to get a permanent staff, particularly a cook and someone in the office to answer the telephone, but everybody has been so kind and our visitors are perfect guests. They look after their own bedrooms, wait on each other in the dining room and have organized themselves into regular working units."

Only about a third of the girls living at Branksome were Sherborne girls, but Diana Reader Harris was acutely aware that Miss Read was going to a great deal of trouble and expense on their behalf: "Miss Read was there the whole time. She was awfully generous. She had no holiday at all." Miss Stuart, fortunately, abandoned her plans to send more girls — the danger of ships being torpedoed by German submarines was far greater than the threat of invasion — and on July 27, 1940, Stuart, as she called herself, cabled LC Reed, as she called Edith MacGregor Read: "We find it difficult to express adequately our gratitude."

Miss Read and Diana Reader Harris agreed that the Sherborne students and staff would integrate with Branksome Hall classes in September and that the Sherborne staff would be paid the equivalent of their higher English salaries. To cover this cost, the girls' parents paid £150 annually to Sherborne School in Dorset, on the understanding that the money would be forwarded to Branksome Hall as soon as permitted. The Sherborne girls would wear their English uniforms, attend St. Paul's Anglican Church and live together in their own house.

On August 3, 1940, Diana Reader Harris noted in her diary, "Perfect house, oil heating, electric stove, couldn't be better, rent free." The empty house at 40 Maple Avenue was also being sought by another English school, St. Hilda's College, and it must have taken all of Miss Read's persuasive skills to get a two-year lease at the end of August. It was unfur-

Sherborne students, 1940s (Diana Reader Harris in centre wearing dark coat).

nished, and Miss Read pleaded with friends, neighbours and alumnae to scour their basements and attics for chairs, carpets, curtains and dishes. Eaton's supplied double-decker bunk beds.

"We do the washing up and cleaning of the rooms ourselves," Angela Riddell wrote in her diary the day she moved in. "The house is big with lovely large rooms. There is a large garden with two tennis courts and a lot of flowers. In the afternoon we sat and wrote letters in the greenhouse which is attached to the house." In her diary, Angela listed "New Things Learned in Canada": "Petrol is called gasoline, ie, gas; food rubbish is garbage, lorries are called trucks, chemists are called drug stores, comics are funnies, lifts are elevators, prams are baby carriages. . . ." Angela also noted that "There are a lot of mosquitos in hot, damp weather."

As well as learning to understand Canadian English, the girls had to adjust to unfamiliar food — peanut butter, maple syrup, hot dogs, hamburgers, watermelon, and drinks like Coca-Cola and Honey Dew — and their food was often served in such huge portions that some girls, knowing how strictly food in England was rationed, were shocked. "If we felt uncomfortable about the lavish food and luxurious life, this was often just a part of feeling guilty for being away at all," said Elva Parkinson Carey, a Sherborne student who arrived in Toronto at age eleven. Some of the English girls were troubled by secret doubts. Were they running away? Shouldn't they be in England to help out? Did their parents not want them? Forty years later, compiling *A Very Hard Decision,* her documentary history of the English war guests at Branksome Hall, Elva discovered that, while most parents had cited fear of invasion as their reason for sending their children to Canada, other factors had played a part: "First, personal ones, including family deaths, illness, rocky marriages and the desire to be free to do war work. It could be convenient that we went."

Both Branksome and Sherborne girls came from upper-middle-class professional families, but they were separated by a cultural chasm. Angela Riddell described her first encounter with Branksome students on September 10, 1940: "We got up in djibbahs [Sherborne uniform] and went over to the school after breakfast. All the day girls were there arranging their lessons. The girls in our form were terrifically tall and grown-up looking; actually, they were seventeen and eighteen some of them! They were all dressed up and had piles of lipstick all over their mouths. We were allowed to talk in the passages, and consequently there was a terrific hullabaloo. We got some exercise books and when we got back took some very nice Branksome girls 'round the house."

The Sherborne girls were one to three years younger than their Canadian classmates. They were young for their age, naïve about boys and shy with adults. At the same time, they were fiercely competitive in games — they ran Branksome's best athletes off their feet — and self-confident in class. On September 16, 1940, Angela wrote, "We had terribly boring lessons as none of the Canadians seem to ask any questions. I am right in front so I have to behave myself." Their accents set them apart, and their shapeless uniform — green jumper, white blouse and beige cotton stockings — made them feel frumpy. "We were conspicuous too for our brown felt pudding basin hats," said Elva Parkinson Carey, "but the hats had a way of 'blowing away' on the bridge across the ravine."

The "little England" enclave of Sherborne girls at 40 Maple Avenue was unusual. Some of Branksome's one hundred war guests boarded in the school, but most were day girls living with Rosedale families. Jean Ingham, who arrived from Staffordshire at age fourteen in August 1940, was billeted with two unmarried sisters, Ann and Margaret Laidlaw, at 32 North Sherbourne Street. Jean wrote home regularly, and her letters give an intimate glimpse into the daily life of a war guest. "Last Friday the Sherborne girls entertained quite a lot," she wrote on September 30, 1940.

> First, in the afternoon, they gave a demonstration lacrosse game to show the Canadian girls how it was played and quite a lot of them are keen on learning. Then at night they gave some sketches and a play. They were about the war, the blackout, the air-raid shelters, and one was about a German girls' school. The girls in this all came in marching goose-step after their teacher and sat down in a row of chairs. They were asked various questions, such as "Who discovered the North Pole?" or "Where will Hitler be tomorrow? Where will he have dinner?" To these the answers were: "Hitler, London and Buckingham Palace." They stood up to answer each question all together, and when it was answered the teacher said "Sit." They also did a play called "The Scarlet Coconut" which was very good. By the way, did I tell you that I am to learn to play lacrosse and Miss Read the headmistress is arranging special swimming lessons for the English girls who can't swim so I am going to be quite energetic especially if I play basketball as well.

The Battle of Britain was raging, and while Canadians anxiously read the newspapers and listened to the radio, having the English girls in the school gave the Canadian students a much more personal appreciation of the threat of German victory. "Miss Stuart saw that it was to Branksome Hall's *benefit* to take in Sherborne students," said Elva Parkinson Carey. Certainly, Diana Reader Harris, a glamorous and charismatic English teacher, left a lasting imprint on her students, and she encouraged Branksome's tradition of writing and performing plays. The highlight of the 1941 school year was a performance of *1066 and All That.*

"We had decided to let outsiders come and take a silver collection afterwards so we played to a packed hall," Jean Ingham wrote home on October 19, 1941. "Everything went well and I think that the audience just loved it. I wish we could do it again as it was loads of fun. We collected $119.75 which we gave to the fund for sending parcels to war prisoners in Germany. Not bad eh? (Not many gave *silver.*)"

Jean enclosed several newspaper clippings, one of them praising the performance, directed by Diana Reader Harris, as "a masterpiece — hilarious, satirical, musical, colorful and very, very funny." Another clipping showed Princess Alice, wife of Canada's governor general, the Earl of Athlone, surrounded by an honour guard of prefects on Branksome Hall's front steps. "Princess Alice," Jean wrote,

> was a very gracious lady and made a nice, short speech and also gave us a holiday to be taken whenever it is convenient for us (a very nice woman). Then on Thursday a man came to lecture to us about the Jews. It seems that he was a Jew who turned Christian. He is a minister now, I think, and he also helps get the Jews out of countries where they are being persecuted (rather like a Scarlet Pimpernel idea). He gave us a very interesting talk on his experiences.

At a time when Canada was confining Jewish refugees from Britain to concentration camps, it was typical of Miss Read to follow the visit of an English princess with a lecture on the Holocaust, even if the speaker was

Princess Alice with Head Girl Isobel Coulthard (Mary Stuart Playfair front left, Shirly Milner Brown front right), 1941.

a Christian convert. She also saw to it that the girls attended a Toronto concert by the black American bass baritone, Paul Robeson. "The concert was magnificent," one of the English girls wrote in her diary. "He has an amazing physique — the broadest shoulders. His voice is stupendous, and he put so much energy into his singing that at one point a little drop of sweat rolled down his neck, over his collar and down his coat." Canadians were more tolerant of "coloured" people than Americans at this time, but racial discrimination was practised in many ways. Having Branksome students attend the Robeson concert was EDM's way of giving them a subtle lesson in social justice, and it may have been Robeson who inspired Miss Read to take under her wing a young black contralto from Truro, Nova Scotia, Portia White.

Portia, the daughter of a Baptist clergyman, had begun singing in her father's church choir. After his death, she taught school to help support her family, but she continued to take lessons and win prizes in local music festivals. Portia dreamed of becoming a concert singer, and early in the war, she was awarded a scholarship to the Halifax Conservatory of Music to study under its new director, Ernesto Vinci. After a recital in the conservatory's concert hall in August 1941, Portia and Dr. Vinci were greeted by a tiny woman, full of life and sparkle, who introduced herself as Edith Read.

"Dr. Vinci, we must do something about this child's voice!" said Miss Read. "Why is she hiding away in Halifax? It's time people heard her sing."

"When I'm ready, we plan to go to New York," Portia replied.

"I have influential friends there," added Dr. Vinci.

"Why New York, may I ask?" said Miss Read, turning on Dr. Vinci. "Portia White is a Canadian. She must begin her career right here in Canada. Toronto! There's the centre of things!"

"But I don't know anyone there," said Portia.

"That's quite all right," said Miss Read. "I know everyone you need. You can stay with my girls."

"Portia is still very young," said Dr. Vinci.

"Exactly!" said Miss Read. "People will love her. I know just the dress she must have. Leave it to me, I'll arrange it."

Returning to Toronto, Edith called her dressmaker, booked the chic, Art Deco Eaton Auditorium for the night of Friday, November 7, and mobilized her alumnae to sell tickets to Portia White's Toronto debut. In case anyone was sceptical that Portia was just another of her Cinderellas from Nova Scotia, Miss Read advertised the recital as a charitable benefit for war work. Who could refuse?

Portia, exquisite in a long gown of eggshell silk, sang songs by Beethoven, Brahms, Schubert and Mozart, closing with a Verdi aria and four rousing spirituals. She caused a sensation. Her successful recital led to a

Mrs. F.R. MacAloney, Mrs. Alistair Fraiser, Portia White, and Dr. Edith M. Read at reception following White's concert at the Lord Nelson Hotel, Halifax.

cross-Canada concert tour capped by a triumphant American debut, sponsored by Miss Read, at New York City's Town Hall. "A wonderfully rich, well-placed, natural voice with great charm," wrote the *New York Times.* Said critic Henry Simon, "She has one of the finest contralto voices to reach New York since Marian Anderson, with whom comparisons are inevitable."

Branksome Hall no longer taught music, but Miss Read wangled free tickets to Massey Hall so her girls could hear Pablo Casals, Yehudi Menuhin, Artur Rubenstein, Jascha Heifetz and the Toronto Symphony Orchestra. They attended operas, ballets and plays, and senior girls were allowed to go, unchaperoned, in groups of three or four. On weekends, they went to jazz and pop concerts, to dances at the Granite Club or Casa Loma and, at every opportunity, to the movies. On Saturdays, they raised money for war charities by tagging passersby at Yonge and Bloor, and older girls helped out at the Red Cross and soldiers' canteens. One or two girls became engaged. They wore their rings on chains around their necks under their shirts.

Branksome Hall had become a cosmopolitan community, a haven for girls whose families had fled the Middle East and Malaysia, South America and the West Indies, and it was bursting at the seams. In November 1941, Miss Read was able to purchase 3 Elm Avenue, a handsome old house across Huntley Street, for a bargain price of $19,000. The house had been put on the market by the Toronto General Trust Company under power of sale — the owner had defaulted on the mortgage during the Depression — and the price may have been reduced to less than half the property's value as a gift to the school. Miss Read named it Sherborne House in honour of her English war guests, and she renovated it as a residence for boarders in their graduating year.

The generosity of the Branksome community toward their English war guests was boundless, and nobody expected a penny in return. The

From the back garden of Sherborne House (3 Elm Avenue), 1941.

girls were handsomely housed, clothed and fed, their fees were paid and their uniforms were purchased. They were inoculated, treated for measles and mumps and taken to the dentist free of charge. They were sent to summer camp, given private skating, skiing and music lessons and taken shopping. The girls were grateful but embarrassed, and they felt constrained to be always on their best behaviour. "It was not a normal way to grow up," said Bridget Gregson Lawson. "There was nowhere we could go and slam a door or have a good cry. We had to be polite all the time since we were guests." They couldn't turn to their mothers for advice — letters home were lost, late or censored, phone calls were forbidden — so when it came to those two urgent adolescent problems, boys and clothes, they were on their own.

"On February 7 is the Branksome Hall School Dance," Jean Ingham wrote home in January 1941,

> and I'm not sure whether to go or not for these reasons. First, you have to take your own partners (boys) and second it is in long dress. Both these really can be remedied because I can have a blind date. That's a date with a boy without having seen him. I think Miss Read is getting some for the boarders who do not know anyone to ask. Then I have had three offers from girls at school to lend me a dress if I go, and just the other day the mother of an English girl at Branksome who is staying with some friends of the Laidlaws said I could borrow a dress which Hope had grown out of and as she has reddish hair it will suit me I suppose though I have not seen it yet. I am not sure that I like the idea of the blind date but I still may go.

On February 9, Jean wrote again:

> Since the other letter there has been the School Dance which I am very glad to have got over with. You know that it was my

first big dance and I am not very used to mixing with boys? Well for the last few weeks I have been scared stiff thinking of it and I used to nearly dream at night about what I was going to talk to the boy about. I had to put my name down at school for a blind date, but I did not really ask about the boy's name or anything until about the day before. When I did, I found they had lost the list of "blinds". The girl said that she would phone me at about 4:30 on Friday, the day of the dance, but a girl came up to me while I was still hovering around and said, "You're going to have Larry Rogers, aren't you?" I said, "I don't know, am I?" She told me to wait a minute and went up to the girl who was arranging the dates. Then she said, "Oh Jean, you will have Larry Rogers." I was then told that the girl he was going to go with had come down with the measles so they were trying to get someone for him. Hope Davie, the English girl, had lent me a dress. It was white net with red ribbons on it and it was really sweet. I had curled my hair and it really looked quite nice.

Well I got ready to go by 8:30 and I went to the school to Doreen and Daphne Martin's room. I had been told to meet the girls who would introduce me to Larry Rogers at 9 o'clock. He was rather a queer boy, quite nice looking with fair wavy hair but he had a rather high voice and was a little bit girlish. He was a very good dancer so that was all right. He didn't really talk much and though at first I tried to keep a conversation up I at last said, "I hope you don't mind me being silent but I really don't know what to talk about." He said he didn't mind as he liked to dance in silence sometimes, so that was all right. We still talked a bit between times. The supper wasn't really bad. It was a kind of jelly with meat and peas and stuff in it with a piece of lettuce as well (a Canadian salad).

> I didn't eat all of it as I wasn't very hungry but I ate the icecream and drank the coffee. We also drank two glasses of fruit punch (that isn't an intoxicating drink, it's just fizzy fruit stuff). When I got back I just went straight to bed (it was 2 o'clock) and went to sleep. The next day I went skiing so I have really had a very strenuous weekend.

Jean loved the ski trips to the school farm, Clansdale Heights, especially after supper when they skied by moonlight, and she didn't tell her parents that on Saturdays they shared the trails with handsome Norwegian airmen who skied without their shirts. Jean ended her letter with "Yours til the bobby pin gets seasick on a permanent wave. P.S. Bobby pin means hair pin here."

Blind dates and pincurls, twin sets, pearls, short shorts, Max Factor makeup and perms — the English girls, like it or not, were growing up Canadian. The Sherborne School girls were graduating and returning home, going on to the University of Toronto or becoming integrated into Branksome with the other English war guests.

Jean Ingham's next coming-of-age experience was a summer job: "It seems that girls are wanted in the summer for picking fruit," she wrote on March 15, 1942, "and so camps have been built where they can stay and the farmers come each day and carry off the required number in trucks. It all sounded very exciting and an awful lot of girls wanted to go." Picking fruit on the Niagara peninsula, usually done by itinerant workers, was now under the direction of the Department of Labour, and Miss Read encouraged girls age sixteen and older to sign up. The job was made to sound very glamorous: "For working," Jean wrote,

> we wear overalls — slacks with a bib up the front — white blouses and either *red* bandannas or cow's breakfasts (don't you think that's a lovely name for those big straw hats?). If we go into town we wear royal blue dresses (the colour put

> quite a lot of people off) and little caps and low heeled white shoes I think.

In June, Jean and Mary Smith, another English girl billeted with the Laidlaws, joined Branksome Hall's corps of teenage "farmerettes." Jean was posted to a YWCA camp near the Cudney farm at Saltfleet, Ontario. On September 6, 1942, she wrote,

> When I first went there we thinned peaches and I got my first experience at climbing ladders. We were paid 22½ cents an hour. Next came the cherries — sweets and sours — with and without stems — the price per basket varied according to the latter. We did these for ages and ages. We hoed weeds and pulled weeds, picked up potatoes. This was kind of hard. There didn't seem to be any really comfortable way of doing that. Other jobs were picking plums, pears and apples and then came the blackcurrants. The job itself wasn't unpleasant but it was not at all profitable. Next came the peaches, and they continued right up to the day I left, yesterday, so now I feel as though I don't want to see another peach for ages. You see, if the skin of one peach is a little bruised or torn it can't be put in, and if it is a specially ripe one as well as big it looks so tempting that you feel you couldn't possibly throw it away so — down it goes.

Jean lived in a school gymnasium with sixty other girls. They were awakened at 6:10 a.m. and worked a nine- or ten-hour day in the hot sun. After a bath and a cafeteria-style meal, the girls made their sandwiches for the next day. "Everyone," she said,

> was supposed to be in camp by 10 p.m. and lights out at half past, while on Saturday you were allowed out until twelve. Usually on Saturday nights we hitchhiked into Hamilton and either window

> shopped, did a bit of ordinary shopping or went to a movie. Sometimes we missed the last bus back and had to hitchhike home again. It's quite safe if there are at least three of you.

Canadian girls were learning to do a man's work, being paid for it and liking it. They enjoyed a freedom that had been almost unimaginable before the war, yet for many Branksome girls, the school's greatest asset was its safety. "Branksome seemed a reasonable, fair world," recalled honours student Patricia Morrow Morley. "I couldn't imagine violence. There was respect for teachers, parents and rules and a sense of decency. The feeling of security was unconscious, taken for granted, like breathing."

Canada was now at war with Japan as well as Germany. The Japanese bombing of American warships in Pearl Harbor, Hawaii, in December 1941 had brought the United States into the war, and there were fears that the Japanese would attack the west coast of North America. In August 1942, Canadian troops had suffered heavy casualties in an ill-conceived raid on the German-occupied French port of Dieppe, and hundreds of ships and lives were being lost to German submarines in the Battle of the Atlantic. The Canadian war effort was grinding into full gear, and the Misses Laidlaw had more urgent obligations to worry about than two self-sufficient adolescents.

"I must tell you the rather startling news we received from the Laidlaws last night," Jean announced to her parents.

> They told us that they had thought things over very carefully this summer and that they had come to the conclusion that it would be better for us if we lived with girls of our own age and so they had decided to send us to Branksome as boarders! We were flabbergasted and confidentially we didn't like it very much but we are now just about recovered and await our fate with placid resignation (rather good that?).

If Jean felt hurt or rejected, she concealed it, even from her parents. "You had to protect yourself," said Jean's friend Kathleen Hinch Conrad, a fellow boarder at Branksome. "You cannot let yourself worry." Kathleen was an only child, and her parents, stationed in Singapore, had been taken prisoner by the Japanese. "It was a time of great anxiety," she said. "I kept trying to find out where my mother was." England was being bombed, the newspapers were full of atrocity stories and letters from home often contained bad news.

"People's brothers and fathers were killed, families split up, as mine did, many things happened that were quite traumatic," recalled Bridget Gregson Lawson. "It was emotionally hard. We derived a great deal of strength from our friends." Some English girls, including Bridget's sister, retreated into a cocoon of misery and homesickness, and a few, like Doreen Martin Evans, rebelled. "A friend told me later that I was the naughtiest girl in the school," said Doreen. "I was very difficult. I cried a lot. I was a nervous, sensitive child, an upset child."

Many British parents assumed that their children would be welcomed by distant Canadian relatives they didn't know, but after the first flush of enthusiasm, some relatives threw up their hands. Doreen had been taken in at Branksome Hall by Ainslie McMichael after two guardians had given up on her. "Miss McMichael was enormous, frightening to us," said Doreen, "but she had a sense of humour. She'd say things like 'I suppose you come from a village called Egg on Toast.' We didn't get any sympathy. She was tough on us. I was always in trouble with Miss McMichael." Doreen was a bright student, and her infractions — skipping classes, hiding in cupboards, rude remarks — didn't rank with a Newfoundland girl caught with a bottle of Scotch in her room. Miss Read used on Doreen her tried and true strategy for problem girls: she made her a prefect. "She was turning poachers into gamekeepers," Doreen laughed. "It must have been hard on the well-behaved girls." Doreen loved the music appreciation classes and worshipped Diana Reader Harris, who gave her a lifelong love of Shakespeare. "I was largely rehabilitated by a wonderful *French* teacher of French," she said. "She encouraged me to speak the language (we had a French table in the dining room), took me out to dinner in some posh Toronto restaurant and gave me the best role in the French play that year, *Ces dames au chapeau verts* I think it was."

Diana Reader Harris was under unreasonable pressure from Miss Stuart to return the Sherborne School girls to England exactly as they had departed. "We got the feeling that Diana Reader Harris didn't want us to change," said Elva Parkinson Carey. "I remember her saying to a girl who cut off her long hair, 'I brought you out from England with plaits, and I'm taking you back with plaits!'" The Sherborne girls attended St. Paul's Church, prepared for confirmation and wrote entrance exams to English universities. They had extra lessons in sewing, first aid and "housewifery" to make up for the absence of maternal examples. Most of the Sherborne girls were glad to have a corner of this foreign field that was a bit of England, but others, like Elva, grieving for a brother killed in combat, felt lonely and unloved. "One girl became distraught over her house being bombed," Elva recalled. "Diana Reader Harris simply told her to shape up and get over it. Miss Reader Harris was not a motherly person. We all suffered for that." Recalling her years at Branksome, Elva reflected, "There was no pressure to be clever or good, but there was pressure to be happy."

Edith Read had no patience with girls who whined or complained. "It was a do-it-yourself school," said Mary Alice Burton Stuart, a day girl who graduated in 1945, "and you were supposed to do it with energy, hard work, self-discipline and respect for others. We were never allowed the luxury of pinning the blame for disappointments on others than ourselves. We were free to try to succeed at anything."

Branksome girls were free to smoke too, although the school officially forbade smoking. "We could go for a walk in the afternoon, instead of playing games," said Nancy Geddes Poole, a fifteen year old from London, Ontario, who boarded at Branksome for a year, "so we hid our cigarettes and lighters in our bloomers. We went to the park past Sherbourne Street and smoked behind the bushes. It was *very risky.* We smoked Players and Black Cats. That's what our mothers were smoking." The safest place to smoke was the Royal Ontario Museum: "On Sunday afternoons, we could walk to Bloor and Sherbourne or to the museum. The museum was open on Sundays, and that's where most of us learned to smoke, in the cafeteria. We spent *a lot of time* at the museum. We were the most *museumed* people. I never got caught there, but I got caught one night in residence. My roommate and I hung out the window, and we should have known that our cigarettes were glowing in the dark. Suddenly, there was Miss Shaw at the door, and the place was *reeking* of smoke. We were gated for two Saturdays."

Nancy resented having to recite five Bible verses to Miss Read every Saturday morning before she could go out. "It did not endear Miss Read to me," she said. "She increased my scepticism. Miss Read used girls as 'war workers' so she didn't have to employ a large staff. I would do *anything* rather than garbage duty. The garbage was just *alive* with rats."

For some girls, Branksome's laissez-faire style was simply lazy, but the war years brought important innovations. In 1944, the Branksome girls challenged the boys of the University of Toronto Schools to debate the topic "For the good of Canada, the CCF party should be put in power at the coming election." The girls, arguing the affirmative, lost, but the debate became a yearly event. They also created their own in-house radio station, the Branksome Broadcasting Corporation, and broadcast skits and concerts from the common room to students listening in the gym. Unlike other girls' schools, Branksome allowed all senior students to write the provincial matriculation exams, even if they were likely to fail. Some girls did fail, then tried again and again until they passed.

"Miss Read admits to a soft spot in her heart for the student who tries hard even though unsuccessful," journalist and Branksome graduate Margaret Aitken wrote in *Saturday Night* magazine on March 11, 1944. "It is her belief that diligence, honesty and fair play are to be prized above scholarship. A lazy lump she cannot abide, but an all-round pupil gains Miss Read's highest regard."

Branksome had reason to be proud of Margaret Aitken, one of Canada's best journalists, and it could be proud too of Mary Barker and Margaret Eaton, who had achieved senior officer rank in the Canadian Women's Army Corps. Branksome alumnae were driving trucks and ambulances for the Red Cross, running soldiers' canteens, working in war industries and serving in the women's auxiliaries of all the armed services. To free up young mothers for war work, Miss Read had persuaded Ruth Hamilton Upjohn to start a kindergarten in the basement of 14 Elm Avenue. "We started in 1940 with eight children, including boys," Ruth said. As the kindergarten population grew, and expanded to include a nursery school, it moved into an old house where the school's caretaker lived. Ruth was paid $50 a month, and the fee for each child was $50 a year. In 1943, Dot Seixas joined Ruth to play the piano for singing and musical games.

Dot Seixas and Ruth Hamilton Upjohn, in the 1990s.

On December 5, 1944, Edith Read celebrated her sixty-fifth birthday. Or perhaps she didn't celebrate it. Edith was secretive about her age, and she appeared ageless. She had been principal of Branksome Hall for nearly thirty-five years. Her do-it-yourself school, unlike many of its competitors, had survived two world wars and the Great Depression, and it had developed a reputation for integrity and independence. Branksome Hall had nearly four hundred students. The Branksome Hall Corporation owned five houses in Rosedale, the fifty-acre farm, Clansdale Heights, and, since the board of directors had capitulated in 1942, the vacant acres — increased to twenty — in Hogg's Hollow, North York, that Miss Read had bought in 1939. In May 1942, Dalhousie University had recognized Edith Read's contribution to education by awarding her an honorary doctor of laws.

Edith still considered Halifax her home. She owned two adjacent houses, 396 and 398 Tower Street. She rented out rooms to cousins and friends and kept a suite for her own use during her vacations. Her Halifax life was private, and her guests were rarely connected with the school. Edith travelled during vacations, and as she grew older, she became preoccupied with Bible study, an interest she shared with English teacher Jennie MacNeill. Edith liked to do things in style, and with an Allied victory in the wind, the spring of 1945 must have seemed an ideal time to retire.

Chapter Four

EDITH READ HAD EVERY REASON to feel happy, even triumphant, when she presented her state-of-the-school report to the annual meeting of the board on November 20, 1945. Germany had surrendered to the Allies in May, and Japan, after the United States dropped atomic bombs on the cities of Hiroshima and Nagasaki, had surrendered in August. Canadians, after years of sacrifice, were looking forward to peace.

Branksome's English war guests had enhanced its academic reputation, increased its prestige and raised its public profile. Enrolment now stood at a record 477 day girls and boarders. The highest praise for the school came from Diana Reader Harris, who later arranged for an annual exchange to permit a graduating Branksome student to spend a further year at Sherborne School. Branksome reciprocated, and an exchange program with Sherborne School was established and lasted for twenty-five years.

Miss Read had learned from her guests that British independent schools for girls, dedicated to plain living and high thinking, were ancient, spartan and threadbare. Space was so limited at Branksome Hall that Miss Read was forced to turn away applicants, but she saw the school's cramped, Victorian quarters as an asset. "For many years, I envied the wealthier schools their large expansive buildings, with everything under one roof," she told the board, "but I have completely changed my mind. If I had the decision to make and a wealthy friend handed us, say, two million dollars for a new school, I would build along the same lines as we have at present, and I know every member of our staff would agree with me. The separate buildings are invaluable not only for the work of the school and various departments, but also for the development of the character of the girls. Our school may look old-fashioned, but its equipment is most modern so that everyone connected with it can feel justly proud of our equipment as well as our high scholastic standing."

Having dropped a broad hint that she needed money, Miss Read went on: "Now the time has come for me to be thinking of a successor. I want you to know that I am ready to leave at any time or ready to remain for as long a time as is necessary. We have always said that the Bible was the centre of all our teaching, and our crest is the open Bible. I feel sure that every member of the board will want that policy to be continued, and it is my dearest wish. I consider that the chief qualification for my successor would be that she is one for whom the whole Bible is the inspired Word of God and who has an evangelical belief. If she is one who agrees with the statement of faith of the Inter-Varsity Christian Fellowship, and one the fellowship would like to have as a member of their board, then I would gladly at any time turn over the principalship to her."

Edith's religious views had come to resemble more closely those of the school's founder, Margaret Scott, and among the school's thirty-five teachers, only one, Jennie MacNeill, met Edith's qualifications. The offer to resign, however, was a mere formality. Edith told the board that she looked on them "as my greatest friends," and as far as they were concerned, Miss Read could remain principal as long as she wished.

Edith was in good health, although she had been slightly injured in a car accident in February 1942. Behind the wheel of the school's huge, seven-passenger Plymouth, she had collided with a Bell Telephone truck at the corner of Yonge and Gerrard Streets. The car had been a write-off, and Edith had been cut on the forehead. The accident appears to have been her fault — she drove like a maniac — but, undeterred, she had sued Bell Telephone for damages. The company had settled out of court for $3,000 and a new car.

Miss Read could hardly think seriously about retiring before her long legal dispute with the City of Toronto over taxing 16 Elm Avenue was resolved. The Ontario Court of Revision had exempted from taxation all of Branksome's houses used by staff and students but not Miss Read's private rooms. Branksome had appealed to York County Court, and Judge Barton delivered his judgement on December 11, 1945: "A girls' school cannot be carried on without a resident principal or head," he ruled, "and in my opinion the occupation of the premises in question is occupation by the school, and they are therefore exempt."

Edith owed her victory to her tough, tenacious lawyer, Clive Thomson, a partner in the Toronto law firm of Gibson, Thomson and Gibson. Thomson knew everybody in the city's legal community, and like his client, he was clever, industrious, frugal and opinionated. Thomson, a Presbyterian and Director of the Upper Canada Bible Society, had joined Branksome's board of directors in 1941. He had acted for Edith, in her personal affairs, and for the school since 1924. Now that Miss Read's three original mentors, W.D. Ross, F.H. Deacon and S.J. Moore, were becoming too old and ill to attend board meetings, Clive Thomson assumed the role of her advocate and advisor.

Like Caesar conquering Gaul, Miss Read was determined to own all of the west side of Elm Avenue between Huntley Street and the Rosedale ravine. Colonel Deacon had promised to sell her his ravine estate, Glenhurst, for $100,000, the price he had paid for it, but there were two thorns in Edith's flesh: 4 Elm Avenue, a single-family home, and, on the lip of the ravine, 1 Elm Avenue, an artists' colony owned by Edna Breithaupt, President of the Wakunda Art and Community Centres of Canada.

On behalf of the school, Clive Thomson offered to purchase 1 Elm Avenue "for a fair price and payment in cash." Miss Breithaupt, suspecting that Miss Read was after her property, replied that, to her, the house was worth at least $50,000. Thomson advised Miss Read to wait: it was unlikely, he said, that any rival would pay such a price for "a big, expensive, old-fashioned white elephant."

Miss Breithaupt, however, apparently brought to the attention of the city's commissioner of buildings, K.L. Gillies, the fact that Branksome Hall seemed to be illegally occupying an old coach house at the rear of her property. On November 19, 1945, Gillies sent Miss Read an ultimatum:

> RE: REAR, NO I ELM AVENUE.
>
> Dear Madam,
>
> Our Inspector reports that extensive alterations have been made to the two-storey brick garage at the rear of the above mentioned premises and the second floor has been converted into a classroom, with a fire-escape constructed to the ground, and a window has been cut in the east wall without a permit from this department; also the south-east section of the first floor adjoining the garage portion is being used for a classroom having accommodation for 28 children; furthermore this building is not suitable for the purpose of a school and does not have adequate fire protection; furthermore this building does not have an elevation fronting upon a street in which suitable means of entrance and exit are provided, contrary to By-law 9668
>
> You are hereby notified to discontinue using said garage for the purpose of a school and remove fire-escape and place the building in its original condition forthwith. For your information, I beg to point out that By-law 11474 prohibits the use of a building in this area for any other purpose than for a detached private residence.

Branksome Hall's contractors had in fact renovated the old garage into space for the kindergarten and nursery school without a building permit, and while Thomson objected that the city's demand to restore the garage to its original derelict condition "was utterly unreasonable and ridiculous," the city persisted. Finally, Miss Read persuaded the city council that, since Branksome contributed more in educational and financial investment than Toronto lost in taxes, the school should be exempted from the detached private residence by-law.

Now it was up to the building commissioner to determine whether 3 Elm Avenue and the garage behind were safe enough to be used as a student residence and classrooms. Gillies decided they were not. Neither Miss Read nor Clive Thomson backed down from a fight, and it took nearly a year of inspections, correspondence, political lobbying and the intervention, on the school's behalf, of Ottawa's parliamentary deputy fire marshall before, on May 2, 1947, the problem at 3 Elm Avenue was solved by installing a fire escape on the west wall and two smoke screens on the staircases.

"I would suggest that you try to find out the reason why Branksome Hall has been pestered with vexatious litigation and proceedings of one kind or another ever since you moved to Rosedale in 1912," Clive Thomson wrote to Miss Read.

> Now what does this mean? Why is this vendetta carried on? Who is egging on the city authorities now? It would seem that Miss Breithaupt may have been responsible for starting this last affair. But it also seems as if there were certain people in some of the departments who are very ready and willing to take proceedings against Branksome Hall. Why is this? Is it just a result of spite — i.e., having failed in previous litigation have they a spiteful desire to try to win some victory against you? I suggest you try to get to the bottom of this, if you can.

The motives behind Toronto's hostile, or at best uncooperative, attitude to the school may have been more political than personal. In 1946, the city was drafting plans to build a four-lane expressway, the Clifton Road extension, through Rosedale to link Jarvis Street on the south with Mount Pleasant Road to the north. At Elm Avenue, the expressway would run along Huntley Street, effectively cutting Branksome Hall's property in two, and Toronto may have been trying to push Branksome Hall out in order to expropriate the property cheaply. The school did lose some land on the east in front of its Scott House infirmary, and the expressway came within yards of both Sherborne House and the gymnasium.

Colonel Deacon had fought unsuccessfully to stop the expressway on behalf of Glenhurst, Branksome Hall and the South Rosedale Ratepayers' Association. With their children grown and away from home, the Deacons no longer needed a large house like Glenhurst. In the spring of 1947, bedridden as a result of strokes, Colonel Deacon decided it was time to fulfil his promise to Edith Read: he would sell his estate to Branksome Hall for $100,000. The offer was made by his son, Coulter.

Edith jumped at the opportunity. Branksome's buildings were bursting, and for the first time in its history, the school had money in the bank. Branksome girls had been using the Deacons' lawns for sports, games and graduation garden parties for so many years it seemed as if the estate already belonged to the school. Although the yellow-brick mansion was eighty years old — it had been built in 1867 by Edgar Jarvis — the building inspector reported everything but the plumbing to be in good shape. Situated on a knoll facing west toward Park Road, shaded by a magnificent elm, Glenhurst was solidly built, with stained-glass ornamentation, a walnut central staircase and fireplaces in nearly every room. With two storeys and a large attic, the house provided bedrooms, a kitchen and bright, sunny classroom space.

To Miss Read's shock and chagrin, Branksome's board of directors, dominated by John A. Tory, J.S. McLean and a new member, E.G. Baker,

Readacres (formerly Glenhurst) and the giant elm tree, from the west lawn, 1948.

President of Moore Corporation, flatly refused to offer the Deacons more than $80,000 for their property. On July 14, 1947, Coulter Deacon coolly returned the school's $1,000 deposit, saying "all members of the family consulted consider the offer much too low." In a letter to Clive Thomson, Deacon refused to consider a bid lower than $100,000, adding

> We have had inquiries from more than half-a-dozen other associations, schools, religious and charitable organizations quite capable of meeting our price. Where else could one find a block of seven acres within eight minutes walk from the corner of Bloor & Yonge? We are sorry if the Board of Branksome Hall do not see fit to meet our terms but we feel that the property has much greater value than the price at which we would have

> been willing to sell to Branksome. We are now negotiating with others on a basis of $120,000, which incidentally is far below the figure of $200,000 which my father turned down in 1930.

Deacon's rejection failed to intimidate the three executives on Branksome's board. "Mr. Tory says that he *knows* that Coulter Deacon is saying that we are determined to get this property at any price," Clive Thomson wrote to Miss Read in Halifax on July 29. "He, Mr. McLean and Mr. Baker all believe that *no one* will offer the Deacons more than $70,000 — and that they *must* accept our offer. They all three believe that we are 'being played for a sucker' — (as Mr. Tory expressed it)."

The most serious objections came from J.S. McLean, who considered the school's offer of $80,000 to be "far too much." In an irate phone call to Thomson, McLean said that the buildings on the Deacon property were "no good at all, absolutely worthless for classrooms or anything else," adding "no one in his right senses would want such buildings." The land, McLean said, wasn't worth more than $40,000, and no board would ever buy it if they were not insane. Moreover, McLean stated, the school was too big. Miss Read did not have enough support staff for five hundred students; he would prefer a maximum enrolment of three hundred.

McLean's objections were based on more than financial concerns. The school had outgrown Miss Read's ability to run it single-handedly, and in spite of the board's urging, Edith had not found or trained a successor. She had broached the prospect of becoming Branksome's principal to Diana Reader Harris, but after serious consideration, she had declined. Finally, on September 15, 1947, the board approved Miss Read's recommendation that Jennie MacNeill be appointed Assistant to the Principal or, in effect, Vice-Principal.

Jennie MacNeill had been teaching English literature at Branksome Hall since she had graduated from Mount Allison University with an honours B.A. in 1926. Since then, in her spare time, Jennie had earned an

M.A. from the University of Toronto. As Miss Read told the board, Miss MacNeill was "very capable and efficient and highly regarded by all the staff." Born Jane Elizabeth in Prince Edward Island in 1902, the only daughter of A.J. MacNeill, a Presbyterian minister who preached in Gaelic throughout the Maritimes, Jennie was as shy and reserved as Edith Read was brash and gregarious. An intellectual with no enthusiasm for sports or games, Jennie set high moral and academic standards for herself and others.

"Miss MacNeill was the one teacher who really challenged us," recalled Dodie Robinette MacNeill. "In our final year, she assigned us a three-thousand-word essay. We thought it was *impossible. Three thousand words!* We screamed and pleaded, 'Oh, Miss MacNeill, we can't possibly do that! It's too hard!' But she stuck to her guns, and we did it. The next year, in university, we were so thankful!"

Jennie MacNeill may have had qualms about her promotion to the role of sorcerer's apprentice, but it mollified Miss Read's critics on the board, and on February 2, 1948, as John A. Tory had predicted, the Deacon family sold Glenhurst to the school for $80,000 cash. The purchase came in the nick of time; five months later, Miss Read's dream of building a new Junior School in York Mills ended when the City of Toronto expropriated the school's vacant twenty-acre property for $30,000.

Glenhurst, renamed Readacres, was designated to become Branksome Hall's Junior School for Grades One to Eight, but it wasn't until May 18, 1948, that Toronto city council finally passed a by-law permitting Branksome to use its west campus for school purposes. Readacres needed upgrading, including an addition for classrooms and a gym, but problems getting building permits and postwar shortages of construction materials caused exasperating delays. By 1949, Branksome's students and teachers were putting up with weeks of dust, mud and noise as jackhammers and bulldozers cleared the way for the Clifton Road extension right under the school's rattling windows. The elm trees on Huntley Street were cut down, the boulevards and sidewalks torn up. The school's

Readacres and Junior School addition, 1953.

motto, "Keep well the road," acquired a new layer of meaning. Some of the younger girls believed that they were personally responsible for the maintenance of the new expressway.

However worried, annoyed and exhausted Miss Read must have felt, she never allowed politics, or her own feelings, to disrupt the regular routine of her school. She insisted that the school be inspected by the provincial Department of Education, and in 1948 the inspector had described Branksome as "an unusually good school and staff," praising the girls particularly for their "good posture" and "clear enunciation."

Allison Roach, a Junior and Senior School student from 1944 to 1951, found Branksome Hall an "oasis." Allison had switched to Branksome from Whitney public school in Grade Seven. "Whitney was a punitive place," she said. "There was a lot of strapping. I was terrified, and I wasn't doing well. At Branksome, we could talk and laugh and make noise and walk in any door we wanted. We were told to express ourselves, speak our minds, be honest, direct, down to earth. I loved that school. It was a joy. It saved my life."

Allison Roach as a Branksome student.

Academically, Branksome Hall followed the rigid provincial curriculum, with emphasis on drill, memorizing and the three Rs, but Miss Read did her best to lighten the mood with clan games and student skits. In 1949, the drama club performed Oscar Wilde's comedy *The Importance of Being Earnest,* and each form wrote and presented a short play. "Fourth form opened the series with IV A enacting a satire on 'Julius Caesar' entitled 'God Caesar,' and IV B by presenting a Mock Trial," the *Slogan* reported.

> In a joint effort, the fifth forms presented "Lena Rivers," a comedy-drama which Mary Louise Edmonds completely directed, produced and acted in the title role. (A Laurence Olivier in our midst!) II A tried a new idea and held a "Noihsaf Wohs" ("Fashion Show" spelled backwards) at the height of which Miss Read "brought down the house" when she appeared dressed as a typical "school Marm" of fifty years ago. Teen-age problems were aired by I A in their play, "For Whom the Telephone Rings."

Miss Read's theatrical flair would stand Edith in good stead when the Clifton Road extension, popularly called Mount Pleasant Road, opened on May 17, 1950. "NEW ROAD SAID RUSH HOUR FLOP," headlined the *Toronto Star* the next day. "The first day of the opening saw cars lined up from Jarvis St. almost bumper to bumper to St. Clair Ave. at the peak of the heavy traffic between 8:30 a.m. and 9 a.m."

Some responsibility for causing what the *Star* called "one of the worst traffic jams in many years" lay with Miss Read. City planners had known that hundreds of Branksome students would have to cross the expressway several times a day to get to their classes, gym, dining room and residences, but in spite of the obvious risk that girls would be killed or injured, they had ignored Miss Read's pleas to install a traffic light at the corner of Elm Avenue. Well, if the city wouldn't stop the traffic, Miss Read would do it herself. Joyce Robinson Morris, a Grade Ten student, remembers the scene vividly: "I lived in Moore Park and took the Greyhound coach to school every day. When the extension was opened, we took a new route, and as the coach drew up beside Branksome and I stepped off, there was Miss Read in her academic robes in the middle of the street, stopping traffic for each and every girl who needed her. I was told the police downtown couldn't understand what had happened to all the new traffic they were expecting — it was all jammed up north of Elm Avenue while Miss Read shepherded her girls safely to and fro."

Miss Read, a fierce elf in her long, crimson doctor of laws gown, soon attracted the attention of the police, who were in favour of stoplights, and the newspapers. Muttering "hideous, hideous," Miss Read told Monroe Johnston of the *Star* that "I intend to take a group of angry citizens before the board of control on Monday." Calling the intersection "a fearsome spot where terror and tumult mingle," Johnston reported on May 20 that

> One morning this week an actual count showed 1,200 children had crossed the highway. If a patrolman or school employee is in the vicinity, the trip can be done in comparative safety. Failing this, however, one of the students waving a makeshift

> "STOP" sign will lead her chums across. As witnessed yesterday, this is a hazardous occupation. The lead girl steps from the curb. An approaching motorist can't make up his mind. Finally, with an extra push on the accelerator, he swerves around the breathless girl and continues on his way.

Many times a day, Johnston reported, Miss Read "will jump into her large, comfortable car, pile the youngsters in and drive them to another section of the school. Two station wagons also act as armored cars for the girls."

After Miss Read and her deputation of parents and children appeared before the Board of Control on Monday, May 22, the commissioner of city planning meekly advised that "he favours the installation of traffic lights as requested by Miss Read." It was June, however, after the school had closed for the summer, before the lights were finally installed at Elm Avenue and Mount Pleasant Road. The lights were Edith Read's final, decisive victory in her long feud with city hall.

The road, accompanied by the construction of a subway beneath Bloor and Yonge Streets, brought Branksome Hall into the heart of the city, but fears that the noise and traffic would destroy the school's ambience and popular appeal proved groundless. Branksome Hall was now more visible, easier to reach by car, and later by subway, making it more accessible to girls from other parts of the city. By 1951, Miss Read felt secure enough to recommend that school fees be increased to $900 for boarders, $275 for senior day girls and $150 for juniors.

Branksome's greatest strength was the core of seasoned teachers Miss Read called the "backbone" of the school: Jennie MacNeill and Jean Livingston in English, Margaret Sime and Hélène Sandoz Perry in French (German had been dropped during the war), Jean Claxton in science, Dorothy Phillips in mathematics, Ruth Craig in Latin, Ruth Upjohn and Dot Seixas in the kindergarten and Jessie Johnston from Edinburgh, Scotland, as head of the Junior School.

"Miss Johnston was handsome, a smart dresser in tweed suits and

Jean Claxton.

Hélène Sandoz Perry

brogues," recalled Diana King Hore, a pupil of Miss Johnston's from Grades Five to Eight. "She was a no-nonsense Presbyterian with a sense of humour, a Miss Jean Brodie in her prime without the sexual innuendo. There was no fooling around in Miss Johnston's class. She adored kids, although she had an inexplicable dislike for certain people. She never preyed on anyone who was vulnerable; she'd just be a little grimmer. Once she gently whomped me over the head with a book. I was standing at the blackboard being stupid, and I darn well deserved to be shaken up. I didn't mind at all. I thought she was wonderful."

A Branksome graduate who entered the Junior School in 1950 remembers Miss Johnston as "a fabulous teacher, fair, sound, strict and kind. I had trouble in math, and she was so patient with me, so encouraging. If I got 64 on an exam when I'd gotten 62 on the last one, she was full of praise for me."

Outside class, however, this girl had a much less happy experience: "I

Back: Mrs. Eaton, Mrs. Carson, Mrs. Cook, Mrs. D'Alton, Mrs. Allen, Mrs. Bowker, unknown. Front: Miss Howie, Miss Johnston, Mrs. Dowie. 1962-63.

was a wimp. I had been a very overly protected little kid, and I was terrified of thugs in the schoolyard at Rosedale public school. Mum decided to switch me to Branksome. She thought it would be a gentler scene, and it was considerably worse. All the way through Junior School, I was razzed, teased, bullied, harassed verbally and physically by the same group of girls. They were out to 'get' new girls. It was Mum's mistake to make me wear ribbed woollen stockings on cold winter days. Branksome was the only private girls' school that required bare knees in winter, but it was fatal to be different. They saw me as weird. They'd lurk in corners, leap out at me, call me names, insult me. Sometimes they tore off my tam or got me down in a wrestling match on the ground. One of the girls hated the way my mum did my hair. It was cute. What was it to her?" The bullies, she said, hid in the trees and underbrush of the Readacres grounds, unsupervised by the teachers: "The teachers turned a blind eye.

They didn't want to hear about it, and they didn't want to see it. It was the old Etonian English public school attitude. It was viewed as character building. It was *not* character building."

The wartime ethic of cooperation and self-sacrifice was being replaced by a more aggressive Cold War culture based on individualism, competition and materialism. Miss Read scorned child psychology, and professional counselling for students with emotional, psychological or family problems was almost unheard of in the entire Ontario school system. Children who misbehaved were "delinquents," and "guidance" amounted to little more than directing girls toward suitable, or unsuitable, academic courses or careers. Ainslie McMichael, in her role as school secretary, probably provided a more sympathetic ear and sensible advice than anyone else in the school, but "Sitting Bull," as Ainslie was now called, lacked authority. Miss Read relied on the girls themselves. She increased the number of prefects to fourteen and added an equal number of subprefects; the eight clan chieftains were joined by eight subchieftains, and while there was still no student council, each Senior School class elected a president, vice-president and secretary-treasurer.

In the spring of 1953, Branksome Hall's fiftieth anniversary golden jubilee, happily concurrent with the coronation of Queen Elizabeth II, provided a perfect opportunity to emphasize the school's traditions and its four moral cornerstones: truth, honesty, justice and purity. In honour of the occasion, Miss Read decked herself out in a brilliant blue-and-yellow Nova Scotia tartan suit with matching hat, blue gloves and blue Brevitt shoes. She could be seen for miles, and as Joyce Robinson Morris recalled, "she moved at a fair pace, covering the distance between her house and the main school with quite a long stride for someone so small." Edith Read had tiny, childlike feet, and when she spoke at prayers, she stood at the very edge of the stage, rocking back and forth on the balls of her feet as the girls held their breath in the expectation that she would tumble off.

The year-long jubilee celebration kicked off on Robbie Burns night, January 12, 1953, with a formal, candlelit banquet for the teachers and boarders honouring Diana Reader Harris, now Headmistress of Sherborne School. Miss Reader Harris presented to the school an early edition of Sir Walter Scott's poetry inscribed by the laird of Branxholme Castle, the Duke of Buccleuch, and the speeches were followed by Scottish dancing to reels played on the bagpipes.

Edith Read and Dame Flora MacLeod, 1953.

On Thursday, April 23, a school open house included full inspection of all classrooms, bedrooms and kitchens as well as demonstrations of cooking, sewing, basketball, swimming and handicrafts. A thanksgiving service at St. Andrew's Church on Sunday morning followed a formal dance at the Strathgowan Club Saturday night, but the highlight of the jubilee weekend was a gala banquet at the Royal York Hotel on Friday, April 24. Portia White sang the doxology in the Scottish metrical rendition, and after dinner, while the boisterous guests sang "Up and On," Ainslie McMichael cut a four-tiered birthday cake decorated with fifty candles. Reminiscences by Alexander MacMillan, who had named the school in 1903, were followed by anecdotes of the early days told by alumnae Katharine Boyd and Lillie Shannon Plant, a pupil when Branksome Hall had opened its doors fifty years before. Isabel Adams McIntosh proposed the toast to Miss Read, accompanied by a rousing version of "For She's a Jolly Good Fellow," and in short, witty speeches, alumnae Constance Cann Wolf, the school's only balloonist, Joan Mitchell Flintoft and Head Girl Jean Wahlroth brought the school's history up to date.

Clan Chieftains with the Duke of Buccleuch, 1953. L to R: Molly Hewitt (Head Girl), Ann Farmer, Barbara Graupmer, Sue Savage, Marilyn Earl, The Duke of Buccleuch, Anne Sheir, Sandra Maxwell, Jacqueline Oldham, Margot Thompson.

Branksome hosted Dame Flora MacLeod of MacLeod, Chief of Clan MacLeod, living proof that women could be chiefs, at a school assembly on October 8, 1953, and on December 2, the Duke of Buccleuch himself presented the school with a leather-bound copy of *The Poetical Works of Sir Walter Scott.* Flattered, if perhaps bemused to find himself idolized by five hundred Canadian schoolgirls, the duke generously agreed to Miss Read's request to have stonecutters in Scotland make for Branksome Hall a replica of the lintel, with its motto, over the door of Branxholme Castle. Harrogate House, 14 Elm Avenue, was renamed Buccleuch House.

Branksome, vying with BSS and Havergal to become the largest girls' school in Canada, was financially secure. Choirs, directed by a musically gifted English teacher, Eunice Coutts, were winning prizes at the Kiwanis

Music Festival, and alumnae were making headlines. Margaret Aitken had been elected to the House of Commons as Conservative MP for York-Humber in August, and the following February, figure skater Frances Dafoe, with her partner Norris Bowden, won the World Pairs Figure Skating championship.

Miss Read had reached the pinnacle of her career, and at seventy-three, she was becoming profoundly deaf. No one argued with her, especially when she wasn't wearing her hearing aid, and her opinions had become dogmatic. "Towards the end of her career, Miss Read's mind seemed to become blurred by her personal relationship with God," said Diana King Hore. "She was very vulnerable to religious nuts and pious hypocrites who had us down at the People's Church being saved. She fell for them. Heaven and hell were pretty clear-cut for Miss Read." Some students appreciated the missionaries Miss Read was hiring as teachers, while others resented them. One girl learned to take advantage of their zeal. "I was always breaking all the rules, but I could work off my demerits by memorizing Bible verses," said Nancy Ruth Jackman, the school's most notorious hellraiser during the 1950s. "So if there was a party on the weekend, I would work off as many demerits as I needed to be allowed to go. Everybody would laugh when *I'd* win the Scripture Prize. It was not a good foundation in love or charity. I learned how to work a system."

In politics, however, Miss Read remained Liberal and liberal. Branksome students took part in model United Nations assemblies at Queen's Park, and Edith was the only woman among fifty distinguished sponsors of Cyrus Eaton's Second Pugwash Conference of Nuclear Scientists, gathered to discuss "The Dangers of the Atomic Arms Race and Ways and Means to Diminish Them." By the time the Soviet Union launched its Sputnik space satellite in 1957, Branksome had built new science facilities, and with the arrival of Edwina Baker the same year, it acquired a university-calibre mathematics teacher.

Miss Read's views about education, however, had become conserva-

New science wing, 1957.

tive. "At present she is crusading against progressive educationalists who place self-expression ahead of discipline," Shirley Mair reported in *Maclean's* magazine in March 1957. "'Send the product of progressive education to me,' she suggested recently, 'and I'll straighten the brat out with little difficulty.'" Miss Read had also become an autocrat about dress. "There was a rule against wearing strapless gowns to the formals," recalled Donna Bull George, who came to Branksome from St. Clement's School in 1955. "When one girl turned up in a dress 'without visible means of support,' she was made to put two straps of masking tape over her shoulders."

Miss Read had forceful opinions on everything from fashions in fur coats (unflattering) to jazz. "By scanning the newspapers, Miss Read determines which events are suitable for her students," wrote Shirley Mair.

> Amazed at the number of girls who signed up to hear one pianist, she decided to go along to find out what the attraction

> was. It wasn't until she was in her seat that she learned that Oscar Peterson was a jazz pianist; Miss Read disapproves of jazz. She left the audience and stalked up and down the foyer until his performance was over.

Miss Read had even less tolerance for rock 'n' roll musicians, especially Elvis Presley. "We were not allowed to mention Elvis's name in school," recalled Jane Rapp, a "lifer" who spent fourteen years at Branksome as a day girl. "We hid behind the coats in the cloakroom and whispered about him." Boarders were forbidden to play Elvis's records, and when Elvis played Maple Leaf Gardens in 1957, his concert was off-limits. "Four of us went," recalled Nancy Ruth Jackman. "It was a lark. At the concert, we bought little pink sunglasses, that was Elvis's big colour, pink, and we came back on the Carlton streetcar, bebopping along with our programs and these pink sunglasses. Well, the school dietician was on the same streetcar. She saw us and told Miss Read. We were hauled into the Blue Room. All of the prefects were lined up along one wall, this long row of red kilts, and Miss Read was standing in front of the fireplace. She really took us down. Elvis was of the devil, that's what she said, he was diabolical. It was a terrifying experience for a fourteen-year-old kid like me, but it was that lineup of red kilts that really got me. We'd seen half of them there at the Elvis concert, we *knew* they'd been there, and not one of them had the gumption, gall or sisterhood to stand up for us. It was a lesson in betrayal and the absolute power of Miss Read."

Beneath her crusty exterior, Edith, who now looked like a doll made of dried apples, had a soft spot in her heart for her family and friends. She was proud of her brother John, who had been appointed to the International Court at The Hague, but no one was closer to her than Ainslie McMichael. Edith and Ainslie had grown old together at Branksome Hall. To generations of students, they *were* Branksome Hall. Ainslie, who lived in a room at the school with her cats, was the only staff member who sat on Branksome's board of directors, and after her appointment as secretary to the Alumnae Association in 1954, she had an office of her own. On May 27, 1958, Ainslie got up from her desk and dropped dead.

Chapter Five

THE SCHOOL GRIEVED for Miss McMichael, but Edith Read had suffered a devastating loss. "As you know," she wrote later to Ginty Sinclair Powell, President of the Alumnae Association, "Ainslie's death was such a very great shock to me that I could not pull myself together as I should have done." This was as close as Miss Read ever came to a confession of weakness, but on September 15, 1958, she informed a special meeting of the board of directors that she "felt the need to be relieved of some of the onerous and unceasing work falling upon the principal of such a large school." Miss Read proposed that Miss MacNeill become principal, and she would take the title of honorary principal. According to the minutes, "Dr. Read also explained that she intended to retain oversight of finance and business for the present." She would remain president of the Branksome Hall Corporation and chairman of the board, and while she donated her personal china, silver and table linen to the school for the principal's use, she made no offer to vacate her residence at 16 Elm Avenue for Miss MacNeill.

Jennie accepted this unorthodox, unworkable relationship with Christian humility and deep misgivings. During her eleven years as vice-principal, she had been given no authority — Miss Read had contradicted her every initiative — scant thanks and little public recognition (the 1957 *Maclean's* story failed to mention Miss MacNeill or that the school had a vice-principal). Her health had suffered from overwork, and she had been forced to give up her Ph.D. studies at the University of

Dr. Jennie E. MacNeill.

Toronto. Her commitment to scholarship had been her greatest gift to her students.

"Miss MacNeill taught us all the prickly minutiae of literary criticism," recalled Pat Gordon Bishop, a senior in Miss MacNeill's class in 1957. "She opened a little window into higher learning. I loved what she could give me, but she was scary. Jennie was fat, and she blew hot and cold. She'd flush beet red and blow in a quiet, threatening way and go back to normal. She seemed cold, forbidding. I thought she hated me. Then one afternoon she invited us to her apartment over the coach house for scones and tea. I was thrilled. I felt so madly 'in,' so Oxford. I was carrying a box of cakes across Mount Pleasant Road, and I fell on the ice. 'She'll kill me!' I thought. But Jennie put her arms around me and said, 'Pat, darling, are you hurt?' There I was sitting in the middle of Mount Pleasant Road with all the traffic going by, and all I could think was 'She loves me! Jennie loves me!'"

As principal, Miss MacNeill was given a room in 16 Elm Avenue with Miss Read. "Miss Read started becoming unstuck," history teacher Mattie Clark recalled in a later interview. "She was convinced there were burglars in the house, and Jennie had to calm her down." At the October 1958 Installation of Prefects, Miss Read, not Miss MacNeill, marched at the head of the procession and gave the principal's address to the school. "I felt awfully sorry for Miss MacNeill," said science teacher Jean

Claxton. "Miss Read didn't retire. She was always looking over Jennie's shoulder. It was *very difficult.*"

Jennie MacNeill had no vice-principal — her former position remained vacant — and her administrative staff consisted of one house mother and the school's only secretary, talkative, temperamental Sadie Scotland. Miss Scotland was wonderful with the girls, capably solving the myriad daily problems they brought to the office, but she had a high sense of her own worth and refused to do anything she considered beyond or beneath her. Miss Read had always protested that she couldn't afford to hire more staff, raise teachers' salaries or start a pension plan, and it must have been a revelation for Miss MacNeill when she saw the school's financial statements.

In 1959, with revenues of nearly $400,000, Branksome Hall had a surplus of $88,000. The school was virtually out of debt, and over the years more than $200,000 had been socked away in an "Extension Fund." These profits had been achieved in spite of the fact that, within the past three years, Branksome Hall had purchased all the remaining property on the west side of Mount Pleasant Road, including 1 Elm Avenue, 4 Elm Avenue and 120 and 126 Mount Pleasant Road, for more than $250,000.

Branksome Hall's teachers had been begging for raises and pensions for ten years. They were paid, on average, $1,970 a year, ranging from a few hundred dollars for a part-time teacher to $3,200 for a senior teacher. There was no salary scale, and the amount each woman earned was kept secret. As far as Branksome's board was concerned, a pension plan was "unworkable." Miss Read had refused to raise salaries until the school's debts were paid off, but as soon as one loan or mortgage had been paid, she'd borrowed again. Branksome's teachers, including Jennie MacNeill, had unwittingly financed the school's expansion.

With 590 students and a waiting list, Branksome Hall was thriving. Jennie's priority, however, was to raise academic standards, and to do this she needed more money to hire the best teachers — the starting salary for a qualified teacher in the public school system was $4,000. Canada's public schools were embarking on an era of aggressive modernization, especially in the sciences, and ambitious young women who came to Branksome Hall out of teachers' college quit as soon as they found better jobs. Branksome's teachers were ageing, and they faced an impoverished retirement.

It took more than a year, but by December 7, 1959, Jennie had persuaded Miss Read and Clive Thomson to ask an insurance company to draw up a pension plan. More remarkably, Miss Read had been persuaded to retire as president of the Branksome Hall Corporation, on the condition, however, that Thomson, who acted as the board's secretary-treasurer, take her place. Miss Read remained a director, but frail and increasingly confused, she retreated into 16 Elm Avenue with her nurse companion. She never attended another board meeting.

Miss MacNeill, spurred on by Grade Seven teacher Margaret Dowie, immediately demanded "substantial increases" in teachers' salaries. Mrs. Dowie had tried in vain for years to persuade her colleagues to demand raises, but the unqualified teachers were fearful they would lose their jobs, and the best teachers couldn't find equivalent jobs elsewhere. Male teachers in the public school system had cautioned Edwina Baker and Jean Claxton that, because they were women, they would never be hired to teach a graduating-year class in mathematics or physics.

Miss Johnston and Mrs. Dowie were the only certified teachers in the Junior School, and when the raw new gym teacher blurted out her salary, Mrs. Dowie realized "She's earning more than I am! I was *so* furious! I went to Jennie, and I said, 'Jennie, I'm not angry. I'm *absolutely furious!*" Branksome Hall could not afford to lose a teacher as devoted to her work and as beloved by students and staff as Margaret Dowie, and she was allowed to put her case to Clive Thomson. "Mr. Thomson said to me, 'In the public schools, teachers sit up until one and two in the morning marking papers.' I said, 'Mr. Thomson, in Branksome teachers sit up until one and two in the morning marking papers. If you pay us a very low salary, you may get that amount of work from some of the teachers.'" Thomson got the point, and the teachers got their raise. As head of the Junior School, Jessie Johnston would be paid $4,500. Miss MacNeill's salary as principal was $7,500.

It was a victory, but Jennie's troubles were only beginning. Miss Read, obsessed with cost cutting and indifferent to her surroundings, had been oblivious to the deterioration of the school's buildings. Sherborne House at 3 Elm Avenue needed expensive repairs — the back porch was literally falling off — and the ground underneath the swimming pool was giving way. And 10 Elm Avenue, an overcrowded, antiquated rabbit warren, was a firetrap — the school had no fire alarms — and the Blue Room looked so shabby the alumnae were raising money to redecorate it. The housekeeper had reported that the drapes were too worn to be washed again. The basement dining room hadn't been expanded or upgraded since 1924, and the cafeteria next to it was so small most day girls brought bag lunches and ate in their home rooms. This unhealthy practice encouraged the school's thriving population of mice, and small, furry corpses often had to be retrieved from under floorboards and behind radiators.

In February 1962, after the school had spent almost $75,000 in repairs and renovations, including a fire detection system, the board made the bold decision to build a modern three-storey residence, including a new dining hall, kitchen and cafeteria, on the vacant northwest corner of Elm Avenue and Mount Pleasant Road. At an estimated cost of $500,000, MacNeill House, as it would be christened, was by far the most expensive building program Branksome Hall had ever undertaken. It would house twenty-five girls and four teachers, and it included a $50,000 glassed-in concrete bridge over Mount Pleasant Road.

Edith Read had had the foresight to buy the corner lot in 1957 — the bridge would be named Read Walk in her honour — but the residence was still under construction when Edith died on April 15, 1963, at the age of eighty-three. A simple funeral at Knox Presbyterian Church was followed by burial in Mount Pleasant Cemetery. Everyone had assumed

Read Walk looking South, with MacNeill House on the right, 1963.

that Miss Read was a wealthy woman, and she had repeatedly assured the board that she would leave the bulk of her estate to the school. In her will, however, she bequeathed to Branksome Hall, in addition to her $50,000 life insurance policy, $17,500.

It was a stunning disappointment, and the school was desperate for money. By the time MacNeill House, a bright, boxy, red-brick building decorated in brilliant colours, opened in February 1964, it had cost $732,000, nearly fifty percent over budget. Branksome Hall had liquidated all of its bonds and securities and spent $192,000 of current revenue, and after Miss Read's $67,500 bequest, it still owed the Bank of Nova Scotia $264,000. In May 1964, the board sold the fifty-acre school farm, Clansdale Heights, unused for the past ten years, for $35,000, $15,000 less than Miss Read had paid for it in 1935. The board had no plan in place for fund-raising, and its endowment fund, started by a $1,000 gift from the alumnae in 1955, amounted to less than $20,000.

Miss MacNeill urged an increase in school fees. Branksome's fees, $50 to $200 below those of Havergal College and Bishop Strachan School, gave it, she thought, a reputation as a "poor" school. She was determined, too, that teachers would not pay the school's debts, and when the board approved a fee increase, it allocated $30,000, half the estimated new revenue, for salary increases. A small pension plan had been initiated in May 1962. The teachers paid in five percent of their salaries, and the school contributed $9,000 a year, about $180 per teacher. For teachers past or approaching retirement age, or those unable to work, the plan was worthless.

"Miss MacNeill then brought before the meeting the matter of Miss F.L., a former teacher at our school," the board minutes reported.

> Because she has now retired on account of old age and illness and is not eligible for the new pension plan and because she has served the school faithfully for eleven years and is in need of financial aid, Miss MacNeill recommended that Miss F.L. be paid a retiring allowance of $65 a month and this allowance be paid until Miss F.L. reaches the age of 70 years.

At seventy, Miss F.L. would be eligible for a government pension.

Jennie, acting with compassion and courage, had established a precedent: from now on, Branksome teachers in financial distress could expect to be looked after. The monthly "bonuses" they received from the school, however, were so pitifully small the money did not compensate for the loss of a proper school pension.

Miss MacNeill had even less success with the school's facilities. Having bought up large, ageing houses, fearing, justifiably, that developers would surround the school with apartment buildings, Branksome Hall had no idea what to do with them. One Elm Avenue had been rented out to tenants since Miss Read had bought it for $45,000 in 1954; the rent had barely covered the taxes and mortgage. Now it was vacant, and it would cost at least $130,000 to renovate it for school purposes. Four Elm Avenue was rented out, and 120 and 126 Mount Pleasant Road were rooming houses.

There was no maintenance budget for any of the school buildings. Miss Read had not believed in long-term plans. When something broke, she had fixed it; when more space was needed, she had built it. Miss Read had thrived on crisis management. Miss MacNeill suffered the consequences.

"The usual trouble with pipes occurred off and on, and that is an old story," Jennie reported to the board on January 12, 1965.

> This year I had to have a staff bedroom and the general office re-papered during the Christmas holidays as a result of plumbing trouble one night. I always like to have the exterior of at least one building painted each summer, but this year we did nothing but the new section of Readacres, which had not been touched since it was built. The major change has been the conversion of the old dining room and kitchen into new quarters for the commercial and household economics departments. Securing equipment for the latter has been quite a job. The Department of Education inspectors were not pleased with our old quarters, and I hope this will satisfy them. They are used to seeing so much extravagant new equipment in the new public schools that they sometimes over-emphasize its importance.

Branksome Hall was not accustomed to receiving critical reports from school inspectors. Miss Read had always charmed them with cookies and chatter, but school inspectors were no longer looking for good posture and clear enunciation. Miss MacNeill warned that the school was struggling to keep up:

> The gift of last year's graduating class was a new phonograph to the French department, while the parents of one girl gave

> me a cheque for $300 for the library. There has been a heavy drain for science and mathematics, as books of reference are needed at all levels, and all books are very expensive. Gym equipment has been thoroughly tested and repaired, but replacements have been made in some sections. A good deal has been spent and much more could be done. Laboratory supplies will be approximately doubled in the chemistry section next year, Miss Claxton tells me, and they were up considerably this year.

Miss MacNeill, scrambling to find qualified teachers, housemothers and, particularly, a residence matron, relied, as always, on the staff. Miss Claxton, who acted as vice-principal, taught physics and chemistry to Grades Eleven, Twelve and Thirteen, a punishing load, and Miss Craig and Miss Sime, without extra pay, took responsibility for curriculum, timetables and exam schedules. "The staff are always willing to cheerfully do extra work in emergencies such as the present," Jennie concluded her report, "and I feel that I have much for which to be thankful." Jennie was so exhausted she had done the unthinkable — she had split an infinitive.

Fire inspectors, unimpressed with the school's new alarm system, insisted on improvements. The new alarms were so sensitive they could be set off by lightning, burnt toast or an iron, and hardly a day passed without fire trucks clanging up to the school door. In February 1966, the foundations under the old kindergarten building collapsed. It was condemned and demolished, and while the board dithered about the cost and location of a new building, the kindergarten spent the next eighteen months in the school cafeteria on the lower level of MacNeill House. Department inspectors warned Miss MacNeill that the school's art and home economics programs were not up to standard for accreditation, the science labs needed equipment and the library was inadequate. Branksome Hall had never had a librarian, and the books had been donated by alumnae and parents. They weren't catalogued, and their educational value was marginal. Borrowed books were checked in and out by prefects at lunch and after school, and books were often not returned.

Costs of running the school were rising, and Branksome was losing students, especially in the Junior School. Students were the school's only source of income, and when revenue from fees fell from $525,658 to $496,113 in 1966, Branksome ended the year with a deficit of $4,000. Miss MacNeill took the blame.

"Jennie didn't know anything about business!" complained Mattie Clark. "Frankly, I thought Jennie could barely add. She never owed anybody a cent in her life because she wouldn't spend anything she didn't have." Jennie's conservative attitude toward money, however, was appreciated by her board of directors, and they raised her salary to $11,000 a year. Jennie dryly described the qualities of a good headmistress: "You should have the education of a college president, the financial ability of a bank manager, the cunning of a serpent, the wisdom of Solomon, the patience of Job, the persistence of the Devil and the grace of God." In December 1966, Jennie told the board that she would turn sixty-five in January, and she intended to retire in 1968, having completed her fortieth year at the school.

Mount Allison University had recognized Jennie MacNeill's contribution to education with an honorary doctor of laws degree in 1961, and her efforts at Branksome Hall were bearing fruit. The pass rate on matriculation exams had risen from ninety-one to ninety-five percent, and the school continued to produce its share of outstanding scholars. Jennie was disappointed, however, that, apart from $1,000 or $2,000 that the Alumnae Association raised at its biannual bazaar, the school offered virtually nothing in the way of bursaries or scholarships. She reported, too, a new "restlessness" among the students, including psychiatric problems.

"Those of us whose schools are in the big cities are increasingly conscious of the drug problem," she warned the board. "We have

A Branksome bazaar, 1965.

Yorkville near at hand and it would never do to forget it. There will always be problem girls and girls who are never anything but a delight, but the opportunities for the former to create serious situations and have an influence on weaker characters are greater."

Jennie MacNeill was too puritanical to cope with sex 'n' drugs 'n' rock 'n' roll at the dawning of the Age of Aquarius. Yorkville was full of hairy hippies smoking joints, freaking out, making free love and being carried away in police paddy wagons for breaking the law. Miss MacNeill was on the side of the police.

"The year I was a prefect," recalled Pat Strathy Davidson, "Miss MacNeill called us all in and told us 'You have to make unpopular choices. If your friends are breaking rules, you have an obligation to the school to report them.' Well, all my friends were around the corner at the Ranch House restaurant, smoking, desecrating their uniforms! What was

I to do? We prefects talked it over with the head girl, and we decided it wasn't our job. Who were we to judge them?"

Branksome girls were watched. "You couldn't go to Yorkville," said Jane Rapp. "You were afraid of being reported. One day I was walking home with a boy, and a neighbour called the school office. I was told I shouldn't be associating with boys in my uniform!"

Carol Wilton, an honours student who left in 1968 to attend a junior college in Switzerland, found Branksome's code of conduct so surreal it created irreverence for the system. "Here we were in the middle of the sexual revolution," Carol said, "and the two big rules were don't chew gum and don't throw orange peels on the floor of the overpass. It was so trivial, it alerted you to the comical side of authority for the rest of your life. If you wanted to design a system for independent thinking, it wouldn't be Branksome, but that's the way it worked."

For all Miss MacNeill's vigilance — every tip, however malicious or misinformed, was checked out — Branksome was dangerously indifferent to the safety of girls living in residence. There were no security guards or night watchmen and nothing to prevent intruders from climbing up fire escapes and through open windows. One night a girl woke up to find a homeless man snoring on the floor beside her bed, and a group of half-naked college boys partied it up with girls in a boarder's bedroom before Sadie Scotland, who had an attic room at 10 Elm Avenue, raised the alarm. The boys fled, pursued by Miss Scotland and Miss MacNeill in their nighties, and when no one was caught, the incident was explained away as a fraternity prank. The possibility that her boarders might be sexually assaulted doesn't seem to have crossed Jennie's mind.

Sex was on everybody else's mind, and it was at the top of the agenda when *Globe and Mail* columnist Zena Cherry interviewed Miss MacNeill in February 1968:

> "You must have had to adjust your thinking tremendously about young people — regarding sex and such — there have

> been so many changes?" I asked Dr. Jennie E. MacNeill who will retire from Branksome Hall girls' school in June.
>
> "Not really," she answered. "We emphasize that one of the cornerstones of the school is purity."
>
> I bare my bruised soul to you when I admit I was a little embarrassed. I hadn't heard such a square statement for a long time.

Jennie was absolutely sincere but wilfully blind to promiscuity, teenage pregnancy, illegal abortion, the pill and venereal disease. "It's possible the day may come when we teach sex at Branksome," she went on,

> but I feel if parents were doing what they should be doing, schools wouldn't be dabbling in it. The subject must be handled so carefully; otherwise it can do much harm. Branksome parents, on the whole, I'm happy to say, are intelligent enough to cope, but as for this early dating and going steady, I think parents are just plain crazy to allow it.

For boarder Linda Kennedy (now Dee Burnlees), an only child from Owen Sound, Ontario, her two years in residence, 1959–60, were a golden opportunity to learn to socialize with other girls and to develop independence and self-reliance: "My first year was spent in the junior house above the main offices. I shared a small room on the west side of a narrow hall with a round elf resident. She loved to dance around so lightly you didn't hear a sound. She was jolly company and prevented me from being homesick. Not far along the hall was the séance room. That resident went in for hypnotism and cards. The housemother was a tiny elderly lady whom we seldom saw.

"My roommate and I both graduated to the senior residence the next year. Sherborne House had large rooms accommodating four girls each.

We were joined by a passionate Ottawa Rough Riders fan and a girl from Sudbury who horrified me by piercing her ears with a needle and a cork. We would plan extensively for the dance with the St. Andrew's boys and for graduation. We saw even less of our housemother here who always seemed to be hurrying out in her army uniform to some meeting or other. There was a study hall downstairs packed with desks where we did homework, wrote poems, memorized verses or doodled intensely. Memorizing fifty Bible verses earned you a free weekend 'out.'

"You needed a written invitation from an approved relative to take these extra weekends out of school. Most of us were much too far from families to warrant more than holiday visits. The residential students then included girls from Bermuda, Boston, Cuba, Peru, the Maritimes and Ottawa. They included physically and mentally handicapped girls, survivors of divorced parents, orphans and one adoptee fleeing the menopausal rages of her mother. Some shared their stories; others kept their silence, brooding. Others created fantasy families and lives outside. By seeing other girls up close and personal, I learned we all have problems, and we all deal with them in ways that best suit the individual. The kindly housemothers offered support, and the weekend staff provided assorted diversions. Weekend outings were limited to either the Art Gallery of Ontario or the Royal Ontario Museum, returning to school by 5 p.m. These provided wonderful walks in the heart of Toronto. We loved the Swiss Chalet, foreign films and the Imperial movie theatre. Sometimes the school organized a special event such as a trip to see *The Magic Flute.* The ultimate trip was the occasion when the physical education teacher took a group of girls to Bermuda for the spring break!

"I loved Sunday breakfasts of delicious hot currant biscuits with butter and honey, which could be eaten down in the kitchen in a housecoat. Sunday evening often brought a missionary to speak about her adventures in the field. I remember having breathing lessons from the famous singer Portia White. We lay on the floor, and she piled seven books on each abdomen. We were to breathe so as to push those books up and down slowly. There were oil-painting lessons in an artist's studio on Sherbourne Street.

"The main dining hall was a wondrous place of long, dark, wood tables and benches. The staff sat at the middle table, with the principal sitting in a large armchair at the end. Above her on the wall were two round mirrors that worked like Victorian gazing balls, so the staff could probably see everyone in the room behind them. At breakfast, we lined up to get Red River cereal or oatmeal, which is still my favourite. There were sausages too. Dinner was a more formal affair, with bowls and platters of food to be passed around. Most memorable were huge silver punch bowls full of Jell-O or pudding to be dished out by the presiding adults. The kitchen behind the dining room was all tiled and full of stainless steel cauldrons and steam tables. A surprisingly small staff cooked for the many residents. The cooks were helped by a couple of students who were the children of missionaries in far-off fields. I suspect their aid with serving and dishes earned them pocket money or helped defray their fees."

Students who lived at home were not as sheltered from the social upheavals of the 1960s, and there was more to the student restlessness than sex and drugs. Canadians sympathized with Martin Luther King's civil rights movement in the United States; they were impressed by the televised images of mass marches, sit-ins and police violence, and especially among the young, there was passionate opposition to the war in Vietnam. Students were arguing about ethical, racial and political issues, and they were fascinated by a newcomer to the Canadian political scene: Pierre Elliott Trudeau. Canada, still euphoric from the 1967 centennial celebrations, was swept by a wave of "Trudeaumania" in the spring of 1968 as the fey, bilingual, bicultural, bachelor lawyer from Quebec somersaulted into the leadership of the Liberal Party and succeeded Lester B. Pearson as prime minister.

Freedom was in the air, and French was in fashion. Fortuitously, Branksome Hall had chosen as its new principal its senior French teacher,

Margaret R. Sime.

Margaret Sime. There were those who thought the school should have looked outside for a younger candidate — Marg Sime would retire in six years — but no one could doubt her ability. Still lean and dark-haired, Miss Sime had matured from the timid graduate of Victoria College who had come to Branksome, her first teaching job, in 1932. She was respected, even feared, by her students. Her colleagues considered her smart, fair and approachable but cold. Her sharp wit could be scathing, and she suffered no fools.

Marg Sime smoked. In fact, she chain-smoked, in her office, with the windows open (the teachers smoked in the "staff apartment," a dingy room above a garage behind 16 Elm Avenue). And she drank. At a dinner hosted by the chairman of the board, Miss Sime was asked if she would like a glass of sherry. "Why is it," she snapped back, "that everyone thinks headmistresses of girls' schools drink sherry?" The chairman timidly asked what she would prefer. "Scotch on the rocks, please," she replied.

When it came to dealing with her board, Margaret Sime adopted Pierre Trudeau's aggressive, gunslinger pose. In her mission statement, "The Aims and Objectives of Branksome Hall School," submitted to the board in August 1968, she wrote,

> If the Principal is to be, as she should be, an educator in the true sense of the word, directing, counselling, and advising staff and students, maintaining a liaison with parents and with

> other schools and keeping abreast of modern educational research and experiment, it is evident that steps must be taken to prevent her from becoming no more than a glorified housemother with administrative duties. The two obvious measures are the appointment of a Business Administrator and a Dean of Residence.

Miss Sime's demands forced the board to confront some troubling questions. Do we have an operating budget? Where is our plan for the next ten years? Do we know how much it has cost us, per girl, to operate this school over the past ten years? Do we have an inventory of our physical assets, their ages and the costs of maintenance? Why don't we have a salary scale for our teachers? Why don't more Branksome alumnae sit on the board?

Apart from the principal, the only woman at board meetings was, ex officio, the president of the Alumnae Association. The association did not want to come under the board's thumb, as it had been in Miss Read's day, and the board had never thought to recruit new members from among the school's graduates. However, the death of Clive Thomson, at age seventy-eight, in February 1968, and the resignations of two more board members, left three vacancies. The new chairman, businessman Marshal Stearns, was in favour of asking alumnae to fill these vacancies, but the search committee was able to find only one: Mary Alice Burton Stuart.

Winner of the Governor General's Medal at Branksome Hall in 1945, and gold medallist at University College in 1949, Mary Alice had made a career of being a volunteer, bringing her energy, aplomb and acumen to the boards of many of Toronto's arts and charitable institutions. Her daughter Clayton was a Branksome student, and Mary Alice had warm memories of her own school days: "I cannot remember as a Branksome girl ever feeling anything but liberated," she said, "and every ounce of liberation brought its pound of responsibility."

Mary Alice was not going to be a token. She would be heard, as well as seen, and there was plenty to talk about. The publication in June 1968 of *Living and Learning,* the report of the Provincial Committee on Aims and Objectives of Education in the Schools of Ontario, exploded like a bombshell under both teachers and parents. The committee, chaired by Mr. Justice Emmet Hall and public school principal Lloyd Dennis, recommended a "child-centred" education that would allow students to progress through an ungraded, twelve-year school system at their own speed "without the hazards and frustrations of failure." This would require, the report said, new methods of assessment and promotion, more mobile classes and a broader curriculum: "The fixed positions of pupil and teacher, the insistence on silence, and the punitive approach must give way to a more relaxed teacher-pupil relationship which will encourage discussion, inquiry, experimentation and enhance the dignity of the individual."

It was characteristic of the time that the Hall-Dennis report, as it was called, never once referred to a pupil as "she," but its controversial recommendations encouraged Branksome Hall to take a good look at itself. Miss Sime still demanded that the girls stand when a teacher entered or left a classroom and when the girls spoke. "Insist that this courtesy be shown you, always," she admonished her teachers. Students' desks were arranged in neat rows, too, unless mathematics teacher Gwen Boyes dumped them over in a fit of rage. "There were teachers who taught by intimidation," said Pat Davidson.

While Ontario's students and educators generally welcomed the new ideas, parents worried about laziness, lack of discipline and whether their children would leave school unable to read or count. Fearful that the public schools would become egalitarian to the point of chaos, some parents saw the private schools as bastions of discipline and moral authority.

"We got so many girls from the public schools because of the lack of discipline," said Margaret Dowie, who became head of the Junior School in 1969. "There were so many rebels who didn't want to come to

Branksome and who were determined to rock the boat. They were very disruptive, but I told them, 'You'll never defeat me!' In one art class, the girls painted themselves, their hair, their faces, their clothes. I lined them up and got a pail of hot water and a scrubbing brush, and I scrubbed every one of them! 'You're going out of this school *clean,'* I said. 'You're probably going to have a wet kilt and wet hair, but I couldn't care less.' It never happened again."

Branksome parent Adam Zimmerman had become disenchanted with the school's authoritarian style, and in 1969 Zimmerman, President and CEO of Noranda Mines, joined the school's board of directors. "My daughter Barbara was in a class of very independent and bright girls," he said. "They were bored, and they got into mischief. They deserved punishment for mocking their teachers but not excoriation. It made me mad." Zimmerman could cut to the root of a problem like a chainsaw, and when he visited Branksome, he found it, as he said dryly, "quaint beyond charm." The buildings were antiquated, the curriculum was outdated and many of the teachers appeared to be older than the school. "There was nothing there," he shrugged.

Where to begin? Should the school's old houses be renovated or torn down and replaced? How much would it cost, and where would the money come from? Although Branksome had raised its fees sixty-eight percent in the past ten years, expenses had increased more than one hundred percent. The school was selling off property to cover its losses. Miss Ann Laidlaw, who had bequeathed her family mansion, 32 North Sherbourne, to Branksome Hall, would have been horrified to see it rented out, then sold for $72,000 in 1968, and the rooming house at 126 Mount Pleasant Road was sold for $26,000 the following year. Clearly, Branksome could no longer survive on student fees alone, and it could no longer function as a relic of the Victorian age.

At Miss Sime's insistence, the board decided to add a new wing to the east side of 10 Elm Avenue. The addition would house an upgraded library and resource centre, a language laboratory — Miss Sime had

Language lab in the new Sime wing, 1978.

pioneered the practice of teaching French in French in Toronto — and office space for an expanded administration. The new business manager, Harold Hudson, a semi-retired insurance executive, became the first man hired "upstairs" at Branksome Hall. Music teacher Earl Davey would follow in 1973, and among the students, Branksome developed a more relaxed attitude toward boys.

"Debating was attractive because we could debate the boys' schools," said Linda McQuaig, President of Branksome's debating club from 1969 to 1970. "It was sexy, and I was always pushing the limits of what we could debate to make it interesting. One year we debated the topic 'Love without licence is immoral.' In 1968, we beat UTS. Branksome was not considered a big intellectual school, but *we won. We knew we could win!*"

The next year the Branksome debating team of Carolyn Brown, Linda McQuaig and Ann Wilton beat out twenty-two Ontario schools to win the championship Terrance Cronyn Trophy in a tournament at Ridley College in St. Catharines, Ontario, debating both sides of challenging topics such as "Nationalism is a beneficial force in the world today." Linda won best speaker of the tournament. The following year, with Sheila McIntyre replacing Ann Wilton, Branksome won the trophy again, competing against thirty-one schools, and Linda McQuaig won for the best extemporaneous speech. "I had a good time," Linda said. "It was just arguing. It was fun." Linda credits her English teacher, Valerie Collins, for giving her tips on how to seize the audience's attention — Linda opened one debate by kissing the moderator — and speaking in public gave her confidence: "It was enormously creative and stimulating for me, an intellectual flowering. It was absolutely pivotal in getting me into public debates."

A survey of the school's forty teachers found that they were earning, on average, less than seventy-five percent of the salaries paid by the Toronto Board of Education (the average salary in Branksome's Senior School was $6,200, $5,185 in the Junior School). The average age for Senior School teachers was fifty and forty-seven for those in the Junior School.

"A friend of mine thought that Branksome Hall was an old folks home," laughed Susan MacGregor, a science teacher who came to Branksome in 1970. "The school had old, navy blue nurses' capes for the teachers to wear going from building to building, and he'd seen all these white-haired ladies flitting about like witches."

At Adam Zimmerman's insistence, the school raised the teachers' salary benchmark to eighty-five percent of the Toronto scale and gave teachers an immediate raise. Miss Sime began seeking out new young teachers with fresh ideas and lots of enthusiasm: Barbara Healey introduced psychology, sociology and a progressive guidance program, Vesna Davidovac joined Susan MacGregor in the science department and Josie Kizoff began to reorganize health and physical education. In English, Nora McRae and Judith Barker Quigley taught "The Emergent Woman," an avant-garde course focussed entirely on literature by and about women. The writers studied included Margaret Laurence and Margaret Atwood, Sylvia Plath and Virginia Woolf, and reading Plath and Woolf encouraged discussion about insanity and suicide. In 1971, Susan Kenny, a young graduate of Bryn Mawr College, became head of the English department.

After Miss Kenny arrived, Grade Nine students were no longer required to study Scott's "The Lay of the Last Minstrel." Nobody missed it. The compulsory scripture course had already been eliminated for Grade Thirteen. "I was told," Susan said, "that girls had been coming into English class afterwards and slamming their books on the desk. They'd had enough of 'God's Plan.' God's Plan had become a school joke." The plan was the invention of the fundamentalist scripture teacher, Ella Forsyth, who tried to sweeten the boarders' compulsory Sunday-evening services by offering them oranges. "I lived in the school my first year," Susan Kenny said, "and I attended one Sunday meeting because I was interested in the speaker. Miss Forsyth offered to give me an orange if I would come every Sunday." The missionaries' stories and photographs of life in China, India and Africa, however, did broaden the girls' knowledge of countries they would be unlikely to study in class.

Branksome students were demanding rights in return for their responsibilities. After 1970, the prefects were elected by the students and teachers of the Senior School. Previously, the principal's choice of prefects and head girl had always been a mystery equivalent to the Vatican's selection of a pope. Nancy Adams MacDonnell, head girl in 1962, remembers it this way: "My family was at our cottage the week before school started. The phone rang, and my mother had a hasty conversation. Then she dashed next door, obviously to return the call. It was Miss MacNeill, asking my mother's permission to appoint me head girl. My mother told me. That was the first I knew of it. Of course, I was thrilled!"

Miss MacNeill and Miss Read had chosen girls they considered to be leaders (or girls in need of self-esteem), but if their choices weren't popular with the students, school spirit sagged, and extra-curricular activities suffered from apathy. However, the new system was a compromise. Miss Sime reserved the right to assign each prefect to her task and to choose the head girl from the prefects. There was no campaigning. All Grade Twelve students were in the running, and the votes each girl received were kept secret. While the students generally approved of the girls elected, and the girls felt honoured, it could not be called a lesson in democracy.

Academically, Miss Sime's greatest challenge was to introduce the new Ontario academic credit system to the Senior School, a gargantuan task that required reorganizing the entire curriculum and timetable. She made the school more egalitarian by eliminating the A, B and C designations for the Senior School grades, and once the $630,000 Sime Wing opened in October 1971, all the students finally had lockers. The common room, however, could be used only for club and clan meetings, a practice that predated Miss MacNeill's era, and senior girls were expected to spend their spare classes in the library.

Miss Sime, in charge of policing the school uniform since the kilt had been introduced, remained strict. "On my first day at Branksome Hall, my brand-new kilt hung straight down to my knees," recalled Julie Wood Lucas, who arrived in 1969 as a Grade Ten student. "Everyone else had fashionably short kilts. That night I carefully raised the hem, labouring through miles of pleats, and pressed it all neatly.

"On my second day, happy in my short kilt, there was a surprise kilt inspection. While the victim knelt on the floor, the distance from hem to floor was measured — three inches maximum. I alone failed! How could this be?

"That night I dropped the hem again — miles of #@! pleats — and passed inspection (on the stage!) on day three. Now my kilt was long again, and everyone else's was short. AARRGGHH! Then some kind, pitying soul showed me how to roll the waistband, and I was both cool and legal."

Marg Sime gave her teachers optimum freedom in their classrooms, but she could be a stickler for procedure. If a teacher wanted to run off a test paper on the school's gestetner, she had to make her request in writing, and Miss Sime returned it initialled. She also insisted on signing every girl's report card herself, with a handwritten personal comment. "She'd gather all the teachers together, and we'd go through *every* student," sighed Barbara Healey. "The girl's marks were read out, and we'd decide whether she should get excellent, very good, good or satisfactory. No student was ever rated 'poor,' so 'satisfactory' was a terrible thing to get on your report card."

Marg Sime allowed her women teachers to wear pantsuits, and she didn't object to young men with long hair. "She wasn't put off by my beard and garish clothes," marvelled music teacher Earl Davey. "I was married. Maybe that helped a bit." Miss Sime could be a feminist, too, with a sly sense of humour. Invited to one "black tie" party, she arrived wearing a navy blue suit, a white blouse and a black tie. When Governor General Roland Michener officially opened the school's new tennis courts in 1972, Branksome board chairman Nicholas Fodor proposed an inaugural match between Michener and himself. Miss Sime tartly reminded Fodor that the tennis courts were for the *girls* and that he and Michener would play a doubles match with two student partners,

Opening game, 1972: Governor General Roland Michener and Margaret Bartlett vs. Nicholas Fodor and Betsy Kofman.

Margaret Bartlett and Betsy Kofman. "She stood up for what she believed, no matter having people such as me breathing down her neck," said Adam Zimmerman. "She stood her ground and gave it only gracefully. I would describe Miss Sime's style of teaching and management to be to follow the straight and narrow in the traditional way."

Susan MacGregor agreed: "She considered women to be *ladies.* When we raised the issue of salaries at a staff meeting, she told us '*Ladies* do not discuss money!'" Some of Branksome's more casual, laid-back teachers found Miss Sime's concepts of ladylike behaviour absurdly archaic. "We'd have tea out of a little china cup," recalled swimming teacher and coach Joan Lumsdon. "You had your own cup. If you were in the 'in' group, you got invited to Miss Sime's for lunch. Lunch was a boiled egg. You'd write your name on the egg and place it in a pot of boiling water. You'd have your own egg, toast and soup and starve. You wouldn't *dare* call anybody by her first name! Everybody had her own chair. God help you if you sat in the wrong chair! I sat on the floor at staff meetings for eight years. When Rose Westcott retired, she willed me her chair."

Ladies didn't discuss liquor either, but while Miss Sime forbade liquor on school property, everyone knew she enjoyed a nightcap. Why couldn't the teachers have a drink from time to time? When Miss Sime gave the Senior School teachers permission to have a drink with their dinner before Parents' Night, Margaret Dowie made the same request on behalf of the Junior School staff. Parents' Night came with no reply, and since Miss Sime rarely came to the Junior School, the teachers went ahead. "We got a bottle of gin," said Mrs. Dowie, "and we had just proceeded to pour the gin when who should come in the door but Miss Sime! 'Oh, Miss Sime,' I said, 'we do this all the time!' She didn't say anything, so we all had our gin and tonic from then on."

Ladies were calling themselves women now, and women were addressing each other by their first names, but at prayers Marg Sime gave the girls "improving lectures" on manners, morals and the "social graces." In her 1968 mission statement, she had defined the school's chief aim to be

Marg Sime and Marg Dowie share a drink at the 1988 Alumnae Dinner.

"the building of the character of its pupils so that we may send into the world women of courage, discernment and understanding, women devoted to the search for truth, women prepared to be the wives and mothers of Canada's most responsible citizens."

The world was no longer as Miss Sime saw it. Women *were* responsible citizens, and young women were experimenting with the limits of that responsibility. "After the Installation of Prefects, we all went up to one girl's cottage for the Thanksgiving weekend," recalled Sandra Bolté Amell, sports captain and prefect in 1973. "One of the girls was really into marijuana, and she passed it around. Some of us tried it — I wasn't even aware there was any in the school — and, boy, we had a great time! I guess the rest didn't, because on Tuesday morning Miss Sime called us in. She told us she would speak to our parents and that we would no longer be considered prefects." The "smokers," however, were not stripped of their duties, and they continued to wear their red ties and kilts.

Joan Lumsdon remembered Miss Sime writing a skit for prayers spoofing the incident: "We all wore kilts, and to the tune of 'Onward Christian

Soldiers,' we sang 'We're marching off to Jarvis smoking pot.' How was it possible that that old broad would have known about pot? She was very cool, very level-headed. She was a liberated woman, although people didn't think she was. Miss Sime looked stern, but she was a loveable woman."

Branksome's board unanimously endorsed Miss Sime's handling of the pot-smoking prefects, but the miscreants and their parents didn't find much to laugh about. Parents were outraged that their daughters were being punished by the school for something they had done out of uniform, on a weekend, in a private home (did anyone in Toronto *not* experiment with marijuana?), and since their status remained ambiguous, the prefects had been sentenced to a year in purgatory.

"We continued on, but we were a split group," Sandra Bolté Amell said sadly. There were hard feelings between the smokers and non-smokers and toward the prefect who had snitched. "I could lose myself in sports activities, which I loved," Sandra said, "but every now and then I'd think 'What am I doing here?' Miss Sime did not personally acknowledge us, even at graduation."

Running Branksome Hall was a more stressful and complicated business than it had been when Marg Sime became principal in 1968. With a student population over six hundred, Miss Sime had to abandon her attempts to get to know each girl as an individual, yet she tried to interview every student at least once a year about her report card, and she wrote personal letters of recommendation for the graduates. She did all the student admissions and teacher interviews and met with unhappy or angry parents. She handled all the school's correspondence, except for that of the business office, set the rules, enforced discipline, counselled girls in difficulty and, until the school finally hired a dean of residence, supervised the housemothers and boarders. She ate most of her evening meals with the girls, read prayers after dinner and entertained groups of girls in her residence after the Sunday-evening services.

When Marg Sime drew up her own job description in 1972 to assist the search committee looking for her successor, it was clear that she was doing the work of four people. Branksome intended to hire only one. Where would the school find someone willing to take on such a task?

First year of Branksome Hall, 1903–04.

Miss Scott.

Tennis anyone? c. 1911

Back row: Violet Robinson, Mary Hamilton, Frances Grant, Freda Cole, Maizie Tyrell, Christine Raynar. Middle row: (Lucille Shaubert), Beatrice Shand, Edith Read, Miss Gardiner. Front row: Unknown, Ainslie McMichael, Norah Burke. c. 1916

Branksome students, 1919.

The pool, opened 1926.

Florence Downing, Virginia Peers, Donnajean Holmes on porch above porte-cochère, 1934.

Shirley Halsted, Jane Egbert, Mary Holmes, Lucille Dixon, Joyce Phillips '39, with Scott House in background, 1938-39.

In class with then teacher Margaret Sime, 1951.

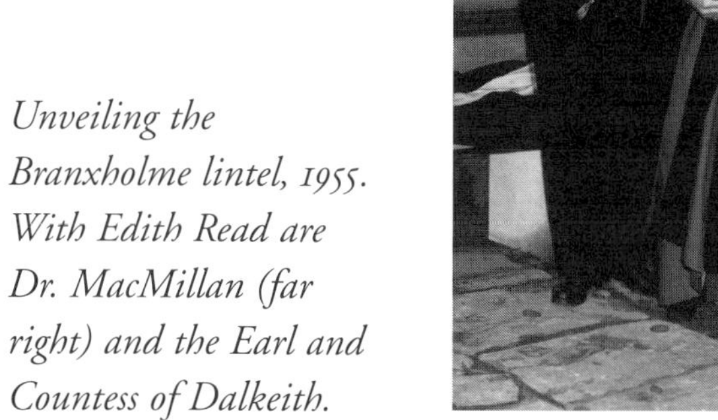

Unveiling the Branxholme lintel, 1955. With Edith Read are Dr. MacMillan (far right) and the Earl and Countess of Dalkeith.

The new library, 1957.

Ceremonial tree planting, 1967. Head Girl Susan Collyer van Tijn '67 and Miss MacNeill.

Staff, 1970-71.
Back row: Mrs. Dick, Mrs. McRae, Miss Keyes, Mrs. Lumsdon, Mrs. Van Fleet, Mrs. Olson, Miss Brough, Miss Snowden, Miss Duperley, unknown, Mrs. Petersen, unknown, Mme. DeHenne, Mrs. Chenoweth, Mrs. Duchemin, unknown, Miss Zimmerman, Miss Vlasinich, Mrs. Naftolin, unknown. Middle row: Miss Baker, unknown, Mrs. Glanville, Mme. Menc, Miss Forsyth, Mrs. Campbell, Mrs. Flett, Mrs. Hay, Miss Barker, unknown, Mr. Hudson, unknown, unknown, Mrs. Gamey, Mrs. Wade, Miss Boyes, Miss Howie, Miss Scotland, Mrs. Westcott, unknown, unknown. Front row: Miss Forder, Mrs. McMillan, Mrs. Coulter, Mrs. Coutts, Miss Claxton, Miss Sime, Mrs. Dowie, Mrs. MacGregor, Mrs. Markes, Miss Brown, Mrs. White.

Dame Diana Reader Harris and Margaret Sime, 1979.

Student production of "You Can't Take It With You," 1982.

Carol Service Pageant, 1982.

Debate, 1983.

Grade 9 History students meet former U.S. President Jimmy Carter at Universal Speakers Luncheon, 1984.

Junior School teachers Robin Medcalf, Dorothy Brough, and Liivi Georgievski, 1986.

Wizard of Oz production, 1980s.

Branksome supports our Community.
A group of Branksome students, alumnae, parents, faculty and friends entered a team in the Heart and Stroke Ride for Heart in the spring of 1991.
From left to right: Pat Strathy Davidson '60 (Board member), unidentified male behind, Sally Adams Medland '66, Andrew Medland, John Medland, Scott Walters (back), The Right Honourable Roland Michener (former Governor General of Canada and Official Starter of the 1991 Ride for Heart), Allison Roach (Principal), Paul Kizoff (behind Allison), Karrie Walsh '91, Tracey Ferriss '91, George Booth (Chair, Board of Governors), Victoria Hartley '91, Mary Lesslie Hallward '74, Graeme Hallward, Bob Medland, Jim Griffiths, Colin Watson and in front, Joyce Walker McKeough '56 (Board member), and Phil MacDonnell.

Math teacher Pam Young.

Staff versus students tug of war.

Students awaiting start of the Terry Fox Run.

Ruth Ann Penny.

Mary Barker '23, niece of W.D. Ross and Branksome teacher 1926-29.

Karen Murton's installation as Principal. Sarah Psutka, Karen Murton, Ann Wilson, Tony Graham.

Rhythm & Truth Brass Band and Stage Band perform at Mardi Gras in the quad, 1998. Heather Cole, Olivia Tischler, Elizabeth Hermant, Megan Snell, Michelle Omura.

English teacher Susan Kenny and students "in the Branksome spirit."

Chapter Six

ALLISON ROACH, VICE-PRINCIPAL of George Harvey Secondary School, a public school with more than two thousand students in suburban Toronto, had no intention of applying for the job of principal of Branksome Hall. She had been at George Harvey only a year, and at age forty-one, she could expect further promotion within the public school system. Allison's closest friends, however, were her old Branksome schoolmates, and they thought Allison would be a perfect match for the school. They persuaded her to meet with board member Joyce Frankel Kofman, a member of the search committee.

"We were certainly interested in someone outside the school," Joyce said. With a master's degree in education from the University of Toronto, years of experience as an English teacher, and a good working knowledge of the public school system, Allison Roach would bring to Branksome a fresh perspective, and it would be complemented by her intimate knowledge of Branksome as a student and prefect. She had the advantages of both worlds, and she had the same energetic exuberance that Edith Read had brought to the school nearly seventy years before. Allison personified the Branksome ideal of the "all-round girl." Straightforward, unaffected and self-disciplined, she was a high achiever with a big laugh and a wacky sense of humour who loved sports and music and appreciated the school's Christian traditions. Miss Roach also had a quick temper, forceful opinions and limited patience.

"Every time I tried to talk to the search committee about education,

Allison Roach.

they shut me up and asked me what my five-year plan was," Allison recalled. "I said, 'I have no five-year plan because I don't know anything about the school, and you know absolutely nothing about me!' I didn't know what they were looking for, and they certainly didn't know what they were getting. I took the job because I loved the school, and I wanted to go back into teaching. I didn't like administration very much compared to teaching."

As principal of Branksome, Allison would be able to teach a senior English class, and before she took over in June 1974, Marg Sime reassured her that when it came to teachers' salaries, the Junior School and the residence, everything looked after itself. "Of course," said Allison, "these were my great problems." Salary increases were lagging well behind raises for public school teachers, pensions were pitiful, Junior School teachers were leaving en masse — Miss Sime had at one point proposed closing the Junior School altogether — and residence was a nightmare.

"I remember being taken up to the second floor of Buccleuch," Allison shuddered. "The floors were all dirty-coloured beige linoleum that had great rips in it, and this was the same at Sherborne House and on the second and third floors of 10 Elm Avenue. The walls were a dirty yellow, and the rooms had iron beds that were white, and they were chipped. They had khaki army blankets and for light one bare lightbulb hanging from the ceiling. I was horrified. I wouldn't show people through the residence, I was so ashamed."

As soon as Joyce Frankel Kofman and other board members toured the residence, they committed enough money to redecorate and refurnish all the rooms. Branksome, with more than one hundred girls in residence, could not afford to lose boarders, but the Dickensian decor was only part of a larger problem. Residence rules had changed little in fifty years. Boarders no longer had to memorize Bible verses to go out on Saturday afternoons, or to take an early morning walk around the block, but crowded into tiny rooms, they resented their lack of privacy. Use of a single, communal telephone, located in a hall, was restricted, permission slips were required for petty errands and their behaviour was constantly criticized. Punishments were unjust and excessive. Branksome's boarders had become rebellious, and they probably accounted for most of the one hundred girls, fourteen percent of the student population, who regularly did not return the following year. The situation improved in 1975 when Allison appointed a diplomatic, warm-hearted Scottish widow, Anna McMillan, a retired teacher, as dean of residence.

Joyce Frankel Kofman.

Anna McMillan.

"The biggest thing you needed was common sense," said Mrs. Mac, as the girls called Mrs. McMillan. "If you spoke to them as human beings, they would understand. They didn't like to be bossed. I wouldn't be after them all the time." She involved the girls in running their own houses by setting up residence councils, and she met with them informally every Thursday night. She got rid of rules she thought hidebound and irrational, and while the girls were still confined to residence at night unless invited to a family home, Mrs. Mac tactfully slept through their pyjama parties. She understood how girls who had been sent to the school against their will could be angry and miserable: "They hated being in boarding, and I had to feel sorry for them."

Some nights Anna, tipped off by the girls, would check out the Yorkville and Bloor Street coffeehouses for girls who had sneaked out. "There were plenty of back doors," Anna said, "and a lot of girls did sneak out. We'd find them. None of them got into any trouble. I'd say, 'Get to bed, and I'll see you in the morning.' If I spoke quietly, didn't make a fuss, I found the girls very reasonable. I had to make them understand my responsibility for them. You have to see the funny side to put up with it. They thought they were being so clever!"

Mrs. Mac was a wise, compassionate housemother, but she couldn't fix the plumbing. Toilets blocked up, bathtubs overflowed. "I walked into MacNeill House, and the floor of the residence upstairs was flooded with water from overflowed toilets," Allison recalled. "Students and I mopped up. Some water had seeped into the kitchen below. The dietician, Miss Kawano, and I cleaned the kitchen thoroughly until after 1 a.m. That's what you did. I came into 10 Elm Avenue one morning, and I saw Anne Bedard sitting at her desk in the guidance office writing away, and she had an umbrella over her head. I said, 'What on earth?' And she said, 'I'm trying to protect myself from the leak.' The pipes used to freeze. I'd come into 10 Elm, and there would be mist everywhere. I remember Nora McRae walking through the mist, saying, 'A Japanese landscape! Isn't this wonderful, it's a Japanese landscape.'" When the water pipes broke in the basement locker room, the teachers waded in to rescue the students' possessions. "There was Edwina Baker down there directing the evacuation of the students' lockers. It was like the London blitz. There was a wonderful esprit de corps. The working conditions were appalling, but the teachers didn't complain. They took things with good humour, rolled with the punches." Edwina Baker said crisply, "You always have to be prepared for the unusual to happen."

Anne Bedard, 1979.

Years before, Miss Read had conceived the idea that a monster boiler in the basement of 10 Elm Avenue could, through a network of underground pipes, supply hot water to all the school's properties east of Mount Pleasant Road. Not only had the pipes rusted, but also if the residences wanted hot running water in warm weather, classrooms had to put up with hot radiators. In cold weather, maintenance man John Preston slept on a cot beside the old furnace, ready to jump up if it turned off, and swimming instructor Joan Lumsdon cautiously tested the pool every morning, fearful that the first girl to jump in might be boiled alive.

Joan Lumsdon was developing a swimming program that would soon dominate competition among Ontario's independent girls' schools. Joan had begun full time in 1969, working in the narrow, twenty-yard pool with girls who found the school's bathing suits repulsive. Branksome provided a bin full of shapeless, blue-grey, one-size-fits-all cotton suits, and as soon as the suits got wet, they sagged down to the girls' knees. "No wonder the

Joan Lumsdon with a kindergarten class.

girls hated swimming," Joan said. She solved the problem by ordering stretch suits in Branksome colours for the students to buy as part of their uniform. She also abolished the practice of having the girls step into a basin of chemically treated water before entering the pool area. "Not long after I started," Joan recalled, "the nurse, Miss Forder, arrived with a brown shopping bag full of bottles and a blue plastic tub, like a baby's bath. 'This is a footbath,' she said. 'A what?' I said. 'They're illegal. They went out with the dark ages.' I took a brown bottle from the shopping bag. It was formaldehyde. 'What are you doing,' I said, 'embalming them?'"

Vera Forder, along with Gwen Boyes and Ella Forsyth, had left the school when Miss Sime retired, taking with them much of its eccentricity. Margaret Dowie had retired as head of the Junior School in 1973, but Branksome's Scottish identity was safe in the hands of her successor, Glasgow native Dorothy Brough. Margaret Sime had rarely visited the Junior School, and she had ignored the deteriorating condition of the buildings.

Darcy Bett Sutherland, a Junior School pupil at the time, remembers Readacres as wonderfully creepy. "It had a lot of character. The cloakroom in the basement was dark, and there were rooms full of old doors and desks. We were never allowed to go to the third floor. It was spooky, so we'd try to sneak up the staircase. We'd slide down the banister. I loved that staircase, with its stained-glass window, and the big windows in the classrooms, fabulous windows, with shutters that you could close, and the long oak table in the library with its huge, carved legs." Darcy had plenty of time to study the school's furnishings since, as punishment for misbehaviour, she had to sit quietly, hands folded in her lap, while her classmates were playing outside. An athletic, independent girl, Darcy had trouble staying still, but while she found Miss Brough and teacher Lillian Howie strict disciplinarians, she loved her teachers and her classmates. "My best school friends were boys," she laughed.

Dorothy Brough, Head of Junior School.

Since 1940, when the kindergarten had started accepting boys, some boys had attended the Junior School until Grade Three. Integration raised the possibility that Branksome could become a co-ed school. Miss Sime had already polled parents about the prospect of co-education. She had found them strongly opposed. Applications from boys were dwindling, and Branksome stopped admitting them.

Allison Roach continued daily prayers in the gym — the school did not have, and she did not want, disembodied voices barking out of an intercom — but she quietly dropped the school song, "Up and On," so full of sexual double entendre girls had giggled over it since her own schooldays. She lengthened class periods and the school day. Branksome girls would work harder, and except in gym class, where they played in their bloomers, they wore their kilts three inches above the knee.

Allison expressed her vision for the school in the 1975 *Slogan:*

> Branksome is a small school. I see it as a school with a real sense of community. We assemble together every morning, we know each other and where we belong, we are aware of what activities are going on in the school and have the opportunity to participate fully. The buildings, in a sense, belong to the students. There are few locks and few places in the school which cannot be fully used throughout the day. It is a school where most activities are actually run, and run well, by the students themselves. It reverberates with chatter and laughter. Finally, it is a place where grievances and suggestions for improvement *can* be heard, discussed and quickly acted upon if possible. I would like to see Branksome grow as a result of increased student involvement, of their taking more responsibility for the excellence of their school as a place of learning and recreation and as a place of residence.

The contentious issue of what kind of school Branksome Hall would become had preoccupied the Branksome community since the board of directors had formed its first planning committee in 1968. The committee commissioned D.G. Pyper of Dickie Construction company to do an inventory of the school's properties, and his report was worrying. Not only were the plumbing, electrical wiring and interior finishings in all the buildings obsolete, but also the centre section of 10 Elm Avenue was so structurally unsound it would have to be demolished. In February 1969, the committee, chaired by Nicholas Fodor, recommended rebuilding the centre of 10 Elm and, as part of a master plan, eventually replacing the old houses and garages at 14 and 16 Elm Avenue with "a modern academic building."

The alumnae, however, thought that the old houses, with their attics, crannies and squeaking stairs, not only gave Branksome its romantic, gothic personality but also were as homey and comfortable as an old shoe. Students like Laureen Newman Fisher, who graduated in 1977, agreed: "I really enjoyed the oldness, the dented stairs. Those of us in our graduating year felt that it was because of *us* that they had to redo the school." In Branksome's maze of closets and twisting corridors, girls could try to hide from adult scrutiny. "Oh, I can be anonymous here," Sandy Smythe rejoiced when she put on the Branksome kilt. "Then at prayers, Miss Roach said, 'Hello, Sandy.' I had no anonymity. I was 'a Smythe.'" In Miss Sime's era, teachers who had been at the school for generations routinely called girls by their mothers' names. The girls didn't even try to correct them.

Old was great as far as the girls were concerned, but old was unsafe and costly to replace. In 1970, the school had set up the Branksome Hall Foundation to raise money for bursaries and school equipment from charitable donations, but the relatively small amounts of money that trickled in — $185,000 by 1974 — couldn't begin to cover rebuilding costs estimated at $750,000. In November 1972, a long-range planning subcommittee, chaired by Mary Alice Burton Stuart, undertook a thorough investigation of the school's needs. The committee concluded that Branksome should remain a girls' school with day and boarding pupils and an emphasis on academic achievement, discipline and school spirit. Branksome should also, the report said, "retain the old buildings which give the school its unique character." The Stuart report listed as immediate priorities a new gym and larger swimming pool, an auditorium, more classrooms and better facilities for art, music and drama. Submitting the report to the board on June 22, 1973, planning subcommittee chairman Glen Wilton stated, "The school requires money for capital projects, and income from the Foundation and students' fees should not be used for such purposes. The only course is a capital funds program. Such a program should be established without delay."

The capital campaign did not begin, however, until the spring of 1977, and it began, as Pyper had warned, in response to the impending collapse of the centre of 10 Elm Avenue. "Things were in such bad condition that we simply had to fix it," said Allison Roach. "We would not have been able to open the school. We rebuilt and then raised the money." For three years, Allison had patched and painted, washed woodwork and windows — the school couldn't afford enough cleaners — and wondered if she would have enough money to hire teachers for the next year. "I was so worried that the school was going to go under," she said. By May 1977, enrolment had dropped from nearly seven hundred girls to 662. Ed Patrick, who had taken over as business manager after the death of Harold Hudson in 1971, kept a close eye on the bottom line, and by raising fees and cutting costs to the bone, Branksome struggled through.

Adversity inspires ingenuity, and under Allison's leadership, Branksome was blossoming intellectually and artistically years before the building restoration got under way. "It was a buoyant time, very intellectually alive," recalled music teacher Earl Davey. "I was afraid when I went it would be so preppy, but I had a good choir, and I got along wonderfully with the girls. It didn't bother me being the only man on staff, girls received me so warmly. I worked them hard, and they were keen to excel." Davey directed a school choir of forty voices and a chamber choir of ten to fourteen girls. The choirs gave concerts in neighbourhood churches and, with beating hearts, at Lakefield College near Peterborough, where Prince Andrew was briefly a student, but they no longer competed in the Kiwanis Musical Festival. "I asked myself, 'Should we be doing artistic stuff for the sake of ribbons?'" Davey said, "and I said 'no.' You set your own standards for the talent you have available."

The school's big production, involving all the girls, was the December Carol Service. Under the direction of Davey's predecessor, Eunice Coutts, the service had grown into an artistically sophisticated event featuring medieval carols and original compositions that required hours of rehearsal. "The senior goldfish were in the pageant," Davey laughed, but playing an angel or the Virgin Mary remained the highlight of some girls' school careers. Nora McRae, responsible for rehearsing the tableau, is remembered for striding into the school office and saying loudly, "It's hard to find a virgin around here!"

Music teacher Earl Davey, 1978.

Christmas Carol Service at St. Paul's Church. Dan Bickle conducts.

Nora McRae and Susan Kenny.

Mrs. McRae, a striking woman with forceful opinions and a dramatic flair, was one of the school's many well-travelled teachers who enriched students' lives with their personal knowledge of art and theatre, museums and exotic places. For years, Nora and history teacher Aija Zommers sacrificed their own weekends and family time to coach the debating teams and drive the girls to tournaments all over Toronto and southern Ontario.

"The women's liberation movement, the feminist movement, really [was] evident in debating through my twenty-five years," Nora recalled in an interview shortly before her death in 1996. "At first, most of the girls would wilt when the boys put their thumbs under their lapels. They couldn't stand up to them. Then there was no more wilting. It just stopped happening." Part of the reason was probably Nora herself. "Nora was a feminist," said Judith Barker. "She didn't label herself, but she was. She'd say 'Just pay us the same.' It does come down to economics."

Allison Roach had an uncanny ability to find exceptionally innovative teachers, and she believed that the curriculum itself was less important than how it was taught. "It's what you have the kids *do* with that material that counts," she said. Her views were shared by Mimi Hollenberg, who arrived in 1976 to begin a part-time library program in the Junior School. Mrs. Hollenberg, an ebullient person, had a degree in library science from McGill University and first-class experience as a librarian. The Junior School library was a cramped little room in the old Glenhurst section, its collection a hodgepodge of books that had been donated over seventy years. Mimi culled the collection, selling and giving away books that were irrelevant, and since she had no budget, she invented ways of financing the library herself. Searching through publishers' catalogues and trade journals, she chose the books she wanted, ordered them, set up a bookstore-style display and invited parents, students and teachers to buy a book to donate to the library. "Parents would buy books in memory of people or as gifts for teachers," Mimi said. "One parent might buy many books." Donors received a tax receipt, and Mimi's twenty percent profit went into the library's budget to buy more books. Later, in collaboration with a Toronto children's bookstore, Mimi organized a spring sale of paperbacks, with part of the proceeds going to the library.

Ingenuity also characterized Mary Craig Tasker's new art program for Grades Seven and Eight. Mary, Grace Morris Craig's daughter and a Branksome grad, had studied for three years at Toronto's New School of Art, but she had no degree in fine art or experience as a teacher. Her art room was an old bedroom in Glenhurst, her office a closet. "I decided to look at art in a different way," Mary said. "I wanted to pull the creativity out of these kids. We used found objects, pieces of junk, newspapers, clay, string. I focussed on shape, line, colour, texture. We did collage, papier-mâché, calligraphy. The girls were quiet and active. There was a lot of psychotherapy going on while they were working away."

The art class represented only a fraction of the time and energy Mary was giving to the school. Elected president of the Alumnae Association in 1976, Mary was looking for ways to persuade Branksome's four thousand former students to contribute to the school's $1.5 million Restoration Fund. Demolition of the centre of 10 Elm Avenue had begun in the early spring, but by the end of June 1977, the fund, chaired by Mary Alice Burton Stuart, had raised only $102,000. "It was hard to know where to begin," Mary Alice reflected. "We had never before asked for money for capital needs. The school had no computer, no photocopier — we got a copier — and no list of all the alumnae. The school had thrown away all the names and addresses of parents, and there were no records of the graduates."

While fathers regularly wrote cheques to support their sons' schools, the idea of giving equally to a daughter's school was a novelty. Branksome Hall had never cultivated the wealthy women among its graduates, and in conservative social circles, it was still considered indelicate for women to ask for money. For decades, the Alumnae Association had raised thousands of dollars a year to buy furniture, musical instruments and equipment for the school, and they had done this the hard way, through bridge parties, supper dances, an annual art show and a mammoth biannual bazaar. Fund-raising had been a lot of work for a small, loyal group of Toronto women, and they had received little recognition. Only a few hundred of Branksome's alumnae, now dispersed around the world, paid $2 a year to join the association, and most of them were indifferent. Some of the lost girls may have remembered Miss Read's annual alumnae dinner in the basement dining room of 10 Elm Avenue, a menu that featured, year after year, meatloaf, potato chips, jellied salad and lemon meringue pie. During Miss Sime's era, the executive of the Alumnae Association rose to their feet when Miss Sime entered the room. Charlotte Keens Graham joked that she jumped to her feet when she heard Miss Sime's voice on the phone.

When school opened in September 1977, the Restoration Fund had raised less than $300,000, costs were estimated at $2.45 million and construction was still in full swing. "There was an area where there was no electricity, no heat and places where you could see blue sky," Allison Roach recalled. "One of the kids called me and said, 'There's a racoon in the sink.' I went up, and there was a sweet little racoon all enclosed in the sink in its nice little bed. The girls wore their winter clothing to school, but I had only two complaints. It was an adventure for them."

There was nostalgia over seeing the old school ripped apart.

Generations of boarders had descended the main staircase in their formal gowns to be presented to their dates waiting nervously below, and every student must have slid down the banister at least once. "Bye, bye, banister," one girl said, giving it a final hug. "Don't forget to keep the squeak in the stair," Joyce Frankel Kofman had cautioned Bill Grierson, the architect who designed the "recycling" of the school's property. For the girls, the best part of reconstruction was eyeing all the handsome, muscular workmen in hard hats.

Destruction had uncovered attics and cellars full of cast-off chairs, dressers, desks, windows, toilets and clawfoot bathtubs. Mary Craig Tasker hit on the idea of auctioning off the choice pieces and disposing of the rest at a giant garage sale. "For the auction, we had a big bash in the dining room with a cash bar," Mary recalled. "I thought, 'Poor Miss MacNeill, she would not like this at all.' Men were invited, and it was such a good party we ran out of Scotch." The proceeds provided the seed money to start a Parents' Association, and the garage sale, which raised $6,000, was, Mary realized, "a very successful thing for the morale and get-togetherness of the group."

They needed a boost. The worried chairman of the board, Adam Zimmerman, came into the school every morning at eight o'clock to go over construction costs with business manager Ed Patrick, and Zimmerman joked that, if the school didn't raise the money, he and the rest of the board would go to jail. Allison Roach didn't let her own worries affect the cheerful mood of the school. "We had a lot of fun," said Sandy Smythe. "It was a great time." Sandy and her mother, Dorothy, a professional musician, produced and directed the school's first musical cabaret, and starting with *The Sound of Music,* using boys from Toronto schools for the male roles, musicals became an annual event. Sandy was also sports captain, hockey coach and an honours student. "I gave a lot to Branksome, and it gave a lot to me," she said. "I had the opportunity to practise leadership roles, take initiative, develop self-confidence. I loved it there."

The late Pauline McGibbon, Lieutenant-Governor of Ontario, and Branksome Board Chair Adam Zimmerman at reopening of 10 Elm Avenue, 1978.

Completion of the restoration in 1978 coincided with Branksome Hall's seventy-fifth anniversary. Dame Diana Reader Harris, recently retired as headmistress of Sherborne School, was the guest of honour at a birthday banquet in April, and Ontario's Lieutenant-Governor, Pauline McGibbon, cut the ribbon for the official reopening of 10 Elm Avenue in October. The anniversary year was an ideal opportunity to invite the Branksome community, past and present, to tour the school. The alumnae held a gourmet luncheon for the oldest of the Old Girls, women who had attended Branksome Hall between 1903 and 1920. A surprising number of them accepted the invitation, and those who could not come wrote poignant reminiscences. The women who came had such a wonderful time that many classes began to hold regular gatherings such as luncheons and bridge games. The Alumnae Association persuaded the school's new business manager, Keith Sharpe, to give it a computer, and

Dodie Robinette MacNeill began to set up an alumnae database that included, in addition to names, addresses and phone numbers, professions and personal interests.

Branksome, with a record enrolment of 730 girls, was becoming more confident, adventurous and competitive. In 1978, Branksome became the first girls' school invited to participate in the independent boys' schools' debating tournament, the Fulford Cup. The same year, in order to compete against the public schools in sports, Branksome joined the Toronto District Intercollegiate Athletic Association.

The refurbished gymnasium, lengthened by twelve feet when the gallery was torn down and the stage moved to the opposite end, sparked fresh enthusiasm for sports. Physical education teachers Josie Kizoff and Diana Jennings Parker no longer had to store their equipment on the rafters, and they were opening up new possibilities for Branksome athletes. "The girls had been playing basketball in the fall, volleyball all winter and tennis in the spring," said Josie. "How boring. We started baseball and badminton, cross-country running, folk and jazz dance." Diana introduced yoga, power walking through the Rosedale ravine and a course in orienteering — using a compass to navigate around the Branksome campus.

Physical education, including swimming, was made compulsory, but it was divided into units, including health education, so girls could select the activities they preferred. Health classes covered fitness, genetics and anatomy as well as sex, pregnancy, childbirth, marriage, relationships and addictions. "The girls loved to talk about adolescent issues," Josie Kizoff said. "We talked about AIDS when that became a big, scary thing, anorexia, styles of leadership. You don't have to have a red kilt to be a leader. My husband was in the public school system, so I picked up a lot of ideas about where to get videos and guest speakers. I'd bring magazine stories about young people and read them."

Competition among independent girls' schools increased as new schools opened and more boys' schools admitted girls, and now that they

Girls in Lower Field with "Ribbit", the Branksome mascot, 1982.

had proper gym uniforms, Branksome girls were ready to take on the province at the Ontario Federation of Schools Athletic Association's annual meets. Branksome did well in Metro Toronto competitions, particularly in badminton, volleyball and soccer, but three fleet-footed sisters, Kate, Alison and Sarah Wiley, dominated the competition in middle-distance track meets and cross-country races. In 1979, at age fifteen, Alison set a Metro Toronto midget record for 3,000 metres, and in June 1980, the Branksome team of Darcy Bett, Jane Horner and the three Wiley sisters won the girls' championship at the OFSAA meet in Etobicoke. The following year, at the OFSAA meet in Thunder Bay, Branksome took the title again, with Kate Wiley victorious in her division's 1,500 and 3,000 metre races, Alison Wiley at 800, 1,500 and 3,000 metres.

"We were the breakthrough," said Alison. "Here we were, this team of four or five girls from a little school up against teams that were one hundred strong. It was something to be proud of." Alison gives much of the credit for Branksome's continuing success to Allison Roach, Vice-

Principal Susan Kenny and all the staff members who came out to meets to cheer the girls on. "It was a great atmosphere," she said.

Branksome became a power in track and field, especially cross-country running, but while Allison Roach encouraged the girls to go out and cheer, the school's emphasis was on spirit as well as victory. Swim coach Joan Lumsdon put it this way: "Success is a combination of spirit and ability. The swim team makes the coach. If they don't have it, neither do you. You may have some kid who hates the water, can barely swim the width of the pool, but if she works hard, she'll get an A for effort. It's attitude."

By 1981, thanks to pleading letters, arm twisting and the hard work of the school's fund-raisers, the Restoration Fund was reaching its $1.5 million target. Sherborne House at 3 Elm Avenue was being renovated to upgrade the residence and provide ground-floor space for the growing primary school, and the Branksome Hall Foundation, under the direction of graduate Wendy Wilson Lawson, had been put in charge of raising money for a program of continuous property maintenance and construction. Following the practice of women's colleges in the United States, Branksome alumnae were being asked to donate every year, and parents, the biggest contributors to the Restoration Fund, were accepting the school's regular fee increases as a matter of course.

Prosperity and financial stability meant that the school could, at last, plan ahead. A new science wing, a new Junior School and a double gym for the Senior School were on the agenda, but the long-range planning committee, chaired by Nancy Pinnington, understood that Branksome's reputation rested ultimately on the depth of its curriculum and the quality of its teaching. To compete with the popular French Immersion program in the public schools, Branksome introduced extended French in some subjects in the Junior School and expanded all French-language instruction. The Junior School also acquired a music teacher, Dawn Willingham, who started a choir, and the juniors revived the practice of putting on short plays. The young married women on the Branksome

Olive Harris with young charges in the staff day-care centre, 1981-82.

staff were delighted when the school gave them space for a day-care centre for their preschool children.

Teachers no longer lived in the school, but they were expected to live for the school. They coached most of the interschool teams and accompanied them to competitions in Metro Toronto, Port Hope, Lakefield and St. Catharines. They took classes on trips to the Stratford Festival, Chalk River, Moosonee, Ottawa, Quebec City and Washington, DC. They attended prayers every morning and appeared at school functions in the evenings; they rehearsed student concerts and plays, supervised clubs and publications, did duty at lunch hour and made themselves available for tutoring and advice.

Dana Bett fondly remembers Junior School trips led by teacher Marie Hay, including a trip to Greece and Italy: "Mrs. Hay's trips were special — informative, fun and exhausting. Mrs. Hay always managed to get into places other tourists never saw. How she did it I never knew. Her trips always taught me so much about where we were, what we were seeing, about life and other people and their cultures. I am a better and more knowledgeable person today because of Mrs. Marie Hay."

Marie Hay.

The teachers were also role models. Branksome hired men to teach music and drama, women to teach science and mathematics. Ian McVay cracked the history department in 1985, but Branksome has rarely had more than four male teachers at one time. The equality of women was never an issue; it was assumed. No one thought it odd that Jean Claxton, Vesna Davidovac or Jackie Shaver would teach chemistry and physics, and interest in physics grew as more girls contemplated careers in engineering, science and medicine. "I don't think of teaching girls!" exclaimed biology specialist Susan MacGregor. She doesn't believe that girls need to be taught science in any different way than boys, but an advantage of an all-girls' laboratory is that girls are never pushed into secretary roles while boys do the experiments.

In the Junior School, however, mathematics teacher Martha Younger, believing that young girls needed to work harder on spatial relationships and motor skills, encouraged them to make three-dimensional structures and play boys' games. Edwina Baker, who has taught mathematics at co-ed collegiates, is impressed by the number of gifted students she has taught at Branksome. She has found teaching mathematics to girls easy compared to putting up with their practical jokes: "Oh, the students would try something, and I'd think, 'Is this something that will really bother me in ten years?' Humour worked better than a reprimand, and you got to know the students *very well.* One day I tripped over a student's shoes and fell flat on the floor. I was furious, but I knew they wanted me to explode. I could hear whispers: 'Go on, say it!' I lay there and counted silently to myself to keep from exploding. You have to be on the ball the whole time."

Julie Wood Lucas remembers an incident characteristic of Miss Baker's aplomb: "The first snow of the season began to fall during a Grade Thirteen math class. Large, soft flakes floated slowly down outside the windows. We all 'ooohed,' but Woubalem Trzos, who had recently arrived from Ethiopia, gasped. 'Snow!' she whispered, her eyes wide with amazement. Miss Baker, astute as ever, asked, 'Would you like to go outside, Woubalem? Right now, I mean?' We all crowded to the windows to watch as she ran out into the gently falling snow, her hands and face uplifted. When she returned, she said, 'It makes no sound!'"

English teacher Medora Sale Roe found that, by analysing a book such as Virginia Woolf's *Orlando,* girls anxious about homosexuality could explore all kinds of sexual identity issues without becoming confessional or embarrassed. Jane Austen's novels could be taught in a way that encouraged girls to examine a female culture they took for granted. Why were women supposed to be charming and placating? Why couldn't women be angry and manipulative? Once the girls started looking around, they found a world full of angry, manipulative women, including, in some cases, themselves.

"We did a lot of brave new world things," Medora said. "We wanted to send them out into the world so they wouldn't be the people sitting in the corner afraid to open their mouths." Opening mouths at Branksome Hall, Medora found, wasn't hard, and once the girls started talking, it was difficult to get them to listen: "Teenage girls are *noisy.* They have shrill voices. Hysteria spreads."

By 1984, Branksome students had started their own irreverent newspaper, the *Kilt Press,* and they were being defiantly slovenly about their uniforms. Uniform infractions became a running war. Allison figured that, if the girls didn't rebel about their uniform, they'd rebel against more serious rules, but some teachers worried that playing cop would destroy their students' trust.

The girls still sang hymns and Scottish metrical psalms in prayers, and usually Allison read a Bible passage, a poem or a story from a newspaper or magazine. Scripture study disappeared from the entire Senior School, but there was still religious education, including speakers representing a variety of faiths, and a school prayer. The Opheleo Society held contests and fairs to raise money for charities during Ramabai Week, and the teachers cheerfully took part in the fun. Edwina Baker remembers dressing up as a fortune teller and reading palms, coming up with predictions — "I see problems in algebra" — that turned out to be all too accurate. Ramabai Week was capped by a dance called the Ramabai Rout. What would Miss Scott say?

Allison was exceptionally considerate of Margaret Sime, who, in return, gave Allison unequivocal support. Jennie MacNeill had died in 1975, but Miss Sime occupied a place of honour at all school functions. She volunteered to compile Branksome's archive, and when she was too ill to leave her nearby apartment, the school's kitchen sent over hot meals. When Branksome Hall brought in a policy of mandatory retirement at age sixty-five, Allison looked out for teachers who might suffer financial hardship. She kept on Agnes Brown to play the piano at prayers, and superannuated history teacher Rita Coulter was assigned to clang the school bell for class changes. Mrs. Coulter, however, would doze off, or become absorbed in conversation, and forget to ring the bell. Allison abolished the bell and retired Mrs. Coulter, but teachers unmindful of their clocks created havoc.

With the school population climbing toward eight hundred, Branksome was bustling and brimming with optimism. The Branksome Hall Foundation was generating surpluses, and the Annual Giving campaigns exceeded their targets. A new $1.25 million science wing, opened in 1983, provided state-of-the-art laboratories, and the old wing was converted to rooms for music, typing and computer science. In 1984, Branksome began to phase out its general-level course, although some courses would still be taught at the general level. Home economics, renamed family studies, would remain at Branksome until 1999.

The Branksome Hall community had never been bigger, or better organized, but very subtly it had changed. Teenagers were more worldly but not necessarily more mature. School dances were chaperoned by Branksome's teachers, and to them fell the repugnant task of guarding the doors against gangs of boys, confiscating liquor bottles — "We poured more good booze down sinks," one teacher said wistfully — and patrolling the grounds and washrooms on the lookout for kids who were drinking or throwing up.

Allison thought that parents should take more responsibility for their children's behaviour. "We have too often had to phone parents to pick up their daughters who were unable to navigate," she wrote in a letter to all Branksome parents on November 4, 1985.

> Sometimes, though rarely, we've had to clean them up after they have been sick. My first reaction when I hear stories of teenage drunken behaviour is to say, "Not Branksome girls; I know them." I suspect that many parents do not believe that their daughters are drinking, certainly not to excess. The fact is that far too many are, and I worry that we adults will not act on this problem until some young girl becomes seriously hurt.

Once students became adults at age eighteen, however, there was little the school or their parents could do about their behaviour.

Allison began to wonder, too, whether young women who could vote should be dressing as schoolgirls. Branksome was now a "subway school," with girls commuting from all over Toronto, and Allison worried, with reason, that they might be stalked, abducted and assaulted. The school, with its ravine property, was exposed to traffic of all kinds, and Jarvis Street to the south had become the centre of the city's sex trade. Allison broached to the prefects the idea of allowing girls in their graduating year to wear street clothes, but the prefects, having sweated hard for their red kilts, turned the idea down flat. The red kilts could go too, as far as Allison was concerned, but she received no support from the Branksome community.

The students, however, were becoming aware that they had civil rights that extended beyond Branksome Hall, and the school had to respect them. When Edwina Baker told a disruptive pupil to sit down, the girl replied, "Even the most hardened criminal is allowed to have her say." Edwina laughed, but Canada's Charter of Rights and Freedoms, introduced in 1982, was making all Canadians re-evaluate their attitudes and behaviour in terms of equality, discrimination and prejudice. Personal disputes that had once been adjudicated informally, in private, were now being decided in public by human rights commissions and the courts, and these disputes included relationships between teachers, parents and students. Students felt freer to complain about their teachers. Teachers had to justify the marks they gave on exams and be accountable for their own conduct. Canadian parents everywhere were more knowledgeable, critical and personally involved in their children's education.

Branksome's population reflected changes in Canada's family structure as well. More girls came from single-parent homes and step-families, or they divided their time between parents who lived apart. Two-income families were becoming the norm, and both parents often worked long hours at demanding jobs. Parents responded enthusiastically to the school's appeals for financial support, but with annual fees now at $5,000, they wanted value for their money and a bigger say in their daughters' education.

Mothers of Branksome students were often Branksome alumnae as well as the daughters, granddaughters, sisters and aunts of alumnae. The school employed a number of alumnae as teachers and administrators, and some of the teachers had daughters at the school. With the Alumnae

Association and Parents' Association working closely together, the Branksome community became highly integrated. Everyone had an opinion about the school, and opinions differed. Allison Roach, as the principal, a teacher, a board member and a graduate of the school, was caught in the middle.

Allison, a demanding boss, expected her staff to give more than a hundred percent. They did, although at times they felt they worked to the brink of exhaustion. Some members of Branksome's board, however, thought that Allison was too friendly and lenient with her staff. They wanted the teachers' duties defined in a printed manual. She feared, however, that codifying behaviour would encourage teachers to work to rule, and as Branksome's salaries inched toward par with the Metro Toronto public schools, she and the board worried that Branksome teachers might decide to join the union, the Ontario Secondary Schools Teachers' Federation.

Strikes by public school teachers had for years been a major reason why parents sent their children to independent schools. Many teachers, however, felt the need for their own association, where they could meet to discuss school policies, working conditions and their relationships with the administration. Allison, who chaired the weekly staff meetings, insisted on attending these discussions; after all, she was a teacher too. Allison consulted her vice-principals and senior staff members before making important decisions, but she made it plain that the final decision rested with her.

Most of the teachers believed, perhaps secretly, that they should have the right to meet independently. They needed an open, democratic forum to express grievances and critique the principal's performance without fearing for their jobs. They had no contract, only "a gentlewoman's agreement," and they felt defenceless when they were contradicted by the principal at staff meetings or argued with her behind closed doors. As Allison said, "I was sometimes asked to discuss something in private in my office with an individual teacher. Sometimes teachers, of their own accord, would enter my office angry at me for some reason. Most of the time they were met with a discussion to iron out difficulties or an apology. Sometimes I hotly defended myself. I was always pleased that teachers felt free to 'tell me off,' but I felt free to rise in my own defence."

Shirley Duperley, 1995.

To young teachers educated in the consensus-building culture of the 1970s, Allison was intimidating. Her fits of temper, however, blew over like thunderstorms, and when she admonished the girls about rule infractions at prayers, they shrugged off her blasts as perfectly consistent with the school's disciplinary environment. But some girls, singled out for misbehaviour, felt hurt, embarrassed and resentful. Girls were regularly pulled out of their classes for scoldings. Since Branksome had no intercom, Allison dispatched her good-natured, hardworking secretary, Shirley Duperley; when the culprit saw Shirley at the classroom door, she knew she was in for it.

Allison's critics thought that she "squelched" kids, but her admirers appreciated the extra attention she paid to girls who were struggling. Allison had zero tolerance for girls who skipped classes, because she thought skipping led to academic failure, and she made friends with many girls who, like Darcy Bett, got into trouble. Darcy took pride in her uniform and excelled at sports, and while she wasn't a great scholar, she appreciated her teachers. "It was the *consistency* of the school," she said, "the small classes, the one-on-one schooling. The teachers were always *there.* They all had such strong personalities. When we studied *The Importance of Being Earnest*, we laughed a lot, and the teachers laughed with us. I worked hard because I wanted to do well. My graduating year was the best year of my life. We were treated like adults. Going to school with the same group of girls for years is very secure, very comforting. I would trust my best friend with my life. We were all like sisters, a huge extended family."

Branksome also encouraged the girls to set up their own clubs, and by 1987, in addition to the traditional *Slogan,* athletics, debating, Opheleo and Beta Kappa societies, the girls had a new rowing program at the Toronto Argonaut Rowing Club, as well as clubs for music, band, chamber choir, computers, science, public affairs, creative writing, typewriting, library, photography, auto mechanics and even a short-lived Greek club. A cooking club brought together girls from Grades Seven and Eight with students in their graduating year in an effort to bring the Junior and Senior Schools closer together. At the annual closing exercises, the girls' contributions to the school were rewarded by a multitude of prizes, including grade prizes for academic achievement, athletic awards, prizes for enthusiasm, service, citizenship and encouragement of scholarship and the Donald Falconer Cup "to the girl whose participation in and contribution to the activities of the school have most exemplified the spirit of Branksome Hall."

The school's "office lady," General Secretary Peggy Emery, recalled that there was "a great sense of fun." Allison would dress up in fright wigs for skits, and when she found a pair of tap shoes in the lost-and-found box one morning, she danced down the hall. The school's administration offices in the Sime Wing were located directly opposite the front door, and Allison insisted that office doors, including her own, be kept open. Business Manager Keith Sharpe, a retired ordnance officer with the Canadian Armed Forces, wasn't amused when women teachers barged into his office. Sharpe, responsible for the school's buildings, secretaries, housekeepers and maintenance staff, ran Branksome Hall like a regiment,

Business Manager Keith Sharpe.

Staff (including Allison Roach) entertain students at Christmas Assembly, 1982.

and from time to time his scrupulous military methods clashed with Miss Roach's more impromptu management style. Sharpe worked long hours, and when the board developed a new pension and benefits plan for the teachers, he put his job on the line to make sure all the school employees were included.

Allison saw Branksome's personality much as she had experienced it as a student: liberal, broad-minded, pragmatic and unpretentious. "I liked the *humility* of the school," she recalled. "Branksome people were great doers, without fuss." But now Branksome students were, rightfully, pushy and proud. The girls assumed they would go on to university and professional careers. They wanted to go to the *best* universities, and many top colleges were demanding average marks over eighty percent.

Historically, Branksome had acquired a reputation for being less academically rigorous than its arch rivals, and since Branksome hadn't advertised the innumerable women among its alumnae who had made names for themselves in medicine, law, business, the arts, journalism, television, teaching, nursing, scholarship and the social services — one didn't blow one's own horn at Branksome — it had hidden its light under a bushel. The public and parents of prospective students saw the bushel: gyms and a Junior School that belonged in a gothic novel.

"We have to build the school to stay competitive," Allison told board chairman George Booth early in 1988. "How are you going to do it?"

"I don't know," Booth replied.

The collapse of the Toronto stock market in October 1987 had hurt Branksome's expansion plans. Trying to raise money at a time when people were losing it was a daunting challenge, but Booth rallied ten energetic, enthusiastic board members into what he called "the war committee." The committee met informally, often via conference calls on their car cell phones ("We didn't pay much attention to process," Booth admitted), and by July 1988, the school had hired an experienced professional fund-raiser, Sally Marshall of Ketchum Canada, to launch its $6 million Building on Success capital campaign.

The school had also hired the firm of Robbie, Sane Architects, famous for the Toronto SkyDome and expert in school design, to draw up plans for a new Junior School and a sunken double-gym for the Senior School. Some members of the board wanted to tear down the 120-year-old house, Glenhurst, which no longer met fire regulations for use as classrooms, but the majority of the Branksome community replied that it would be over their dead bodies. Glenhurst was living history. It had been part of the school community since F.H. Deacon had bought it in 1918. Generations of Deacons had been associated with the school — Scott Deacon was currently on the board — and before the Deacons, Glenhurst had been owned by the Waldies, another prominent Branksome family.

Rod Robbie and Arun Sane, who had designed the school's science wing and quadrangle in 1983, saw the potential for integrating the old house into an intimate new school building that, like a doll's house, would be scaled to the little girls who used it. The design would, as well, relate to Glenhurst's surviving Victorian coach house. "It's not a question of whether or not it's old," Robbie said, "but is it useful?" Although it would be prohibitively expensive to restore Glenhurst to its original state, Robbie thought its rooms would provide precious extra space for staff, tutorials and extra-curricular activities.

Robbie and Sane designed an elegant two-storey brick addition that wrapped around the north and east sides of the house, and they renovated the rest to remove the ravages of generations of patching and painting. Their design took advantage of the ravine to the south and west — the second-floor library seems to be a tree house — and closed the narrow road that motorists had been using as a shortcut through the west campus.

More than $4 million had been raised by the time construction started in September 1989, but Branksome's enrolment, which had climbed steadily since Allison's arrival, had flattened out at about 760 students. With the population of boarders dropping to eighty-five, the future of the residence became uncertain. The school simply had no more room for day girls, and boarding had become, in George Booth's words, "a prickly pear." Branksome boarders paid double fees to cover the costs of their room and board, and it had become fashionable in Hong Kong for families to send their daughters to North American schools to improve their English. This revenue was attractive, but the girls were often homesick, and their English skills tended to be below the level Branksome's teachers demanded. Branksome did not teach English as a Second Language, offer a course in Mandarin to its Canadian students or hire Asian housemothers. Most of the boarders, who spoke Chinese among themselves, clung together for mutual support. Allison tried to pair day girls with boarders, and she locked the residences from 9 a.m. to 2:30 p.m. to force boarders to participate in school activities, but she despaired. "I used to think," said Allison, "how wonderful it would be not to have a residence. Just take down those buildings and give us some land. The board could never make up their minds whether to keep it or not."

For the boarders, residence was, as always, an exercise in survival. Jackie Szeto, a boarder from Hong Kong, turned it into an opportunity. As head of the residence council, Jackie organized weekend trips and barbecues that included boys from Toronto's Royal St. George's College. The boarders celebrated each other's cultural traditions, especially the Chinese New Year, but their greatest victory was persuading the dining room to serve them familiar East Asian and West Indian food. "I cried for the first forty-eight hours, but I was lucky to go to Branksome," Jackie said. "My cousins went to English schools, and that was *awful.*"

For the first time in its history, Branksome was being asked to measure up to its own ideals. In 1986, the Canadian Educational Standards Institute had been established by the independent schools to evaluate to what extent each member school achieved its goals. Branksome's goals, implicit and assumed, would have to be articulated and documented, and its mission statement had changed very little since Margaret Scott had defined the school in 1903.

What *were* Branksome's goals? How well was it doing? Should it continue to call itself a Christian school? A boarding school? What was its image, its identity? These were thorny issues. The process of self-analysis, which involved focus groups and questionnaires sent to parents, students and alumnae, was complicated by a revolution in educational electronic technology and by Royal St. George's College, which showed a tentative interest in sharing the Branksome campus. Board members began talking about Branksome in terms of governance and process, management models, marketing, value added and product quality. Allison Roach was appalled by what she considered to be a corporate, bureaucratic, Bay Street concept of the school. "A school is different from a business," she said firmly.

But Branksome *was* a corporation, with an annual budget over $10 million and $16 million in assets, and administration had become a profession, with its own ideology, language and codes of conduct. Rather than hire full-time administrators to assist the principal, however, board members rolled up their sleeves and pitched in. Allison was run off her feet trying to attend meetings of a dozen subcommittees, and while she followed directives ratified by the board, even if she disagreed with them, she thought subcommittees' suggestions, often merely expressions of personal opinion, could be followed at her own discretion. Inevitably, the involvement of board members in the day-to-day running of the school led to confusion, tension and misunderstanding. "The lines had become blurred between the administration and the board," admitted Mary Pat Jones Armstrong, a parent and graduate who was elected to the board in 1987. "The board should be setting policy, but it was trying to run the school. Everybody cared so much."

Allison had bought, and rented out, a home of her own in Toronto several years before, and she moved there from the principal's residence at 4 Elm Avenue when construction started on the Junior School. Space was needed for storage, and since 1976, when Allison had moved into the large, graceful house next to the Junior School, she, like her predecessors, had been required to share her home with the school. For years, classes had been held in her basement and dining room, the alumnae and board used the living room for meetings or receptions and the dean of residence lived on the third floor. Allison had the second floor and the kitchen.

With too many cooks stirring the administrative pot, and construction problems on the gym and Junior School pushing costs more than $1 million over budget, the Branksome community split into what one former board member tactfully termed "traditionalists and iconoclasts." Personalities clashed, tempers frayed and rival fiefdoms battled it out behind the scenes. Sally Marshall, hired as Branksome's first director of development in 1990, reported at first to the board, not to Miss Roach. Members of the executive of the Alumnae Association, which now reported to the development office, were furious at being chastised for not raising enough money; the Alumnae Association was already busy with the Annual Giving campaign, which increased its target every year, a newsletter, the annual alumnae dinner, year reunions and a shop that sold school memorabilia. The alumnae's goodwill could not be measured in dollars, and the executive, having lost its independence, thought their hard work was not sufficiently appreciated or respected.

At the same time, Branksome was conducting an emergency search for a new head for the Junior School. At the end of 1989, Dorothy Brough, suffering from exhaustion and poor health, had suddenly stepped aside to take the less demanding role of director of students. Miss Brough, with her quick mind and brisk ways, was Branksome's last contact with the traditions that had inspired her predecessors, Jessie Johnston and Margaret Dowie. "We had a lot of lectures about manners and behaviour," recalled Anne Roe, who was in the Junior School in the late 1970s. "We had to walk up the staircase *properly.* We never had books on our heads, but it was that feel. I remember, when I was six or so, Miss Brough telling us that if we didn't behave we would never grow up to be *ladies.* I thought to myself, how could I grow up and not be a lady? I went home to my mother, and I said, 'Are you a lady?' She replied, *'Yes!'*" Audrey Brown, who taught in the Junior School for eight years, admired the girls' "businesslike" attitude: "Excellence was expected. We had some corkers, believe me, but it was a joy to teach at Branksome."

The board's search committee included Allison, but other committee members made it clear to her that they, not the principal, would choose the successful candidate. Moreover, the new head of the Junior School would report directly to the board. Later revoked, it was an intolerable presumption of the principal's prerogative, regardless of who was chosen, and for Allison Roach, who had devoted the prime of her life to making Branksome a better school, it was a stinging slight. In October 1991, she told board chairman George Booth that she intended to retire in June 1993, Branksome's ninetieth anniversary.

Chapter Seven

Allison Roach described 1991 as Branksome's *annus mirabilis.* The Senior School double gym, which boasted a sprung floor, opened with an Olympic-style parade of the school's sports teams carrying banners and flags, and the bright, spacious Junior School addition, which perfectly complemented the old house, provided, at last, imaginative space for the library, art room and physical education. Old Glenhurst, which could not be used for classrooms, was converted into offices, work rooms and the day-care centre. There was no money for landscaping.

This, it turned out, was an opportunity. A team of consultants, Ecological Outlook, suggested that the ravine to the south and west of the Junior School could be used for environmental education if it were restored to its native Carolinian forest. This idea had been put into practice years before by kindergarten teachers Ruth Hamilton Upjohn and Dot Seixas. In the shady forest area behind the kindergarten, they had planted a garden of wildflowers to teach nature study. The flowers and trees attracted a variety of forest birds, warblers, buntings, nuthatches, and the children learned to identify them from their songs as well as their feathers. After Ruth retired, however, gardeners' crews buried the fragile plants under piles of leaves and trash, and rubbish was routinely dumped in the ravine. (One of Allison Roach's cats is buried there too.) A stand of towering century oaks had been cut down, apparently for safety reasons (the ravine was part of the playground), and Norway maples, an invasive, foreign species, were threatening to choke out the native Canadian trees. The Norway maples, some of them fifty years old, would have to be removed, and this, science teacher Pat Merrilees realized, required educating adults, as well as children, about the school's eco-system. Replanting the ravine with Ontario trees, shrubs and wildflowers would give members of the Branksome Green project an outdoor learning experience to share, but no longer would the girls be allowed to run roughshod through the underbrush.

The Junior School addition was named for Sue Savage Bett, a loyal and popular member of the class of 1952, who had died of cancer in 1988. Both of Sue's daughters, Darcy and Dana, had attended Branksome, and her husband, Ian, made a donation in her memory to the building campaign. Memorial donations, amounting to more than $400,000, came from friends and colleagues of Robin Younger, a senior partner in Dominion Securities, who had died in 1989. Younger's daughter, Martha, a Branksome teacher, had also attended Branksome, and since his wife, alumna Trish Wilson Younger, had chaired the capital campaign to build the science wing in 1983, it was named for Robin Younger. Branksome, like other donor-dependent organizations, was losing its shyness about identifying, and praising, the people who kept it in business.

In its search for a new principal, the Branksome board took an unusual and creative step. It asked committees of parents, alumnae, students and staff to examine the school's strengths, opportunities and challenges in the future, then to draw up a personality profile of a principal best suited to lead the school into the next millennium. "The whole face of education in Ontario was changing," said Patti Thomson MacNicol, a

Martha Younger unveils plaque at Younger Wing dedication, 1990.

Branksome graduate and board member at the time. "The cosy days were gone. It was a very competitive environment. Parents were more aware of what was going on in the classrooms and holding schools accountable." With the economy on the rebound, more parents could afford to send children to independent schools, and they were critically comparing the alternatives. Educators everywhere were confronting the digital phenomenon that would soon be known as the "information economy," a world in which teaching and learning, like all communication, would be increasingly driven by electronic technology.

Where would Branksome fit in? Was this a time for radical change or for caution? Was the school in danger of losing its identity or of becoming musty and old-fashioned? On some issues, there was surprising unanimity: in spite of competition from co-ed schools, Branksome Hall would remain a single-sex school with a progressive curriculum and culture that reflected its predominantly feminine environment. The new principal had to be a woman. In other areas, however, opinions differed. Parents wanted greater emphasis on academic excellence; the students, satisfied with the school's intellectual standards, emphasized career development and more extra-curricular activities. Parents felt strongly that both the curriculum and the quality of teaching should be evaluated and improved; teachers wanted the new principal to encourage staff discussion but minimize changes. The alumnae cautioned that the school should build on its traditions and not abandon its concern for the "whole child."

Certainly, Branksome was facing formidable challenges. The enrolment had flattened out at about 770 girls, and the school was concerned that this population did not reflect the city's multicultural identity. If Branksome did not want to be seen as elitist and insular, it would have to broaden the diversity of its student body. Had its Scottish identity perhaps become a handicap? And should Christianity remain part of a liberal, non-denominational school? These were philosophical questions, but Branksome was facing more urgent financial problems. Money was needed for computers and improvements to the older school buildings, yet school fees alone were insufficient, and the cost of the new buildings had put the school $1 million in debt. Branksome would be looking for a principal with an appreciation of budgets and bottom lines as well as the skills to make the school as prosperous as it was progressive.

In fact, it was looking for a paragon. The search committee's candidate profile envisioned an "experienced educational leader" who possessed a broad liberal education and a commitment to academic excellence; teaching experience; senior administrative experience; knowledge of independent schools; the capability of understanding and maintaining with pride Branksome's traditions and its warm, caring atmosphere; outstanding qualities of leadership and innovation; an affinity for and rapport with young women; excellent communications abilities; consistency in philosophy and wisdom in discipline; knowledge of issues surrounding single-sex education for girls; an approachable manner with all elements of the Branksome community; limitless energy and enthusiasm; and a sense of humour.

The search committee, chaired by Dan Sullivan, was scouring Canada, the United States and Great Britain for a woman who embodied these ideals when, in the summer of 1992, it learned that Rachel Phillips Belash, retired Head of Miss Porter's School, Farmington, Connecticut, was interested. After nine years at Miss Porter's, Rachel and her husband, Alexis, a financier, were looking for new challenges, and Rachel's friend Priscilla Winn Barlow had been hired as principal of Havergal College the year before. Branksome had been described to Rachel as "a nice school," and she found the idea of living in Canada attractive. Branksome was bowled over by her qualifications.

Born in Wales in 1934, the daughter of a headmaster, Rachel took her undergraduate degree in modern languages from Oxford University and later earned her Ph.D. in Latin American literature from the University of Kentucky. She had taught at Vassar College and, in addition to her scholarly publications and translations of Latin American literature, had published numerous articles on girls' education. For four years, she had been a vice-president of the First National Bank of Boston, with responsibility for financial planning and marketing. Rachel was, as well, on the executive of the New England Association of Schools and Colleges and a founder and co-chair of the Coalition of Girls' Boarding Schools (now the National Coalition of Girls' Schools). Passionately committed to achieving excellence in girls' education, Rachel Belash was widely known as an outstanding educator as well as the retired head of one of the most prestigious girls' schools in New England.

Rachel Phillips Belash.

Rachel brought a varied life experience to the job: as a single mother, she had supported her four young children from her first marriage. She was widely praised as a woman of exceptional enthusiasm and intelligence, a strong leader who worked by consensus, an accomplished public speaker blessed with a banker's head for business. She was also described as impatient, critical and aloof, a woman of determination who did not tolerate tedium. In person, Rachel was slight, almost fragile, unassuming and direct. Her credentials and her style ideally suited a school anxious to shed its reputation, a legacy of Miss Read's, for valuing character ahead of scholarship.

In November 1992, Rachel Phillips Belash agreed to become Branksome Hall's sixth principal. "I jumped into it," she laughed. Little did she know what she was jumping into. Rachel, disguised as a prospective parent (the identities of the candidates were kept secret), had paid one brief, hurried visit to Branksome, and, apart from the members of the search committee, she had spoken only to the school's director of admissions, Karrie Weinstock. "The buildings were in rotten shape," she said. "I had seen the financial statements, and I knew they were in a mess financially, but I hadn't met a single teacher, and I hadn't talked to Allison Roach."

Apart from a formal one-day introduction to the school in February 1993, Rachel spent almost no time at Branksome Hall until she took over as principal on July 1. There were delays in getting her visa — filling top jobs in Canadian schools with Americans was not popular in some political quarters — and it would have been awkward to have Rachel, described by one board member as "a turnaround artist," hovering in the wings during Allison's farewell celebrations, especially when, privately, Rachel saw herself as "a cat among the pigeons who would churn the place up and bring it into the modern age." Rachel was impatient with Allison's views about the school, and Allison, ignored, felt rebuffed.

Confident that she had a clear mandate to bring a fresh, critical perspective to Branksome, Rachel quickly realized that she had not been thoroughly briefed. "Two days after I started," she said, "I was asked, 'What are you going to do about the Carol Service?' I didn't know there *was* a Carol Service. Nobody had mentioned a Carol Service. I said, 'What Carol Service?'" Amazed that plans for Branksome's December Carol Service had to be finalized in midsummer, Rachel asked, among other things, why a school that no longer defined itself as Christian was having a Christmas Carol Service. Branksome Hall had students who were Jewish, Muslim, Buddhist and atheist, but unless they voiced religious objections, all girls were required to participate. Some staff considered the need for girls to opt out discriminatory, rehearsals took hours out of precious class time and increasing numbers of girls were skipping rehearsals and the concert. Rachel was not alone in thinking that it was high time to review the Carol Service. The "religion issue" had been high on the school's list of challenges facing the new principal.

Then Rachel was asked about the pageant. What pageant? She didn't know anything about the pageant. When it was described to her as infantile, Rachel agreed. "Oh, my God, no, for heaven's sake *not,*" she declared. "So word went around that this ferocious new person had cancelled the pageant," she laughed. "I got this delegation of senior students, practically in tears. They had waited all their school lives to be in the pageant. 'We know it sounds strange,' they said. I said, 'You mean you want to dress up as angels and the Virgin Mary?' And they said, 'Yes, we do.' I said, 'I'm not going to stop you. I think this is extraordinary, but if you want to do it, you do it.'"

Too late. The false rumour, accepted as truth, that Rachel Belash had cancelled the Carol Service was rocketing through the Branksome community. The traditionalists, some of whom had attended the Carol Service for sixty years, were outraged. For many, not only was Christianity part of Branksome's identity, but also the Carol Service was a rare opportunity for members of the entire Branksome community to gather together in celebration. The alumnae, in particular, had fond memories of singing in services past and a deep attachment to Branksome's traditions, and the alumnae had included "Christian" among the new principal's desired attributes. In advertising for a new principal, Branksome had given her commitment to maintaining the school's traditions precedence over academic excellence, teaching ability and administrative skills. Students and staff had also expressed strong opposition to dramatic or radical change.

Invariably pleasant and polite, Rachel was as opaque as Allison Roach was transparent. The first Branksome principal to be married with a family, Rachel also made it plain that she intended to have a private life. She needed time to read, go to plays and concerts, entertain friends, play her cello, be a wife and mother. The principal's residence would be regarded as her private home, not communal school property, and while she would be on the spot in emergencies, she didn't intend to be at everyone's beck and call.

It was her nature to quiz and question until she understood *why,* and with an unsentimental eye, Rachel was questioning *all* of Branksome's traditions, including the prefect system, the clans and prayers. She reduced daily prayers to an assembly three times a week and eliminated all hymns and prayers except the school prayer. "Assembly was the worst part of the day as far as I was concerned," she said. "I am not a cheerleader type. I'm not a ham. I don't like to get up in front of many people and hold forth. That's not my strength. That Senior School gym filled with six hundred girls sitting on the floor, with the teachers sitting around, it was a nightmare."

Miss Porter's, a bucolic rural boarding school of 260 girls, had not prepared Rachel for a rambunctious urban school three times the size where most of the students were day girls. Rachel also had to learn to deal daily with anxious or irate parents on the phone or in her face.

"She wrote wonderful letters to parents," recalled Shirley Duperley, the principal's secretary who immediately took Rachel under her wing. "She explained the school's mandate, its educational goals. She never couched anything in angry language. I remember one angry father who completely changed his mind once he'd read her letter."

With individuals, or in small groups, Rachel was frank, funny and companionable, but in public she preferred to be unobtrusive, a facilitator rather than the focus of attention. She wasn't shy, however, about letting Branksome know where she stood as a philosophical feminist. Rachel believed that a girls' school could only justify its existence if it were run from a feminist, or womanist, point of view. She had expressed her views earlier in an article, "Girls' Schools: Separate *Means* Equal," published in *Independent Schools, Independent Thinkers,* edited by Pearl Rock Kane. "When the student body is female and more than half the teachers are women," Rachel wrote, "there is an unspoken validation of female norms and their consequences." In a co-ed environment domi-

Alexis Belash, Rachel Phillips Belash and Mary Pat Armstrong at Rachel's installation as Principal, 1993.

nated by male values and assumptions, girls, she said, often feel alienated and disconnected. "Girls' schools faculties," she argued, "are more invested than their colleagues in co-ed schools in making changes in form and content if these may be of benefit to girls — gender-balancing the curriculum, for instance, or downplaying competitive behavior in the class room."

Rachel tried to express her philosophy in a scholarly speech to the school's 1993 annual general meeting titled "Separate AND Equal: Mary Wollstonecraft Meets Carol Gilligan." Her audience struggled to understand how Wollstonecraft's eighteenth-century treatise, *Vindication of the Rights of Women,* was relevant to a contemporary psychologist's theory that adolescent girls in the United States experience a "loss of voice" and what message either of them had for Branksome Hall. Loss of voice? At *Branksome,* a school famous for speaking up? What would Miss Read say? Branksome had for years enjoyed an international reputation for excellence in debating and public speaking, students in the drama courses researched, wrote and produced docudramas about social and political issues and feminist opinions were freely expressed in the *Kilt Press.* Students like Shirley Brown, now a corporate lawyer and a Branksome board member, had vigorously challenged conventional wisdom, and if the girls thought the principal had done something silly, they said so.

"Our principal recently made a request of the students which caused a notable amount of speculation," Swith Bell had written in the *Kilt Press* in October 1990.

> She asked that we do not drink pop in uniform off school property. With an attitude like this, the uniform begins to look like a sexist symbol of the Victorian era. It is hardly feminist of us to pretend that women do not *eat* or *drink.* This is the first step to making impressionable young girls ashamed of their bodies. Miss Roach uses pop as the sinful item — but what about *juice boxes?* What about *Evian water?* Let's go one step further. . . . Have we the right to pick our noses in uniform off school property? The question here is similar to the abortion issue: do we have the right to our own body and what we put in it? Or are we to be denied even *that?*"

Allison Roach was only trying to prevent the girls from tossing their empty pop cans on neighbours' lawns. In the next issue of the *Kilt Press* — in a column titled "Is God Male?" — Swith Bell angrily denounced the Lord's Prayer, recited daily at prayers, as "an anti-feminist mantra." Allison was so delighted with Swith's outspoken views that she awarded Swith the Principal's Prize at her graduation in 1992.

In February 1993, Branksome students had attended a co-ed conference at Upper Canada College called The Gender Challenge: A New Hope for Women and Men, featuring radical American feminist Robin Morgan as the keynote speaker. Earlier, Branksome prefect Lynda Collins had organized a co-curricular women's issues group in the Senior School where girls discussed issues of equality, violence, racism, self-esteem and sexuality.

Sarah Hunter and Swith Bell, 1992.

Lynda, searching to define her own sexual identity, had become a feminist at fifteen. "I heard a speaker, an Israeli woman, talk about body image in a political context," she said. "I realized that it was a political act to accept my body." Lynda, an outstanding student, musician and school activist, began making speeches at prayers about how issues of hatred and inequality were mirrored in daily school life, and she read books of feminist theory. At seventeen, she was comfortable with the fact she was lesbian, and she thought it was imperative to "come out" at Branksome: "It was a political act. Silence is a powerful form of oppression. There was a certain amount of internalized homophobia. We had to pretend that we *weren't* lesbian." Lynda talked it over with Allison Roach, who said go ahead but please don't announce it at prayers. Lynda came out to her friends and brought lesbian feminists to speak to the women's issues group.

"It was received very well," she said. "I wasn't taunted. I was very powerful at that school. I was this *icon.* It was confusing for the students, but it created me as a hero. It was a huge deal, *huge.*" The staff, privately reassessing their own attitudes toward homosexuality, behaved as if nothing untoward had happened, and Lynda sailed through her graduating year blissfully unaware that the men on the Branksome board, oblivious to the fact that Shirley Brown, seated at the same table, was gay, fussed and fretted about Branksome becoming known as "the lesbian school." Lynda's essay on "Queer Theory" won her a scholarship to the University of Toronto, and Lynda was moved to tears by the cheers she received from the Branksome community. "It's important to make change," she said. "It created change for the lesbian students who came after me." Looking back, Lynda is grateful, too, for the freedom from sexual harassment she experienced during her twelve years at Branksome.

Since arriving at Branksome, Rachel Belash had been experiencing a time warp. It became clear to her that, while she and the Branksome community spoke the same language, words had different meanings. "Everybody was talking about 'the installation,'" Rachel recalled. "I thought they meant *my* installation as principal. How naïve." *The* installation, the Installation of the Prefects, had blossomed into a spectacular ceremony, attended by the entire school, held in a church filled to capacity by parents and alumnae. Highlighted by the solemn passing of the school flags to the incoming head girl and prefects, the installation featured speeches of welcome by the principal and head girl and an address by a distinguished guest, usually an alumna.

Standing in front of the choir stalls, watching the horde of girls in red and green kilts walking up the aisle toward her, Head Girl Tessa Akande, an African Canadian, wearing her black velvet Highland jacket and ruffled shirt, the prefects and clan chieftains holding high a canopy of brightly coloured flags and banners, Rachel wondered, "Where am I?" "I thought I had gone back thirty years," she said. "That's how it felt, in every single way." It was closer to seventy years, in fact, since Miss Read had invented the installation ceremony, nearly sixty years since the Branksome girls had donned kilts. The prefect system had been in place since before the Great War.

Rachel, a liberal democrat, thought the prefect system was elitist, and some of the prefects themselves felt uncomfortable with being so visibly segregated from their classmates. It was not uncommon for girls who failed to get elected prefects to leave the school or to sob for days. The

1994 Prefects (Head Girl Tessa Akande far right).

prefects and clan chieftains, however, were so essential to the structure of the school that Rachel kept them in place. Her only change was to make election results public, and the head girl was the candidate who received the most votes.

The uniform was another issue. "If you are trying to encourage girls to be autonomous individuals, and you are expecting them to dress all alike, that's a contradiction in terms," Rachel said. "If you impose a uniform, you would be failing if you did not have expressions of personal freedom — necklaces, pierced noses, socks up or down, underpants that show. If the kids are not doing these things, you're producing a bunch of militarized robots."

Her views thrilled the girls, especially those who wanted to stand out in a crowd, but they did not sit well with parents who believed that, if a uniform is going to be worn, it should be worn properly or with teachers who were confused about what, if anything, constituted a uniform infraction. "Rachel treated the kids like adults," said a sympathetic teacher, "but they weren't adults, and there was no discipline."

Rachel hadn't had to worry about uniforms at Miss Porter's, where the girls wore everyday clothes, and she thought she had better things to do than fuss over girls who were late or skipped class, until absenteeism reached epidemic proportions. At the same time, she moved to democratize the school by setting up a Student Life Committee where girls could air their grievances, and she enlarged the student council. To protect the girls' privacy, and save time wasted in gossip, Rachel ended the practice of discussing individual students' problems at staff meetings, and while she gave teachers and staff exceptional freedom to speak their minds, she didn't put up with the noisy "nonsense" of the school that Allison Roach had cherished. "I tried to model tolerance and respect," Rachel said. "I never lost my temper. That's not my style. I treated the kids with as much respect as I treated the teachers. It did change. I didn't hear voices raised, yelling at children. The climate improved a great deal." Her reserve, however, could be misinterpreted as arrogance or disapproval, especially by the faculty, as Rachel called the teachers, and they were apprehensive.

Any change in leadership is stressful after nineteen years, and the teachers, who worked without contracts, had heard that Rachel had been hired to "weed out the dead wood." She did review teacher evaluations, but she found no dead wood to be weeded. She defended the teachers before the board, introduced the common practice of rotating department heads and welcomed the formation of a Teachers' Association in May 1994. The association, with voluntary membership, was a sensible alternative to unionization. "I got on well with Rachel," said the association's first president, Annice Blake. "She supported people having a voice. We had a perfectly amicable relationship."

The administration, meanwhile, was working on a personnel handbook that included sexual harassment policies, crisis management guidelines, an organizational chart and a code of ethics. In January 1995, teachers' salaries finally reached par with those of the Metro Toronto public schools.

The presence of an internationally recognized scholar and educator as

Branksome's principal brought the school welcome attention and prestige within Canada's relatively small community of independent schools. By 1995, Branksome's fees — $10,650 for day girls — had become higher than those of St. Clement's, Havergal and Bishop Strachan, but Branksome's enrolment reached a record high of 850 girls. Parents, justifiably worried about destreaming, drastic financial cutbacks and teacher unrest in Ontario's public school system, were lining up to get their children into independent schools, and to accommodate booming enrolment in the Junior School, Branksome converted a residence building into classrooms for day girls.

Rachel Belash, like Allison Roach, thought that Branksome Hall should abolish residence altogether. Rachel believed that the boarders, who paid double fees of $21,950 a year, got substantially less than double value for their money, and the school had become too financially dependent on residence revenue. Boarders now accounted for less than twenty percent of Branksome's population, and unlike independent schools in rural locations, Branksome found it hard to provide boarders with a safe, stimulating community of students and adults that included evening and weekend activities.

In 1995, in a compromise attempt to provide a more flexible, home-like environment, Branksome switched to a five-day residence program. Boarders would live at the school during the week and go home, or to a guardian's home, on the weekends. Ninety percent of the girls were already taking off on weekends, and the school hoped that five-day boarding would attract girls from outlying cities and towns in Ontario.

The Ontario boarders, however, did not appear. The opportunity may have been poorly advertised. Toronto is ringed with independent, co-ed day and boarding schools, and the cost of going to Branksome as a weekly boarder, $17,000 a year, was steep. Karrie Weinstock, then Director of Admissions, has another explanation. "Red-blooded Canadian girls are not interested in single-sex boarding schools," she stated bluntly. "They don't see the value in them. They want co-ed boarding schools."

It turned out that Branksome's overseas boarders, almost all of them from Southeast Asia and the West Indies, also wanted the option of staying at the school on weekends. Many felt uncomfortable imposing themselves on their relatives, especially when the "guardian" was a virtual stranger. "The guardians are not always the nearest and dearest," Karrie said. "The girls often didn't feel welcome. It was isolating." Parents thousands of miles away were frightened at the prospect of their daughters being homeless for two days a week and horrified at the thought of them hanging out in Chinatown or a tough, black neighbourhood. After a year-long trial period, Branksome reinstated seven-day boarding.

Traditionally, most girls entered Branksome in Grade Seven and Grade Nine, with some arriving for Grade Thirteen. Now they were applying for Junior and Senior Kindergarten and the primary grades. Margaret Scott, bending over her infant niece's cradle a hundred years before, had been more prescient than she knew. Psychologists were stressing the importance of early childhood education, and highly educated parents wanted to give their children the best start in life. If these parents had limited budgets, wouldn't it be wiser to invest their money in their daughters' first five school years rather than the last five? The introduction of standardized testing at the Grade Seven entry point was a further incentive to enrol children early.

Pressure from the primary grades, however, was squeezing girls in Grades Seven and Eight out of their classrooms. Dismayed to find them thundering from class to class across the overpass, Rachel came up with the idea of creating a Middle School in the old residence, Buccleuch House. The Middle School, headed by a mathematics teacher, Judy MacLellan, was part of Rachel's massive reorganization of the school's administration. Abolishing the roles of the vice-principals, Rachel created an administrative team that included the director of development, the director of finance and administration, the director of admissions, head of the Junior School, a new head of the Senior School, Barbara Healey, and a new dean of students and residence, Nanci Smith.

Rachel Belash and her Administration Team, 1998. L to R: Patti Thomson MacNicol, Nancy Adams MacDonnell, Judy MacLellan, Nanci Smith, Ruth Ann Penny, Rachel Belash, Karrie Weinstock, Susan Kenny, Barbara Healey, Laraine Church.

Rachel, a firm believer in decentralization, liked to call her model "a horizontal web." Her web created initial confusion among the staff about who was to report what to whom, but weekly team meetings integrated aspects of the school that had functioned as independent fiefdoms for generations. "It was a huge step, simply *huge,*" said Karrie Weinstock, who now had virtually autonomous authority over admissions. "You had your own budget, and you managed your own department."

Transforming teachers into administrators absorbed most of Rachel's energy. Rachel met with her team members together, and individually, for days at a time. "It was a wonderful experience working with her," recalled Barbara Healey. "She had a very clear vision of where the school should go, and she had faith in what people could do. She kept the whole school in perspective, and she did a lot of the pulling together. She was the mentor."

Rachel describes herself as an "educational leader, not an instructional leader." By downloading responsibility for the daily managing of the school onto her administrators, she was free to implement policy, promote the school and persuade Branksome's board that, after the debt was paid off, it had to create an endowment fund large enough to provide a constant, predictable source of annual revenue. "For a school of this calibre to have an endowment just exceeding $1 million is a sad, sorry fact, and we are working hard to change this," Rachel said at the school's closing exercises in 1996.

> A non-profit organization without an endowment is like a family with no savings. This may be the situation many of us find ourselves in, but it is not enviable. Come the day when one wage earner loses a job, or another child is born, or the roof leaks after a storm, then indeed hard times are upon us.

Rachel was particularly concerned about the urgent need to introduce expensive electronic technology throughout the school and to provide time for the teachers to research new software resources. One of her priorities had been to draw up a three-year plan to introduce technology in an orderly and integrated way, but computers had to compete for dollars with musical instruments, athletic equipment and other more humble necessities. Many parents saw themselves as the school's "customers," and they were demanding value. Branksome could no longer afford to take pride in doing without or "making do."

Here Rachel found an ally in Patti Thomson MacNicol. A chartered accountant who shared Rachel's concern with the state of the school's finances, Patti became Director of Finance and Administration in 1995. She introduced economies and efficiencies and, for the first time in Branksome's history, drew up detailed projections for anticipated revenues and expenses over the next ten years. Looking at Patti's charts, the board could see exactly where and when every dollar had to be spent and how many dollars they had to raise. Administrators and department heads could now make plans with some expectation that the money would be there to implement them.

Crisis management had become a thing of the past, and the board, spearheaded by chair Mary Pat Jones Armstrong, streamlined itself by adopting the Carver Model of Governance. Committees vanished. The board worked out a comprehensive strategic plan, and unless asked to help, individual members learned to keep out of the principal's hair. The principal, as an employee of the school, became an ex-officio member of the board. Miss Read must have spun in her grave, but, in return, the principal's authority and independence as chief executive officer were strengthened.

Pat Davidson, a member of the search committee, supported wholeheartedly Rachel's full-steam-ahead and damn-the-torpedoes approach: "Rachel came in and shook up a school that had been in a groove for a long time. Her thinking was absolutely sound. The process of shaking up the school was in itself refreshing and healthy. Rachel is confident in her ability and understanding. She doesn't look over her shoulder to check and see. She doesn't stroke people and say 'There, there.' It's a very cavalier approach. I find that appealing."

For faculty and staff in the thick of the fray, however, the process of constant change, exhilarating as it was, became exhausting. Teachers needed to settle in, plan ahead, but Rachel was always fired up for a new project. Her team approach meant meetings, and meetings created committees and subcommittees that held more meetings. Every aspect of school life was up for discussion, and Rachel's conviction that everyone should be allowed to have a say meant long meetings that frequently tried the patience of the less verbose. "Rachel was a free thinker," said Shirley Duperley. "She'd listen to both sides of an argument."

Rachel insisted that the academic departments re-evaluate their goals and performance, although they had already undertaken this time-consuming exercise in 1991 for the Canadian Educational Standards

Institute. Rachel restructured the student body into advisor groups of ten to twelve girls. Each group meets with a teacher/advisor once a week for twenty-five minutes. It is an unstructured time to make friends, talk about world affairs, plan a project or ask for advice. Kids bring munchies and shoot the breeze, but some teachers who would prefer more instructional time fail to see much value in these sessions.

Branksome's teachers were struggling to find their feet in the shifting sands of the school's power structure, but Rachel became upset when teachers were argumentative, and she was offended when they failed to come to her "conversations," monthly after-school get-togethers intended to discuss broad educational issues. But when the teachers weren't coaching or supervising students, they were staying after school to give them extra help. They didn't live on campus, and they wanted to go home, have dinner, relax and prepare the next day's lessons. Rachel decided that the faculty had no intellectual curiosity, and her friendly brown-bag lunches with groups of students failed to stimulate the kind of free-wheeling discussion she had hoped for.

Head Girl Robyn Thompson, 1995.

Robyn Thompson, Head Girl for 1994-1995, recalled that there was no particular dissatisfaction with the school or clamour for change among the students. They were generally happy with their uniforms and the school's traditions, preoccupied with girls' usual concerns, friends, popularity, appearance and boys, and busy with their crowded daily schedules. There was concern that feminism had become identified with lesbianism, and senior girls were interested more in learning about career opportunities than in theoretical debate. As Dean of Students, Nanci Smith was now responsible for the elected student council, the prefects and the head girl, and it was she, not the principal, who met with them frequently and listened to what was on their minds. The principal was still a formidable figure. Girls who had been sent to Miss Roach, or whose mothers and grandmothers remembered the terror of being sent to Miss Read, Miss MacNeill or Miss Sime, minded their manners and kept their opinions to themselves. Rachel found them "docile."

Her relationship with the executive of the Alumnae Association, profoundly suspicious that Rachel was going to axe the Carol Service and everything else they held sacred about Branksome, was cordial but strained. Now that alumnae affairs were handled by the staff of the development office, headed by Nancy Adams MacDonnell, Rachel encouraged the Alumnae Association to play a more visionary role in the school's future. She was bored by talk of craft and flower sales, and at alumnae social events she seemed stiff and reserved. "I am not," Rachel said firmly, "a cheery, back-slapping, coffee-drinking chatterer." The role of the Alumnae Association, however, included, in addition to fund-raising, choosing the Allison Roach Alumna of the Year and responsibility for one of Rachel's pet projects, the Branksome Archive.

Rachel believed that the school should know more about its history and that it should constantly scrutinize its assumptions and priorities. She had been dismayed to discover that Branksome allocated only one percent of its budget to scholarships and bursaries. In the United States, as many as forty percent of independent school students are subsidized. How could Branksome tap the intellectual and creative riches of Toronto and southern Ontario without offering financial assistance? And wasn't it the school's social responsibility to offer girls an opportunity?

Many parents, however, sent their children to Branksome because it *was* exclusive, elite and socially homogeneous. Charles Brown, retired director of two Toronto-area school divisions and a Branksome board member from 1973 to 1987, has seen both sides, and he believes that attending an elite, homogeneous school can be an advantage because the curriculum is academically focussed and the students are highly motivated.

Increasingly, however, parents were looking for a school that would equip their daughters to compete successfully in a global, multicultural economy. Apart from agonizing over the cultural isolation of the boarders, now almost exclusively Asian, Branksome had never taken a hard look at how well it was meeting the needs of its entire student population. In December 1996, the Task Force on Racial and Religious Diversity, co-chaired by Junior School Head Ruth Ann Penny and board member Susan Duncanson Pigott, began to examine four major areas of concern: the curriculum, English as a Second Language, residence life and the Carol Service. After six months of surveys and intensive discussion, the task force recommended a thorough review of the curriculum and how it was taught; a senior course in world religions; recognition of religious holidays other than Christian and Jewish; introduction of ESL; international exchanges; more open and consistent ways of discussing racial issues and dealing with racist behaviour; and a review of the practical and philosophical aspects of the Carol Service. Its final recommendation was to create a steering committee to co-ordinate all these areas of action.

The task force's thoughtful, wide-ranging report was not published or broadly circulated to the Branksome community, and as a result of rumour and misinformation, the Carol Service became the sole passionate issue, a "flashpoint for criticism," as one board member described it. Some in the Branksome community suspected a plot to abolish the Carol Service; others wondered why religion, a matter of personal belief, should be examined at all. As for diversity, the school had always had black students, including head girls, from Canada, the United States and the West Indies. It was impolite to inquire about a student's racial background, and identifying students by race or religion might violate Canada's Charter of Rights and Freedoms. Branksome had historically diversified itself by its admissions procedure, and in the girls it selected, the school tried to achieve a variety of interests, talents, backgrounds and personalities. Increasing the diversity of Branksome's population, including teachers and staff, now became a clearly stated goal, and the board eventually agreed to allocate five percent of its tuition revenue to financial aid for students.

In any institution as venerable as Branksome Hall, change takes time and doesn't happen without criticism, reaction and hurt feelings. Rachel Belash, on a five-year contract, was moving quickly on all fronts, and she felt no need to justify or explain herself. Controversies intensified, and some members of the Alumnae Association, in particular, were furious that a principal they thought was committed to building on Branksome's traditions was calling into question their very existence.

But what *was* a tradition? "If Rachel Belash were to define a tradition, it would be a commitment to learning, not a red kilt," said Adrienne Willis, a prefect from 1996 to 1997. "If a tradition is not relevant, get rid of it. Get rid of the red kilt." Adrienne admitted, however, that hers was very much a minority view. "Traditions may be funny, goofy, old-fashioned," said parent Monika Stevenson, "but people remember them. The women who created these traditions were radical in their own way. As long as the school moves forward philosophically and intellectually, some of those old dinosaurs are wonderful. Perhaps Rachel was too 'cool,' as the kids say in a complimentary way, to appreciate that."

Disappointed to find Branksome more conservative, perhaps more stubbornly Canadian, than she had anticipated, Rachel stopped trying to push things she thought were impervious to change. She put up with, even endorsed, rituals and traditions she privately thought were meaningless. She stopped talking about feminism. Besieged by complaints, she toed the line on uniform violations. Participation in the Carol Service became optional. The pageant remained. "It was not a comfortable place," Rachel said, "and it was tremendously hard work. It doesn't make one popular. I did what I could without creating more fuss."

Exhausted, eager to move on to fresh challenges, and aware that remaining more than five years would have a detrimental tax impact on her family's assets, Rachel refused the board's invitation to remain another two years. "I think the board didn't understand how tough it would be for her," reflected Dan Sullivan, "but she got people thinking. It's better to try and find there is resistance. At least you've tried. That's healthy for the school to know. She tested the school's tolerance. That's very healthy."

Enrolment, at capacity, was healthy. The school's appearance reflected its renewed self-confidence and financial stability. The west campus had been landscaped, the playing field had been rebuilt and the buildings had been spruced up. The administration team, for which Rachel had unqualified praise, was humming. "Rachel had a vision about girls' education she could articulate," said Mary Pat Jones Armstrong, "and she was extremely articulate about the benefits of Branksome. She opened up discussion of ideas and gave us the confidence to go forward."

In her public capacity as ambassador for the school, Rachel Belash welcomed every opportunity to speak in praise of independent schools, girls' schools in particular. She defined independent schools as unique, highly focussed, creative communities. Of girls' schools, she said "We need to be hard to please, while supportive of risk-taking, because self-respect often comes only when exacting standards have to be met. In a girls' school, teachers are responding to no demands but those of young women. Yes, indeed, they get a better deal."

Words like "self-respect" and "exacting standards" might have been spoken a century earlier by Branksome Hall's founder, Margaret Taylor Scott. While Miss Scott and Mrs. Belash would no doubt have differed heatedly about the role of scripture in a young woman's education, they shared a decorous professional style and, like all of Branksome's principals, complete dedication to the ethical dimension of education.

One of Rachel's earliest speeches to the Parents' Association was titled "Educating for Virtue," a concept Rachel defined not as purity, in the sexual sense, but as a truly *good,* or excellent, life. For her, the basic components of virtue were self-discipline, accountability, and storytelling or making sense out of one's life. Uninterested in arbitrary rules imposed from without or above, Rachel, like her predecessors at Branksome, abhorred behaviour that let others down: cheating or plagiarism, late or missed assignments, irresponsibility, failure to come through in a crunch.

Rachel was willing to penalize girls who failed to meet high moral standards, but she wasn't a stick-in-the-mud. "The ability to play is a very important part of the life that girls develop for themselves in schools of their own," she wrote in "Girls' Schools: Separate *Means* Equal."

> In an era when we deplore high-pressure parents and the early advent of adulthood, we should appropriately foster environments that allow teenagers to let childhood linger a bit and learn to distinguish between being childish and childlike. Before they enrol in a single-sex school, girls seem unsure that anything worth calling "fun" can take place without the opposite sex. Once acclimatized, they become aware of new possibilities, of a freedom to deal with their own changing self-image, to explore who they are and who they are becoming. And behind it is the camaraderie, the relationships, and the encouragement to creative, productive play. When all is said and done, the case for girls' schools rests on the importance for young women of a place of their own.

Chapter Eight

SINCE 1995, BRANKSOME'S INTERNAL debate over the school's direction and identity had been taking place against a background of crisis and confrontation in Ontario's public schools. The educational policies of the new Conservative government's "Common Sense Revolution" involved massive restructuring and downsizing of school boards, drastic cost cutting, government directives as to how schools should be run and vigorous efforts to make teachers spend more time in the classroom. Since smaller budgets meant fewer programs and shabbier schools, parents became anxious, and teachers grew angry and alienated. The consequence was a school system destabilized by political squabbling, work-to-rule campaigns and strikes. In this climate, independent schools emerged as safe havens of calm, continuity and quality, and they offered all the co-curricular programs that were being sacrificed in the public system.

In the autumn of 1997, Karen Murton, Principal of A.Y. Jackson Secondary School in North York, responded to Branksome's search for a new principal. At forty-one, Karen was head of a large school with a strong academic reputation. She had been at A.Y. Jackson only one year, following three years as vice-principal of Victoria Park Secondary School and a year as vice-principal of Lawrence Heights Middle School. Karen, however, had developed a philosophy of education she thought went beyond the protocols and policies of running a large public school.

"Being with the North York board was a terrific learning experience," she said. "It broadened my horizons, and its excellent approach to education was significant in the development of my own. I thought I might be interested in having my own school some day, starting something that really supported the beliefs that I had about education. I have always felt that there was too much administration, too much government and political influence. There were too many barricades standing in the way of what I would call 'good learning' for many people. You are so strongly affected by the government of the day and the Ontario Secondary Schools Teachers' Federation. I don't believe that unions have a place in education."

As a member of the OSSTF, Karen had to keep her opinions to herself. When the union went out on a long, emotional strike in September 1997, Karen found herself in a difficult position: "For the first time in my life, I was doing something I *strongly, strongly* disagreed with in principle. I strongly disagreed that we should shut the doors to students and not allow them to enter a school to learn. As principal, I was forced to lock the doors and then go out and picket. I came *this* close to quitting my job. I thought, 'I can't do this.' I felt real pain. To me, the union mentality supports the lowest common denominator. What I want is to provide an environment where everyone can go beyond their wildest dreams, as teachers and as students."

Having taught physical and health education at Havergal College from 1988 to 1992, Karen had visited Branksome often for team games and had had a positive experience with an all-girls school: "There was a wonderful feeling of confidence and independence that emerged at Havergal, particularly in middle and junior years, a sense of knowing themselves and supporting other girls and the strengths they gain from those friendships. It was a different approach — 'We do it all!' When parents worry that a girls' school is not the 'real world,' I reply that they have a lot of time to be in the real world, and a girl is more prepared for the real world because she's feeling very confident."

Karen is confident. Married in 1988 to Michael Murton, a marketing specialist, she epitomizes the woman who can combine a career with a family:

the birth of their son, Michael Jr., in 1991 did not deter her from taking on new professional challenges. Born Karen Jurjevich in Sudbury, Ontario, she grew up in Sault Ste. Marie and moved to London, Ontario, in 1975, where she obtained her B.A. and bachelor of education degree from the University of Western Ontario. A masters of education degree in curriculum and administration from the University of British Columbia followed in 1984 while she was on leave from teaching in Tillsonburg in southwestern Ontario.

Karen Murton.

Tall, intense, with an expressive face and dramatic gestures, Karen enjoys the virtually superhuman energy Branksome expects of every principal. This energy became apparent soon after the announcement of her appointment in January 1998. Karen would often jump in her car and tear down to Branksome with a long list of questions for Rachel Belash. Karen recalled, "Rachel said, 'Make your questions. When you feel you have enough, give me a call, and we'll talk about things.' Rachel knew how to make a seamless transition." Giving unstintingly of her time, Rachel invited Karen to alumnae events and board meetings, set up interviews for her with members of the administration team, involved her in teacher interviews, introduced her to parents and gave her a personal tour of the principal's residence at 4 Elm Avenue.

"Rachel was the perfect person for the school at that time," Karen said. "She told me, 'Karen, it's time to fine-tune.'" First, however, Karen had to deal with the unexpected resignation of Patti Thomson MacNicol, who left to take over as director of finance at Upper Canada College. "It was a big hole to fill," Karen said. "It was *huge.*" Patti had left her department in such good order, however, that her successor, Stuart Ferrie, could begin to implement the plans in place.

Then, inevitably, there was the uniform. Said Karen, "There was a *universal* opinion among the administration and the board members that the students' appearance and deportment weren't what they should be. They warned me, 'Don't be surprised at what you see.' In my first assembly, the girls straggled in talking and laughing, didn't sit down. I said, 'Good morning,' and they just kind of looked at me. I was surprised. So I said, 'Would you please sit down?' So they sat down. They were curious, and I was able to get their attention because I was new, but they *talked* while I was speaking or while the head girl was speaking."

Karen found allies in the prefects, who had come up with a fresh school motto: "Respect, Unity, Pride and Spirit." "They felt things needed to improve," Karen said. "There was no respect for the student speaking at the microphone, for the teachers or for the principal." Coming from public schools with thirteen to fifteen hundred students, Karen was a reasonable but firm disciplinarian: "I told them, 'How you look represents the whole school. It's important to you how I look, so I expect the same of you." She expected them to wear plain, flat, black shoes, no jewellery or nail polish and their shirts tucked in. In return, Karen wore tailored suits appropriate for her multiple roles as the school's principal, superintendent, director of education and CEO.

In an October letter to students and parents, she also expressed herself clearly on the Carol Service. Quoting from the school's policy paper, "Tradition, Religion and Diversity," Karen stated,

> At Branksome, girls must attend assembly so as to participate in our coming together as a school; they are free to sing or not sing, to meditate during our moments of silence. Except in cases of religious scruple, we expect attendance at the Carol

> Service in order to preserve the integrity of the tradition and the quality of the musical performance. First and foremost, all who join our school belong in our community and are honoured and respected for their personal uniqueness. We actively try to understand and support the feelings and views of all our students no matter how young, as well as the views of their families. Our values are grounded in how we treat each other, how we respect each other's differences, in short how we continually recreate the caring community that is Branksome Hall.
>
> Given these observations, I wish to tell you that the Carol Service is definitely happening again this year — and the majority of students are expected to attend and participate. We plan on having rehearsals that will give you an opportunity to truly enjoy singing. I also understand that there are students who will choose not to attend the Carol Service because of their religious beliefs or their ethno-cultural traditions. This is an acceptable, personal choice.

The letter was accompanied by a form for parents to indicate whether or not the student would be taking part.

But curriculum, not carols, was uppermost in Karen Murton's mind. Branksome, as always, was committed to following the provincial curriculum, and it was undergoing massive revision. As well, the elimination of Grade Thirteen meant restructuring the entire Senior School curriculum while continuing to add depth and breadth to the basic subject material. Teachers' "guidelines" for course content were being replaced by provincial policy documents dictating specific expectations and achievement levels, but Karen's primary concern was not with what was taught but with *how* it was taught.

"I instil in my teachers that education is not a game," she said. "It's not a challenge to keep knowledge away from kids and 'trick' kids.

Education is what you want to share with young people. My job as a teacher was to take everything I knew and impart it to these students, allow them to challenge, allow them to look at what I was telling them, then discuss it critically in a way that enriches the learning experience. When it comes to testing, I believe that we must show students what it means to get an A. Let's give examples, then show students how to get there." Influenced by her young son's experience at a Montessori school, Karen's goal was "the independent learner." She said, "Through independence, the child gains dignity, and that dignity can be with a child who's four and five years old. Give that child the recognition and confidence to move forward." She believed that the key to achieving this ideal at Branksome was to enhance the use of information technology throughout the school and to develop new models for evaluating both students and teachers. One of her first acts was to hire Rosemary Evans, a curriculum specialist with both public school and university teaching experience, as Branksome's first director of academic studies.

Fortunately, a full enrolment accompanied by a booming economy enabled the school to surpass its fund-raising goals and finance major renovations. In the summer of 1999, the offices and senior common room at 10 Elm Avenue were redecorated; the cramped library was expanded into a sunny, spacious resource centre equipped with computers, comfortable chairs and classroom presentation space; and with the elimination, after ninety-six years, of cooking and sewing, banks of computers replaced the stoves and sewing machines in the family life labs. Teachers who not long ago cranked out lessons and tests on a gestetner now communicate by e-mail, research software, use computers to integrate various subjects and struggle with problems of electronic incompatibility. Students are learning to keyboard in Grade Two.

Although the pageant was quietly dropped from the Carol Service, the girls' passion for dressing up and putting on plays was acknowledged by the transformation of the old gym into a professional-standard performing arts centre complete with an expandable stage and movable,

Judith Friend with Prefect Adrienne Willis, 1997.

banked seats that, after seventy years, enable parents to actually *see* their daughters perform. Named in honour of Allison Roach, the greatly enhanced PAC is a boon to the extremely popular drama program, headed by Judith Friend.

Judith was the last exchange student to come to Branksome Hall from Sherborne School in England (Sheila Macfeeters was the last Branksome student to attend Sherborne School) before the program ended in 1975. Judith stayed on at Branksome as a residence don after entering university; then, having completed her B.A., M.A. and B.Ed., she returned as an English teacher. Later she was Branksome's dean of residence and, since 1989, head of drama. She has encouraged the girls to supplement musicals with serious plays, some as ambitious as *She Stoops to Conquer,* in addition to their own docudramas on social issues, but the real emphasis of the drama program is on movement, sensory awareness, vocal and writing skills, critical thinking and, since drama requires students to work together, cooperation. "My goal has never been to produce stars," she said, yet Branksome theatre graduates are acting, directing and studying drama all over the world. Said Dean of Students Nanci Smith, "We've taught them to speak up for themselves, be articulate, do their research, advocate and lobby, and now they're doing it all!"

On December 8, 1999, not long after the PAC opened, the students and advisors of the Multicultural Society celebrated Branksome's diversity by presenting Infusion, a spectacular, sold-out, two-hour evening of songs, dances, poetry and costume modelling, including an intermission feast of exotic foods, involving sixty performers, their families and friends, who represented fourteen nations from Sweden to Sri Lanka. Infusion was such a hit it was invited back for a repeat performance and celebrated again the next year.

Infusion gave Branksome's fifty-five residence students an opportunity to take centre stage with performances that included Caribbean dances, a Chinese lullaby, two Japanese songs and a Korean fan dance. Routine in residence was still strict — out of bed at 7:15 a.m., lights out at 11 p.m. — but the atmosphere had become more homey. Visitors were welcome, especially in the dining hall, and boarders were encouraged to bring personal possessions. They were divided into four "families," each headed by a live-in adult don (a member of the Branksome faculty). As well, each house, Ainslie and MacNeill, elected a student head of house to sit on the Student Life Committee. This group, along with the residence prefect and junior dons, elected from the boarders, formed the residence council. A student "home sweet home" committee decorated the common rooms for major holidays, a food committee planned theme dinners and helped the kitchen staff to prepare meals that reflected the cultural backgrounds of the boarders and a social committee organized parties, holiday celebrations and weekend outings — some to boys' schools — and involved the boarders in school-wide social events. Several girls were trained as peer support counsellors, and English as a Second

Scenes from Infusion. Lauren Hezikiah above.

Clockwise from front centre: Alicia Hwang, Hannah Kang, Anny Kim, Eun Hyun, Helen Park (hidden by fan), and Woo-Jin Kwak.

Language classes were held twice a week. The residence population remained predominantly Asian, but new students were coming from Russia and Europe.

On February 2, 2000, a real-life student drama prompted a sudden and visible change in the school. Shortly after noon, a dark, scruffy-looking young man entered Buccleuch House, 14 Elm Avenue, home of the Middle School, and touched the thigh of a Grade Seven student. She was startled and frightened but unhurt. The intruder fled on foot. He was arrested by police two days later. A repeat offender, with a history of addictions, he pleaded guilty and went to jail. Branksome immediately increased security to provide coverage twenty-four hours a day, seven days a week. By the time school reopened in the fall, an unobtrusive electronic security system was in place. While the campus remains open to the public from Mount Pleasant Road, the gates on Park Road are locked except, under supervision, when students are arriving and leaving, and the pathways and locked entrances to school buildings are equipped with video surveillance cameras. Students swipe their identity cards to open the doors; visitors ring a buzzer and identify themselves to the office staff.

The security incident threw the spotlight on the Middle School, Grades Seven and Eight. When its first head, Judy MacLellan, succeeded Ruth Ann Penny as head of the Junior School in 1999, Karrie Weinstock, Vice-Principal and Director of Admissions, was appointed head of both the Middle and Senior Schools. The Middle School has tremendous energy. The girls are encouraged to take initiative in co-curricular activities, in community service and in running Buccleuch House, which they do in the Our House Committee. The Assembly Committee organizes the Friday Middle Division Assembly, which is a highlight of the week. The girls pioneer within the school the three-year Outward Bound program, a three-to-five-day wilderness camping expedition designed to encourage self-reliance. The curriculum in the Middle School is highly integrated to reduce the number of teachers the girls must encounter in a day.

Robin Brebner, Debbie Lucas, and Heather McLuskie.

Senior students complain about a heavy load of homework, a consequence of Branksome's commitment to academic achievement in an intellectually competitive society, yet they seem to find time for more clubs, societies, sports teams and socials, including a new composers' club and a revived classics club. Branksome girls continue to shine at interschool athletic events, but they compete with so many schools, both independent and public, that the ancient, proud rivalry with Havergal and Bishop Strachan has faded away. The kilt, green or red, remains as fashionable as it was when it was introduced in 1939, and in 1999 matching blazers were reintroduced as compulsory formal dress. The school still has no intercom, but assembly continues to be held three days a week. With an expanded student council that includes advisor group representatives, a council of club leaders, a Student Life Committee and intraschool e-mail, the logistics of gathering six hundred girls together in a cavernous gym make less sense than in the days when the whole school marched in for daily prayers to the stirring chords of "Onward Christian

Soldiers" pounded out on the piano by Agnes Brown.

As Branksome has become more decentralized, and the afternoon hours spared long ago for clan games, cakes and sticky buns have disappeared, the clans are struggling to find a purpose. Should they integrate with the advisor groups? Become agents for charitable and community service? Bridge the communication gaps within the student population? Or does this aspect of Branksome's Scottish identity conflict with the school's recently articulated commitment to ethnic, religious, cultural, intellectual and socio-economic diversity? "Reflecting the diversity of our world" is the fifth of seven "initiatives" announced in a school strategic plan adopted in January 2000. This initiative includes not only tangibly representing the wider community among Branksome students, staff and teachers but also actively embracing the extraordinary range of opportunities provided by the school's downtown location and incorporating them into the curriculum and co-curricular programs. As an example, Karen Murton has initiated the Horizons program at Branksome Hall that was founded by Upper Canada College, in partnership with the Toronto public school boards and Frontier College, to provide free, year-round mentoring, including class tutoring and a summer camp, for academically talented elementary school students who live in Toronto's inner-city neighbourhoods.

The overall goal of the strategic plan is to define Branksome as a "community of learners" committed to excellence in scholarship and all aspects of school life. But how is excellence measured and achieved? Implementation of the plan requires developing objective standards and criteria, assigning responsibilities and setting deadlines for evaluation. The bottom line is "accountability," and Karen considers herself as accountable for her performance as anyone else. She is frank and pragmatic. She welcomes constructive criticism and encourages open, informative communication; she submits a detailed report to the board of governors at every meeting, sends frequent letters to parents and polls parents, alumnae and students regarding their level of satisfaction with the school.

Karen works a twelve-hour day, attends after-school events, hosts regular breakfasts for the prefects and, in the middle of the night, jumps out of bed at the sound of sirens or screeching tires. "If there's a false fire alarm, a car accident, I'm out there on the street," she said. "It's my responsibility. It's good to live on campus. The girls know 'She's here for us.'" Her relations with the Teachers' Association are forthright and amicable, and the development of a new teacher evaluation model has been a co-operative effort.

Teachers are evaluated regularly not by the principal but by teams of two faculty members and the head of the school. Performance is measured on a scale based on specific elements, including knowledge of curriculum, effective delivery and evaluation, classroom management, innovative practices, individualized instruction, organization, professional growth, contribution to the school and community and healthy relationships with students and parents. Professional development for all teachers is an ongoing priority.

Karen likes to solve problems by negotiation — in the spring of 2001, she persuaded the head girl and prefects, in the interest of safety, to tone down the traditional all-night initiation of their newly elected successors — but some issues aren't negotiable. One is cleanliness. "I check the property," Karen said. "If I see garbage, I call maintenance. I want the campus to look good." After the Senior School Common Room was refurnished in 1999, food and beverages were forbidden in it. Outraged, the girls retaliated with passive resistance, and Karen learned to turn a blind eye to leftover pop cans and crumpled paper bags. Students who defy the *Code of Conduct,* a booklet of school rules given to each girl at the beginning of the year, are reported to the head of Senior and Middle School, who notifies their parents. Miscreants may get detentions, lose privileges, risk suspension or, in extreme cases, be expelled. Today, however, any girl called on the carpet is entitled to be accompanied by her faculty advisor or a guidance counsellor. Since September 2000, when the Senior and Middle Schools adopted an eight-day cycle of eighty-minute classes, the school's halls have become noticeably quieter. It is almost inconceivable to recall that girls once raced each other in the halls, sunbathed in their bloomers on the roof of the porte-cochère and sprayed fire hoses out their classroom windows. There is some nostalgia for bygone days when teachers, as well as students, had spare time to gossip, daydream, veg out or goof around.

"The pace is *frantic,"* sighed Senior School Librarian Jane Moore. "When a space opens up in the timetable, someone says, 'What do we put in here?' I say, 'Let's put *nothing* in this slot.'" With annual school fees ranging from $9,000 for junior kindergarten to $15,850 for day girls and $31,450 for boarders, parents' expectations have risen accordingly. "Now a lot of parenting is expected to be done by the school," said Nanci Smith. "There is a much greater demand for us to be setting standards of discipline, social attitudes and appropriate behaviour. It's a real partnership with parents." Jane Moore, whose daughter attends the school, sees this as a benefit: "The teachers know the students well. I have confidence that my daughter is *known.* I can't ask for anything more. Parents should have confidence in the teacher. If you value the teacher, your child wins."

Excellence in a school, as Branksome has learned, requires a campus that is constantly evolving to meet students' needs. With an annual operating budget of $14 million, a modest yearly surplus and a $9.5 million investment fund raised from endowed and restricted donations, Branksome developed a Campus Facilities Master Plan early in 2001 as a follow up to the Strategic Plan developed under the leadership of Tony Graham, Branksome Board Chair from 1996–2001. Karen Murton said of Tony, "He was important in mentoring me as a new head, just as Rachel had also played a significant role in facilitating the transition from her era to mine. Tony played a major role in building the endowment and worked very closely with me in the development of a new strategic plan and the Facilities Master Plan that grew from it." Spread over a period of eight years or more, beginning in 2002, the plan schedules a series of renovation and construction projects intended to enhance the appearance and functionality of the school's buildings and grounds, cope with traffic congestion, create more open space, build a new Middle School and add an extension to the Senior School in the northeast corner of the east campus.

Dot Seixas and Sally Adams Medland.

Since Branksome has never been zoned "institutional" — a consequence of Miss Read's long war with city hall — zoning changes and official approval may involve substantial changes or delays. Parking and traffic circulation are major priorities, as is the relocation of the kindergarten, which still has its own small building tucked away on the edge of the ravine, to the Junior School. The prospect is an emotional wrench for kindergarten teacher Sally Medland, a former student and head girl who succeeded Ruth Hamilton Upjohn, the school's first kindergarten teacher, on Ruth's retirement in 1982, and for Dot Seixas, who has been playing piano in the kindergarten for sixty years. "I love this place," said Sally, looking around the big, bright room shaded, like a storybook hideaway, by ancient copper beech trees. "As a student, I loved what Ruth and Dot were doing, and I wanted to do it some day. There was a sense of joy, so much enthusiasm for music and nature and art, a love of life. I know I've carried that on. If school is welcoming, exciting and fun, children love coming to school. Learning happens naturally." The kindergarten building will eventually house the staff day care.

If, as planned, a new Middle School is built in 2004, the music department will occupy Buccleuch House, freeing up the current music rooms overlooking the quadrangle for a Senior School lunchroom. Food, and a comfortable place to eat it, remain close to the top of the list of student concerns. No buildings will be torn down, and the cost of the expansion, estimated at $8 million, will be borne by the Branksome community.

At the same time, Branksome will be going through a profound academic reorientation: the adoption, over a period of years, of the International Baccalaureate Programme. The decision, made in the spring of 2001 following more than a year of extensive research and consultation, calls for the IB Programme to be phased in at the Junior School in September 2001, followed by a middle years preparatory programme in September 2002 and the diploma programme in 2006, with the first IB students graduating in 2008. Since each programme is separate, senior students with no previous IB experience can opt for the IB diploma in Grade Eleven. Branksome will continue to offer as well the standard Ontario high school diploma.

Adopted since 1968 by more than one thousand schools in one hundred countries, including schools across Canada, the IB diploma is a liberal arts curriculum that, unlike the Ontario high school diploma, requires all students to study mathematics, a second language, their own language, an experimental science, a social science and a creative art. In addition, students must write an extended essay based on independent research, study the theory of knowledge and participate in cultural, community and social service activities. Exams are marked by IB examiners.

The IB diploma programme has a reputation for intellectual rigour, but the middle years programme stresses a flexible, interactive, thematic approach to subject material, and each school is responsible for its own student assessments. In the primary years, subjects are organized around six themes: who we are, where we are in place and time, how we express ourselves, how the world works, how we organize ourselves and sharing the planet. There are no IB exams, but the program itself must be IB accredited.

Judy MacLellan, Head of the Junior School, believes that the IB's holistic approach will enhance Branksome's own inquiry-based learning philosophy: "It's a common framework we can all build on. There will be more room for children to go in their own directions — what do *you* want to find out about? The idea is to pick concepts, not topics, 'extinction,' for instance, rather than 'endangered species,' 'democracy' rather than 'government.' You start from what the kids know, and they have a wealth of background."

The IB organization, based in Geneva, provides Branksome, for a price, with internationally recognized standards of curriculum and assessment, teacher training and educational information, as well as independent scrutiny and a global perspective that coincidentally fulfils one of Miss Read's ambitions: on June 14, 1950, Miss Read told a *Toronto Star* reporter that she wished Branksome to become "an international school" with students from around the world. Concerns remain, however, that the IB Programme may discourage girls who find it too demanding or prevent girls with talents other than scholarship from coming to Branksome. The value Branksome Hall places on character and ethical behaviour is as high as it has ever been, and Branksome has always wanted to make room for quiet, shy girls as well as "quirky" girls who are up to mischief. Graduates with modest scholastic achievements have often gone on to exceptionally successful careers in business and the arts. While all applicants, after Grade Six, write a standard test common to all independent schools, selection is ultimately determined by an interview with the girl and her parents. The purpose of the interview, which lasts thirty to forty minutes, is to determine first of all whether or not the girl *wants* to come to Branksome. A girl who glares at her mother or slouches in a chair in an uncommunicative way is not a good candidate. What will she get from the school or give to it?

With a record number of applications, an attrition rate that has fallen to seven percent of the student population and waiting lists for every grade, Branksome has an opportunity to create a unique and exceptional community. Fears that the IB Programme will make Branksome a joyless school may be as groundless as Miss Read's gloomy view of Branksome girls in 1950: "The girls don't laugh as much nowadays as they used to," she lamented to the *Toronto Star.*

> I often tell them that if they'd laugh more they'd feel better. Sometimes, I wish they'd play more pranks on me. There was something a group of them did the other day, some silly, foolish little thing that they thought was going to horrify me. I loved it, just loved it. They just don't know how to "carry on" these days. You know what I mean by "carrying on" don't you? I mean having good, clean, innocent fun. The students used to make their own fun; now they're not quite so capable.

In 1994, however, a Branksome graduating class was capable of hiring a male stripper, disguising him as a YMCA social worker and introducing him to assembly to speak to the girls about volunteering. Bumping and grinding to raucous music, he stripped long enough to reveal "Grads '94" painted on his bare chest before he was ushered out the door. Class president Ellie Hawke was grateful that the faculty had the open-mindedness and sense of humour to take the prank in stride.

Digging in the dirt isn't everyone's idea of fun, but on May 9, 2001, Branksome families, teachers and staff turned out in sun hats, garden gloves and work boots for the tenth annual celebration of Branksome Green Restoration Night in the ravine behind the Junior School. Their tasks were to plant and mulch native trees, shrubs and wildflowers and to pull out garlic mustard, a foreign weed that is threatening to take over the undergrowth. Removal of most of the Norway maples and other non-native trees has left open spaces to plant sugar maples, red oaks, chokecherries, Virginia bluebells, wild violets, trilliums and *rosa blanda,* the wild rose for which Rosedale was named. An overgrown vegetable garden behind the principal's residence is being dug up for a tree nursery, but it will be many years, and much labour, before the entire five-acre ravine is restored.

Claire Kennedy and Annice Blake participate in Branksome Green Planting, 1995.

Crumbling stone pillars by Mount Pleasant Road still mark the east entrance to what was once the Deacon family's Glenhurst estate, and on May 26, 2001, Kathleen Deacon, who grew up at Glenhurst, revisited her old neighbourhood for Branksome's annual alumnae dinner. Returning to Canada after having lived for more than forty years in South Africa, Kathleen was seeing the school for only the second time since Branksome bought the Deacon property in 1948. "It's certainly nostalgic," she said. "The banisters are still there. My room was on the third floor. I looked to see if some of the wallpaper still had my autographs, but I didn't see them. We had a wonderful home, always welcoming, always full of young people. We had such fun and happiness. The house *should* have children in it. It is absolutely appropriate for the Junior School. I think it's great."

The location of the alumnae dinner, the Senior School gym, a reminder of the days when the alumnae gathered in the spartan dining room at 10 Elm Avenue, gave the 350 women a feeling of camaraderie. The highlight of the evening was the presentation of the Alumna of the

Year Award by Allison Roach, celebrating the fiftieth anniversary of her own graduation, to Joyce Frankel Kofman, a former chair of the Branksome board, as well as the mother and grandmother of Branksome students, in recognition of her unwavering commitment to the school and to Toronto's cultural and charitable organizations.

The next afternoon, more than a hundred alumnae braved a violent thunderstorm for a buffet lunch and a tour of the school. For all its innovation and multi-million-dollar investment, Branksome is still its familiar, labyrinthine self: halls twist and turn, end in blank walls or open through fire doors onto stairwells that seem to lead to bottomless chasms; stairs climb from the bright Sime Wing, built in the early 1970s, to narrow, dim halls with wooden doors and Victorian wainscoting. A math classroom is equipped with antique wooden desks with initials carved on their slanted tops. One desktop flips up to reveal an inkwell holder and next to it a contemporary chocolate bar wrapper. The rotunda, the Senior School lunch area, looks like a 1950s diner; the girls call it the "airport." Branksome remains a wonderfully mysterious, surprising place, full of ghosts. That day, for alumnae privately reliving their long-ago school days, memories were enhanced by the storm rumblings reverberating through the halls and classrooms.

"Miss Read would be pleased, don't you think?" an elderly woman whispered to her friend after touring the resource centre.

A crackle of lightning and a clap of thunder overhead caused eyes to glance upward. Earlier in the afternoon, a lightning bolt had struck the principal's residence and disabled the traffic light at the intersection of Elm Avenue and Mount Pleasant Road, the location where, exactly fifty-one years earlier, Miss Read had marched out with her "stop" sign and halted traffic until she succeeded in having that light installed. A respectful silence fell. Miss Read's feelings about the school now may not be known, but they appear to run high.

Notes

Introduction

A survey of girls' school alumnae in the United States, "Achievement, Leadership and Success," was published by the National Coalition of Girls' Schools in January 2000. Information about Great Britain is contained in an article — "Girls' Schools: Where Are We Now?" — by Dr. Carol Kirby, Principal of Ottawa's all-girls Elmwood School, in the spring 2000 issue of the school's publication the *Elmwood Edition.* These and other references were provided by Rosemary Evans, Director of Academic Studies at Branksome Hall.

Research sources for this history, which began in 1998, have included the Branksome Hall archive, the Ontario Archives, the University of Toronto Libraries, some existing school administration documents, minutes of the Board of Governors, memoirs submitted by members of the Branksome community and interviews with numerous people who have been participants in various aspects of the school's history.

Chapter One

The primary source for Chapters One to Seven is the Branksome Hall archive, with its collection of *Slogans,* newsletters, photographs, brochures, yearbooks, memorabilia and clipping files, including the written reminiscences of the oldest Old Girls quoted here. Charlotte Keens

Graham contributed Delphine Burr's quotation about men and heaven; Delphine was her mother.

Margaret Sime began to assemble historical material in 1974 following her retirement as principal, and for years Shirley Duperley, the principal's secretary, saved important material in a big box. The collection continues to grow. In 1982, former teacher Mattie Clark and Miss Sime prepared a brief, useful early history, "The Origins of Branksome Hall." Minute books of board meetings are kept in the school's safe.

For historical background on Toronto, I have referred particularly to *Lost Toronto,* by William Dendy (Oxford University Press, 1978), and *Aristocratic Toronto,* by Lucy Booth Martyn (Gage, 1980). *Centennial Story: The Board of Education for the City of Toronto, 1850–1950,* edited by Honora Cochrane (Thomas Nelson, 1950), is a detailed history of the early public schools, and *The Development of Education in Canada* (Gage, 1957) provides an overview. *A Question of Privilege: Canada's Independent Schools,* by Carolyn Gossage (Peter Martin, 1977), provides sketches of many girls' schools, including Branksome Hall, Netherwood, where Edith Read taught briefly, and Halifax Ladies' College, where Edith had gone to school. Appendix G of *The Report of the Commission on Private Schools in Ontario,* by Bernard Shapiro (1985), is a brief, background essay by Robert Stamp entitled "A History of Private Schools in Ontario."

Women Who Taught: Perspectives on the History of Women and Teaching, edited by Alison Prentice and Marjorie Theobald (University of Toronto Press, 1991), provides context for the story of Branksome's first teachers and principals, including a chapter by Prentice on Mary Electa Adams. *Methodists and Women's Education in Ontario, 1836–1925,* by Johanna Selles (McGill-Queen's University Press, 1996), emphasizes the role played by religion in all early Ontario schools. *Havergal: Celebrating a Century, 1894–1994,* by Mary Byers (Boston Mills Press, 1994), illustrates how different girls' schools are from each other. *The Best Type of Girl,* by Gillian Avery (Andre Deutsch, 1992), is a revealing portrait of British independent girls' schools.

Margaret Sime's research into the Scott family history has been supplemented by the Dundas Historical Museum, Dundas, Ontario, and by descendants of the extended Scott family, Susan Crean, Murray Dobbie, Tom Ritson and Michael Ritchie. It is possible, but not proven, that Margaret's ancestors came from Branxholme parish. Her relationship to Sir Walter Scott would have been distant. Miss Sime's research and Merrickville historian Alice Hughes supplied what little information exists about Florence Merrick. Ottawa researcher Sara Wallace located the male principals of the Ottawa Ladies' College.

In 1910, having tossed Branksome out of its Bloor Street home and demolished the house, the Ontario government changed its mind about building a Government House so close to downtown. It chose, instead, Chorley Park, overlooking the Don Valley in east Rosedale, and sold the Bloor Street property to Manufacturers Life for its gargantuan new head office.

Information about Edith Read's background comes from her nephew, Tom Read, and Halifax family history researcher Heather Long. Edith's academic records are in the archives of Radcliffe College, now part of Harvard University. The story of Miss Read's purchase of the school, outlined in the minutes of board meetings, is told by Mary Barker and by W.D. Ross's daughter, Jean Ross Skoggard.

A stained glass window, erected in Eleanor Stanhope's memory by her sister, was installed in the school's gymnasium in 1924. It remains in the east wall of the Performing Arts Centre.

In 1921, the first federal election in which women could vote, Agnes Macphail, a teacher, was elected for the Ontario riding of Grey-Bruce. For more on Macphail and the status of women at the turn of the century, see *More than a Rose: Prime Ministers, Wives and Other Women,* by Heather Robertson (Seal, 1991).

Chapter Two

Information on Branksome's business affairs comes from the minute books of board meetings.

A graphic fictional portrait of Branksome Hall in the 1920s is *Nancy-Rose,* a young adult novel written by alumna Dora Olive Thomson. Branksome is identified as "Glenelm," Miss Read as "the Princ," Ainslie McMichael as "Miss McGregor." Residence, divided into "Upper Skittle" and "Lower Skittle," is the scene of many midnight feasts. Stumbling on one, Miss McGregor tactfully asks the girls to close their eyes. When they open them again, she is gone. *Nancy-Rose* describes skiing and tobogganing trips to Huntsville, a popular destination before Miss Read bought Clansdale Heights. The novel, 256 pages long, was published in London, England, by Girls' Own Paper. A copy is available for study in the Thomas Fisher Rare Book Library at the University of Toronto, call number T56 N26 193. Thompson wrote eight popular young adult novels before she died, very young, in 1935. An endowment from her parents in her memory allowed Branksome to increase substantially its collection of books.

Charles Tisdall went to many Branksome parties until he was banned from Branksome for life. "While I was shy and a bit insecure at that stage of life," he said, "I was not above pranks. At one party, I learned where the master electrical switch was located. At an opportune time, when the party was in full swing, I found the switch and promptly turned off all the lights in the building. Chaos reigned. Unfortunately, in the dark I could not find my way back to the gymnasium. Miss Read caught me in a hall and later informed SAC headmaster, Kenneth Ketchum, that I was never to darken Branksome's doorstep again." Tisdall, however, married a Branksome girl, Diana Gage Griffith, and their twin daughters excelled at the school.

The definitive study of Canada's attitude toward Jewish refugees is *None Is Too Many,* by Irving Abella and Harold Troper (Lester and Orpen

Dennys, 1982). Mackenzie King's admiration for Hitler and Mussolini is expressed at length in his personal diaries. They can be read on microfiche at the Robarts Library.

Chapter Three

Most of the material in this chapter comes from the Branksome Hall archive, interviews with the author and Elva Carey's history, "A Very Hard Decision," based on questionnaires sent to every English war guest who could be located. Jean Ingham's papers were entrusted to Susan Kenny by Jean's husband, Anthony Perdue, after her death.

Many of the war guests' sponsors, including the Misses Laidlaw, continued to support them through university, and the Laidlaws, as well as J.S. McLean and J.A. MacLeod, President of the Bank of Nova Scotia, sponsored several girls. It's unlikely that the identities of all the sponsors will ever be known.

The account of Miss Read's discovery of Portia White is based on a student script written for a Branksome Broadcasting Corporation production.

Not all English war guests returned home. Kathleen Hinch went on to the University of Toronto, married an American and moved to the United States. Bridget Gregson also studied at the University of Toronto, married young and remained in Canada. Widowed, she later married John Duncanson, whose late wife, Mary, was the daughter of Branksome's former doctor, Robert MacMillan (his nephew, also Robert MacMillan, had succeeded him). Susan Duncanson Pigott is the daughter of John and Mary Duncanson, and the Duncansons' granddaughter, Sara, graduated from Branksome with a prize in history in 1998. These MacMillans are not related to Alexander MacMillan, the school's first patron and the father of musician and conductor Sir Ernest MacMillan.

Mary Barker was awarded the Order of Canada in 1999 for her work in physical education, the YWCA and the armed services. Margaret Eaton, who reached the rank of lieutenant-colonel, was awarded the Order of the British Empire for her wartime service.

Chapter Four

The court's decision is contained in *The Ontario Weekly Notes* for 1946, pages 93–94. Miss Read's long squabble with the City of Toronto is documented in the Branksome Hall archive and in the 1947 minutes of the Property Committee of Toronto City Council, City of Toronto Archives. The traffic light dispute is recorded in the minutes of the city's Board of Control for May 22, 1950, and of Toronto City Council, Appendix A, Volume 1, 1950, pages 1310–1311, also in the City of Toronto Archives.

Branksome began its own bus service during the Second World War when gas rationing made it impractical for parents to drive their daughters to the school. The first small bus, described as a ramshackle vehicle with wooden sides, may have been the "station car" built by General Motors of Canada for Prime Minister Mackenzie King in 1929. The bus was driven by an assortment of teachers, secretaries and maintenance men. One of the teachers, Katherine MacLeod, married Toronto lawyer and Branksome board member Keiller MacKay, and, when MacKay became lieutenant-governor of Ontario, it was said that the surest route to social prominence was to drive the Branksome bus.

The Sherborne-Branksome student exchange began officially in 1950 after Diana Reader Harris became headmistress of Sherborne School, and it ended with her retirement in 1975.

The replica of the lintel over the entrance to Branxholme Castle was installed in a curved stone niche in front of 10 Elm Avenue in 1955. The ceremony was presided over by the Earl and Countess of Dalkeith, son and daughter-in-law of the Duke of Buccleuch.

Through her physician father, who specialized in homeopathy, an alternative medicine favoured by the royal family, Edith Read was on friendly terms with court physician Sir John Weir. She sent Christmas presents to the princesses, Elizabeth and Margaret Rose, when they were children, probably in the vain hope that they would attend Branksome Hall.

When John A. Tory died in 1950, mourners at his funeral whispered among themselves, "Who will control Miss Read now?" The answer soon became clear: nobody.

Chapter Five

Jennie MacNeill had a black Labrador dog that she named Poker. When Jennie joked that she spent all her money on Poker, the girls thought she lost it gambling.

Edith Read had purchased a cemetery plot large enough to hold six to eight of her staff, but Jennie didn't want to share space with Miss Read in death as she had in life. Jean Claxton and the staff arranged to send her body back to Prince Edward Island, where she was buried beside her parents. Only two people are buried with Edith: Ed White, her head of maintenance for twenty years, and his wife.

Branksome girls didn't mind playing games in their bloomers or, at interschool competitions, in full uniform. They found it a challenge, and they didn't worry when their ugly black rubber running shoes left indelible marks on their competitors' pristine gym floors.

On February 13, 1968, Portia White died of cancer at fifty-seven. She had enjoyed a distinguished international concert career, including a command performance before Queen Elizabeth II in 1964, and she had regularly returned to Branksome to sing at banquets, Sunday-evening services and memorial events.

In March 1968, a fifteen-year-old Branksome student, Sarah Sheard, made headlines in the *Toronto Star* when she attended a Vietnam war protest featuring folk singer Joan Baez. When Baez urged members of the audience to live according to their consciences, Sarah jumped up and asked, "What can I do? I'm just a schoolkid." Baez replied, "Drop out of school." Her advice shocked the crowd. Sarah decided that doing so wasn't "terribly practical." She eventually became a novelist and psychotherapist.

For single women, teaching and living at an independent school was not entirely slave labour. A live-in teacher enjoyed a cheap apartment, even if it was one room, and plenty of company. As a community, the teachers could share stories, party together and comfort each other during hard times. Married teachers, while few, made a point of inviting their colleagues to their homes, and parents would invite their girls' teachers home for dinner. As chaperones, the teachers attended plays and concerts they otherwise could not afford, and they, too, liked to ski on the weekends at Clansdale Heights. By 1956, however, Branksome Hall was trying to sell the farm. The old house, rented out, had burned down, and skiing had become a competitive, downhill sport.

Ribbit the Frog was created by 1971 sports captain Jane O'Callaghan. Jane thought that Branksome needed a mascot to drum up enthusiasm during games with rival schools, and Ribbit went on to a long life with many incarnations. The original Ribbit was made of green cloth stuffed with nylons; the current Ribbit is a costume. The Ribbit logo was drawn by Mary Wright McPherson, class of 1986.

Chapter Six

Interviews with Allison Roach, Rachel Belash and Karen Murton have been important sources for Chapters Six, Seven and Eight.

Kate and Alison Wiley, both trained by Rodger Wright of Upper Canada College, where their older brother, Hugh, had been a student track star, ran in national meets for the University of Toronto Track Club. At the Canada Games in August 1981, Alison put Branksome Hall on the map by setting a games record in the women's 1,500 metres and smashing the Canadian junior record in the 3,000-metre race. Her time in the 3,000 metres ranked her sixth in the world. The next year, Alison was the OFSSA champion in the 1,500-metre race and placed twelfth at the World

Cross Country Championships in Rome. A year later, as a student at Stanford University on a track scholarship, she finished second in the World Cross Country Championship to Norwegian Grete Waitz. Alison and Kate, however, put their academic careers first. Kate graduated in medicine from Queen's University, and Alison graduated with an MBA from the University of Toronto.

Allison Roach learned to appreciate the power of parental wrath when she was charged with assault by an enraged mother in June 1984. Allison had been playing a Sunday-afternoon game of tennis with friends on the school's private courts in the Rosedale ravine when the parent, whose daughter attended Branksome Hall, engaged Allison in a heated argument about her family's disputed right to use the tennis courts. The parent subsequently laid an assault charge, claiming that Allison had hit her and knocked her down. When the case went to court in March 1985, the judge dismissed the charge as "a tempest in a teapot."

Chapter Seven

Dot Seixas became so exasperated at girls' inability to pronounce her name that she finally said, "Oh, call me Miss Sneezepickle!" Miss Sneezepickle she became.

Sixteen Elm Avenue became a residence for the dean of students and her family.

When Branksome drama students learned in the spring of 1995 that the school did not intend to stage a musical the coming fall, three senior students, Adrienne Willis, Jen Lees and Veronica Liu, asked for permission to raise enough money for the students to put on a musical themselves. Unable to acquire the rights to *Grease,* they decided to finance a production of *Annie* by organizing a *Grease* theme week, featuring contests, food sales and a dance inspired by the musical. Branksome's *Grease* week not only raised the money but also became entertainment in itself.

Shirley Brown pushed strongly for change at Branksome. Her suicide in October 1996 was a tragic loss to the school.

An annual lecture, the Rachel Belash Speaker Series, has been named in Rachel's honour. Speakers have included feminist author Naomi Wolf, archaeologist Maeve Leakey and author-humanitarian June Callwood.

Chapter Eight

The official opening of the Performing Arts Centre and the Resource Centre on November 23, 1999, was marked by a student assembly and later a reception for faculty, parents and alumnae. Rachel Belash and Allison Roach were guests of honour. The Resource Centre was named for R.S. McLaughlin, founder of General Motors of Canada, whose family and charitable foundation have long been benefactors of the school. McLaughlin's granddaughter, Diana Phillips Jackson, is a graduate.

Earlier, in February, 1999, Branksome's reputation for public speaking was enhanced when Jessica Watson placed first in the Canadian National Public Speaking Competition. As a member of the Canadian team, she later competed in the World Public Speaking and Debating Championship, the fifth consecutive year that a Branksome student achieved this distinction and a record unequalled by another independent school.

Branksome Green has received an award from the Society of Ecological Restoration in recognition of its ravine restoration. Located not far below the junior school, beside steps leading to the tennis courts on the ravine floor, a circular, wooden "outdoor classroom" is used in good weather for nature study, drawing and dramatic readings, among many other activities. A plaque commemorates a Branksome teacher, Wendy Wren Rosch, her husband, Phil, a maintenance man, and their young son, Joey, all killed in a car accident in 1992. A nature pathway through the restored woodlot is called "Ribbit's Path."

On Glenhurst's old gateposts, probably built by the original owner,

Edgar Jarvis, the name is spelled Glen Hurst.

The Carol Service, which attracts standing-room-only crowds at St. Paul's Church, continues to provoke debate, including passionate letters, pro and con, in the *Kilt Press.* About one-quarter of the Branksome students choose not to participate.

Principals

1903–1910	Margaret Taylor Scott
1910–1958	Edith MacGregor Read
1958–1968	Jennie E. MacNeill
1968–1974	Margaret R. Sime
1974–1993	Allison Roach '51
1993–1998	Rachel Phillips Belash
1998–	Karen Murton

Board Chairs

1924–1958	Edith M. Read*
1958–1968	Clive Thomson*
1968–1971	Marshal Stearns*
1971–1974	Nicholas Fodor*
1974–1979	Adam H. Zimmerman
1979–1981	Joyce FRANKEL Kofman '45
1981–1984	Nancy SCHELL Pinnington '46
1984–1991	George L. Booth
1991–1996	Mary Pat JONES Armstrong '63
1996–2001	Anthony R. Graham
2001–2002	Catherine FLAVELLE Henderson '63
2002–present	Wendy Cecil

* denotes deceased

Alumnae Association Presidents

1908–09	Gladys STARK*
1910–12	Ethel AMES*
1912–14	Rita CHESTNUT*
1914–15	Daisy ROBERTSON*
1915–16	Lily SHANNON Plant*
1916–18	Marjorie LYON*
1918–19	Gertrude WINGER*
1919–20	Moly PONTON*
1920–22	Grace RYRIE*
1922–23	Helen BALLANTYNE Kemp*
1923–24	Erie SHEPPARD*
1924–25	Aileene MARKS*
1925–26	Jean MORTON*
1926–27	Elizabeth SCOTT Warren*

1927–28	Mary BARKER
1928–29	Helen WRIGHT Walker*
1929–30	Dorothy HARDING Simonds*
1930–31	Catherine HYDE Phin*
1931–33	Phyllis HOLLINRAKE*
1933–34	Phyllis CALVERT*
1934–35	Margery WATSON Tow*
1935–37	Mary McLEAN Stewart
1937–39	Mary HANNA Hall*
1939–41	Margaret MacLENNAN Smythe*
1941–43	Mary WARDLAW*
1943–45	Laura STONE Bradfield*
1945–46	Gladys SIMPSON Brown*
1946–47	Grace MORRIS Craig*
1947–50	Carmen FAIR Capon*
1950–52	Betty WILLIAMSON Tayler
1952–54	Isabel ADAMS McIntosh*
1954–56	Isobel COULTHARD*
1956–58	Shirley McEVOY Bell*
1958–60	Gwynneth SINCLAIR Powell
1960–62	Lois PLANT Barron*
1962–64	Mona Le GALLAIS French*

1964–66	Margaret DONALD Elgie*
1966–68	Margaret ESSERY Andrachuk*
1968–70	Jean MacDONALD Bennett
1970–72	Katherine McLEAN Staples
1972–74	Eleanor HAMILTON
1974–76	Gilda WALWYN Allen
1976–78	Mary CRAIG Tasker
1978–80	Carolyn KLOPSTOCK*
1980–82	Helen GERMAN Read
1982–85	Barbara PATTISON Hepburn
1985–88	Sally ADAMS Medland
1988–91	Carolyn AMELL
1991–93	Nancy FALCONER
1993–95	Lynn HUGHES Clappison
1995–97	Margo CARRUTHERS Hilton
1997–99	Jean BARTLETT Shirreff
1999–01	Louise COFFEY Hastings
2001–	Cynthia GOODCHILD

* denotes deceased

Parents' Association Presidents

1981–1982	Kathy Anderson
1982–1983	Barbara Snively
1983–1984	Mary Britnell-Fisher
1984–1985	Anne Kirkland
1985–1986	Ginger Taylor
1986–1988	Shirley J. Smith
1988–1990	Marg KLEIN Walker '62
1990–1992	Villy Baria
1992–1994	Shirley Domelle
1994–1996	Nancy Mulvihill
1996–1997	Deborah Hugh
1997–1998	Don O'Born
1998–2000	Ginnie Wright
2000–2002	Jane Smith
2002–	Elaine Dimmer

Faculty

Adamson, Christine
1992–1993
Allen, Madge
1957–1967
Allport, Noreen
1946–1947
Alston, Winnifred
1940–1941
Amsden, Edith
1918–1920
Anderson, Avis
1934–1936
Anderson, Edith
1959–1962
Anderson, Eileen M.
1955–1956
Anderson, Elizabeth
1949–1951
Anderson, Margaret
1994–1997
Anderson, Phyllis
1917–1918
Andrew, Lorna
1951–1952
Angstrom, Nadine
1914–1917, 1925–1926
Armstrong, Katherine
1922–1944
Arnot-Johnson, David
2001–
Astington, Janet
1967–1972
Atkins, Joan
1954–1956
Aucouturier, Dominique
1980–
Auruskin '87, Hayley
1995–2001, 2002–
Bacchiochi, Carlene
1999–2000, 2001–
Badali, Bernadette
2001–
Bagot, Helen
1938–1940
Bairstow, Carol
1992–1993
Baker, Edwina
1957–1988

Baldwin, Deborah HUTCHINS '71
1988–1991

Ball, Jo Anne
1973–1974

Ball, Jonathan
1981–1988

Ballard, Violet
1957–1958

Banks, Bette Ann
1958–1959

Banter, Grace
1920–1922

Barker '23, Mary
1926–1929

Barker, Judith
1970–1971

Barnes, Evelyn
1951–1956, 1963–1968

Barnes, Joy
1942–1943

Barnett, Mary RANGER '52
1976–1986

Barr, Rita
1959–1960

Barrett, Doreen
1966–1968

Bate, Margaret
1954–1955

Batt, Mary Jane
1972–1976

Baxter, Elizabeth
1956–1957

Bayly, Judith
1981–1999

Beamish, Laura
1981–1989

Beatty, Stephen
1997–2001

Beck, Vera
1942–1945

Bedard, Anne
1972–1975, 1976–1994

Beech, Sandra
1988–1989

Beeston, Jennifer
1965–1967

Belash, Rachel
1993–1998

Bell, Ferne
1950–1951

Bell, Leonie
1954–1955

Bell, Jennifer POPPER '78
1983–1993

Bell, Shirley
1978–1988

Bennet, Joyce
1975–1976

Bennett, Jackie
1990–

Bennett, Jean MacDONALD '36
1964–1974

Beresford, Diana
1976–1978

Berka, Jana
1976–2001

Bertram, Joyce
1947–1950

Bethune, G.S.
1921–1925

Bickle, Dan
1982–2000

Billings, Gladys
1922–1923

Bincik, Laura
1991–1999, 2000–

Binnie, Lucille
1970–1972

Biss, Sheila
1963–1964

Bissett, Edith
1951–1952

Black, Ruth
1945–1948

Black, Sheila MacMillan '81
1990–1995

Blackburn, Robin
1993–2000, 2001–

Blake, Annice
1977–

Blanchard, Jean
1921–1924

Boiziau-Waverman, Helene
1985–1990, 1991–2001

Bon, Gladys
1941–1942

Bone, Jackie
1989–1990

Booth, Michelle
2000–2001

Bowker, Jean
1957–1958, 1962–1972–

Bowlby, Kathleen
1926–29, 1931–1937

Bowrey, Muriel
1954–57

Boyd, Mabel
1959–1962

Boydell, Olive
1958–1961

Boyes, Gwen
1947–1974

Boyle, G.
1915–1916

Bradshaw, Joan
1949–1950

Bragg, Mary
1958–1959

Bremner, Cathi
1999–

Brennan, Patricia
1966–1967

Brien, Mollie
1951–1954

Brien, Naomi
1955–1956

Brough, Dorothy
1967–2002

Brown, Audrey
1979–1986

Brown, Margaret
1962–1963

Brown, Ruth
1990–1999

Browning, Ann
1959–1960

Buchanan, Kristin
1999–

Buhr, Doreen
1965–1966

Bullen, Gracie
1943–1944

Bunting, Audrey
1976–1989

Burke, Nora
1914–1921

Burns, Elma M.
1910–1911, 1912–1913

Butler, Irma
1957–1959

Cairns, Andrew
1975–1976

Callbeck, Dorothy
1942–1946, 1949–1954

Cameron, Morag
1965–1966

Cameron, Winnifred
1956–1962

Campbell, Dorothy
1933–1936

Campbell, Marion
1959–1971

Campbell-Rogers, Allison
2000–

Carson, Leta
1957–1970

Chalmers, Elizabeth Provan
1981–2001

Charley, Sarah
2001–

Chaubert, Nellie Rose
1915–1919

Cheeseman, Linda
1981–1989

Chenowith, Lucille
1972–1975

Childerhose, Julie
1999–2001, 2002–

Chilton, Daphne
1976–1992

Chipman, Betty de Wite
1937–1942

Chitty, Jerry
1972–1973

Christie, Marjorie
1946–1950

Church, Laraine
1984–1996, 1997–2000

Cinits, Anita
1985–1989

Clare, Margo NOFFICE '65
1977–2001

Clark, Martha
1937–1940

Clark, Rae
1947–1955

Clark, Ruth
1947–1948

Claxton, Jean
1942–1979

Cochrane, Suzanne
1974–1976

Coe, Damm
1955–1956

Cole, Freda
1903–1910, 1911–1922

Cole, Margaret
1960–1962

Cole, Penny
1974–1978

Colleran, Jennifer WILKES '83
1995–2001

Collins, Valerie
1965–1970

Colvin, Beryl
1953–1954

Colwell, Joanne
1997–2001, 2002–

Compondu, Jeanne
1908–1910, 1911–1915, 1919–1920

Congdon, Joy
1956–1957

Cook, Christy
1962–1963

Cook, Marion
1968–1973

Cook, Mary
1936–1938

Coombs, Charlotte
1940–1944

Cooper, Irene
1945–1947

Coulter, Rita
1955–1972

Coutts, Eunice
1949–1973

Cowley, Winifred
1947–1948

Craig, Jean
1923–1929

Craig, Frances
1956–1957

Craig, Ruth
1928–1966

Crawford, Myles
1985–1990

Crawford, Sharon
1991–

Crocker, Myra
1934–1937

Cudmore, Julie
2001–

d'Alton, Emily
1958–1969

Dan, Susan
1973–1976

Danard, Charlotte
1991–

Danson, Margaret
1939–1940

Davey, Earl
1973–1978

Davidovac, Vesna
1970–1998

Davis, Carol
1966–1967

de Freitas, Elizabeth
1999–

de Pencier, Adam
1999–2001

Dean, Mariette
1976–1987

Debeer, Corinna
1975–1976
Dehenne, Lucie
1969–1974
Delaporte, Helen
1915–1916
Denison, Margaret
1958–1962
Dennis, Jenna
2001–
Dick, Louise
1970–1988
Dieudonne, Michelle
1963–1964
Dobson, Anne
1941–1942
Doherty, Ailene
1941–1947
Doherty, la Von
1942–1949
Douglas, Bob
2001–
Douglas-Oliver, Jane
1982–1990
Dowie, Margaret
1950–1973
Dryden, Mary
1967–1968
Duchemin, Irene
1961–1978
Duffus, Margaret
1951–1954
Dugas, Carol
2001–
Duguay, Kathleen
2001–
Duguid, Margaret
1954–1956
Dunlop, Marion
1954–1958
Dutton, Sheila WESTMAN '56
1959–1963
Eaton, Margaret
1962–1964
Edmison, Elizabeth
1960–1962
Edmison, Helen
1937–1967
Edmonson, Mary
1958–1959
el Baroudi, Gail
1984–1992
Ellins, Lucille
1970–1977, 1979–1981
Elliott, Alfreda
1926–1929
Ellison, Maureen
1975–1976
Elmslie, Christine
1933–1934
Evans, Rosemary
1999–
Fabian, Karen
1989–
Farkas, Susan
1989–1999
Farquhar, Margaret
1947–1949

Faulkner, Althea
1924–1941

Fiaver, Natalie
1947–1948

Fiels, Sophie
1906–1907

Fieltsch, Martha
1996–1997, 1998–

Findlay, Marian
1938–1940

Finnigan, Rose
1974–1976

Fish, Priscilla
1945–1947

Fisher, Jean Wahlroth '53
1956–1958

Fleet, Patricia
1950–1951

Fleming, Patricia Murdock
1955–1956

Fletcher, Ruth
1952–1953

Flett, Margaret
1964–1973

Fog, Wilma
1967–1974

Forbes, Florence
1928–1930

Forbes, Heather
1970–1971

Ford, Marjorie
1913–1917

Forsyth, Ella
1950–1952, 1956–1974

Forte, Nicole
1966–1969

Fotheringham, Susie
1905–1907

Foxcroft, Annette
1960–1962

Fraser, E.G.
1919–1922

Fraser, Janet
1938–1940

Fraser, Jennifer
2001–

Friend '75, Judith
1984–

Friesen, Heather
2001–

Fritz, Alma
1954–1955

Frohman, Amanda
1990–

Gaineys, Audrey
1951–1952

Gale, Barbara
1940–1941

Galloway, Nora
1965–1968

Gambin, Lily
2001–

Gamey, Avis
1967–1972

Gandhi, Anita
1990–1991

Gardiner, K.S.A.
1910–1919

Gardner, Nancy Foggo '55
1959–1960

Garneys, Audrey
1950–1951

Gee, Queenie
1958–1959

Georgievski, Liivi
1982–1991

Gerard, Micheline
1975–1976

Gerow, Larry
1994–

Gibson, Marny
1990–

Gilbert, Marion
1950–1952

Gilespie, Ghilen
1965–1966

Gillies, Anita
1990–1992

Glennie, Barbara
1980–

Glennie, Helen
1933–1937

Goode, Margaret
1949–1951

Goos, Lisa
1998–1999

Gordon, Patricia
1963–1964

Gormley, Margaret
1937–1938

Graff, Vicki
1973–1975

Graham, Laura
1943–1947

Granger, Mary
1956–1957

Grant, Marion
1922–1924

Grant, Frances H.
1917–1926

Gratias McCart, Cathy
1983–1991

Graves, Chula
1969–1970

Gray, Ann
1964–1966, 1976–1990, 1991–1998

Gray, Anna
1998–2000

Gray, Margaret
1957–1958

Gray, Trish
2001–

Greig, Jean
1942–1943

Grierson, Dorothy
1926–1928

Groat, Marianne
1997–1999

Guedon, Jill
1971–1973

Gunsaulus, Betty
1939–1944

Haag, Colleen
2000–

Ham, Patricia
1976–1980

Hamilton, Mary
1910–1919

Hamilton, Margaret
1958–1959

Hammond, Jeff
1978–1981

Harle, Sarah
1959–1962

Harley, Margaret
1951–1952

Harris, Audrey
1979–1980

Harris, Grace
1946–1953

Harrison, Margo
1975–1977

Haultain, Irene
1917–1919

Hay, Marie
1969–89

Haye, Henriette
1924–1929

Hayhurst, Cathy
1994–1995

Healey, Barbara
1972–1999

Hebdon, Katherine
1998–2001

Henderson, Anna
1979–1981

Henderson, Irene
1957–1963

Henderson, Margaret
1936–1937

Henderson, Sylvie
1991–1998, 1999–

Herzog, Helene
1919–1922

HEWITT '54, Molly
1961–1963

Hikida, Karen
1990–

Hillary, Nora
1906–1910

Hockin, Heather
1984–1998

Hodgins, Barbara
1976–1977

Hollenberg, Mimi
1976–2001

Hollington, Alison
1940–1941

Holstead, Jennie
1999–2000

Holychuk, Lenore
1998–1999

Horning, Ella
1946–1947

Hoskins, Josephine
1983–1985, 1986–1991

Howie, Lillian
1948–1975

Howitt, Felicia
1940–1943

Huggins, Zoe
2001–

Hugh, Edith
1926–1928

Hughes, Jane
1956–1960

Hughes, Mabel C.
1954–1964

Hulme, Barbara
1975–1980

Hunt, Madeleine
1953–1954

Hunter, Alison
1998–2001

Hutchinson, Martha
1993–1996

Hutchison, Winifred
1907–1909

Hutchison, Dorothy
1953–1956

Hutchison, Edith
1915–1916

Huyk, Nora
1954–1960

Iggulden, Rosemary
1973–1979

Ing, Kathleen
1940–1942

Irwin, Josephine
1974–1975

Izzard, Edna
1922–1925

Jacques, Hazel
1933–1934

Jajecznyk, Oksana
2001–

Jardine, Mildred
1959–1962

Johnson, Eva
1996–

Johnston, Mary
1908–1920

Johnston, Aline
1958–1959

Johnston, Gladys
1960–1962

Johnston, Jessie
1939–1969

Johnston, Kay
1953–1954

Jones, D. Margaret
1932–1939

Jones, Edith
1929–1930, 1932–1934

Jones, Helen
1941–1947

Jones, Mary
1928–1929

Jordan, Ronald
1978–1982

Joselin, V.
1947–1948

Joyce, Elizabeth
1977–1978

Jubien, V. Margaret
1933–1940

Kalyanam, Padmini
1999–

Kamcke, Leslie
1963–1965

Kane, Kathryn
1980–1985, 1986–1990

Kareda, Shelagh Hewitt '62
1972–1973

Karn, Marjorie
1952–1955

Kashul, Judith
1975–1978

Kelly-Murphy, Barbara
1998–1999

Kenny, Susan
1971–

Keyes, Heather
1971–1974

Kilpatrick, Elizabeth
1921–1935

King, Nora
1906–1907

Kinly, Carmelita
1939–1940

Kirloss, Joanne
1999–2000, 2002–

Kizoff, Josie
1974–

Knox, Katie
1995–

Kolpakow, Andrej
2000–2001

Korotash, Elizabeth
1968–1969

Labrakos, Sophie
1998–2001

Lachowicz, Barbara
1985–1986

Lackie, Sheila
1972–1973

Lamb, Dorothy
1959–1960

Lamont, Claire
1956–1957

Lane, Elizabeth
1963–1964

Lawe, Muriel
1971–1972

Lawrence, Miriam
1987–1994

Leake, Michelle
2001–

Ledoux, Madame
1917–1918

Lee, Carmen
1990–1997, 2002–

Lee, David
1997–1998

Leech, Elizabeth
1948–1949

Lee-Evans, Betty
1940–1941

Lemard, Margaret
1947–1948

Lenoir, Nora
1937–1943

Les Pierre, Jennifer
1999–

Lewis, Janice
1998–2001

Lincoln, Margaret
1995–1996, 1997–1998

Lipkin, Beth
1947–1948

Liston, Hilda
1956–1957

Livingstone, Judy
1953–1959

Lomax, Carolyn
1975–1976

Louie, Edith
1998–

Loumanis, Sophie
1998–2000

Lowry, Pamela
1952–1953

Lumsdon, Joan
1969–1998

Luton, Florence
1951–1962

Luus, Hilkka
1997–

Lynch, David
1995–1998

MacCrae, Anna
1903–1905

MacCurdy, Mabel
1905–1906

MacDonald , Mary
1903–1910, 1911–1918

MacDonald, Iris
1943–1945

MacDonald, Marion
1945–1946

MacDonald, Sara E.G.
1921–1928

MacFarlane, Constance
1937–1938

MacGregor, Jean
1919–1921

MacGregor, Jean
1934–1953

MacGregor, Susan
1970–

MacIver, Patricia
1957–1958

Mackay, Nora
1908–1910

Mackay, Norah
1928–1929

Mackay, Margaret
1948–1954

MacKenzie, Diana
1977–1981

MacKenzie, Hazel
1943–1947

MacKinnon, Miss
1903–1904

MacLaggan, Marjorie
1931–1942

MacLean, Estelle
1954–1956

MacLean, Georgina. L.
1925–1927

MacLean, Mrs. A.L.
1921–1923

MacLean, Nora
1924–1926

MacLean, Sara
1939–1942

MacLellan, Frances
1940–1943

MacLellan, Judy Riggin
1978–1998, 1999–

MacLennan, Nora
1922–1927

MacLeod '73, Carolyn
1995–1999

MacLeod, Katherine
1942–1943

MacMurchy, Helen
1906–1910

MacNeill, Jennie E.
1926–1968

MacNeill, Ruby
1942–1943

Macrae, Anna
1905–1906

Maitland, H. Joy
1957–1962

Malone, Rebecca
1991–1998

Manley, Anu
1973–1976

Manley, Joan
1960–1962

Markes, Maria
1961–1987

Marshall, Carolyn
1948–1951

Marshall, Jane
1989–

Marshall, Maude
1952–1957

Marshall, Michael
1975–1976

Marshall, Ruth
1972–1974

Marshall, Shirley
1959–1960

Marshall-Jewell, Norine
1999–

Martin, Jennifer
2001–2002

Mason, Dorothy
1961–1962

Mason, Marguerite
1973–1975

Matheson, Nora
1923–1924

Matthews, Karin
1966–1969

Mattis, Penny
1972–1973

Mawande, Margaret
1973–1975

Maxwell, Ann
1963–1964

Maxwell, Beatrice
1940–1942

May, Gladys
1920–1921

Mazunder, Mandira
1968–1971

McCakell, Evelyn
1954–1955

McCann, Grace
1956–1957

McCann, Heather
2001–

McColl, Ada
1945–1950

McConnell, Joyce
1943–1946

McCurdy, Mabel
1903–1905

McEvoy, Winifred
1936–1939

McFetredge, Audrey
1954–1955

McGonigle, Eileen
1922–1926

McGugan, Laurie
2001–2002

McIntyre, Robin
1986–1990

McKenna, Grant
1998–2001

McLarty, M.
1913–1914

McLauchlan, Judith
1974–1975

McLelan, Frances
1948–1962

McLeod, Janet
1975–1981

McMeekin, Julie
1997–1998

McMichael '13, Ainslie
1917–1925, 1926–1958

McMurdo, Elizabeth
1950–1951

McNiece, Dorothy
1945–1947

McQuillen, Nicole
2001–

McRae, Nora
1968–1972, 1973–1993

McVay, Ian
1985–

Medcalf, Robin
1990–2001

Medland, Sally Adams '66
1981–

Meech, Susan
1990–1998

Menc, Marie-Louise
1964–1981

Mendes de Franca, Debra
1987–1989

Mercer, Elizabeth
1966–1968

Merrick, Florence
1903–1908

Merrilees, Patricia
1980–2001

Merrimal, Elizabeth
1954–1955

Merry, Audrey
1957–1959

Meyer, Heather
1989–1990

Meyer, Linda
1993–2002

Middleton, Beth
2001–2002

Miller, Janet
1907–1909

Miller, Bev
1993–1994

Miller, Dorothy J.
1951–1952

Miller, Janet M.
1951–1954

Miller, Judy
1950–1951

Millette, Nathalie
2001–

Millichamp, Mary
1909–1918

Millman, Margaret
1958–1959

Mills, Judith
1979–1981

Milne-Ives, Holly
1990–1991

Minnes, Eleanor
1918–1921

Mistry, Freny
1999–

Mitchell, L.
1919–1920

Moir, Muriel
1955–1956

Moon, Pierann
1977–1978

Moore, Jane
1988–

Morden '66, Gillian
1974–1978

Morgan, Gwendoline
1948–1953

Morley, Gertrude
1916–1919

Morris, Maureen
1943–1944

Morse, Ruth Ann
1951957

Mortensen, Barbara
1965–1976

Morton, Audrey
1968–1972

Mouftah, Nadine
2001–

Murdoch, Patricia
1954–1955

Murgatroyd, Barbara
1964–1965

Murphy, Barbara
1999–

Murray, Louise
1909–1910

Murton, Karen
1998–

Mustos, Debra
1989–

Naftolin, Betty
1970–1990

Nauboris, Cindy
1995–2001

Needham, Elizabeth
1998–1999

Neff, Ann
1964–1966

Newman, Florence
1981–1982

Newton, Elizabeth
1950–1951

Nguyen-Moreira, Lily
1997–2001

Nicholus, Richard
1975–1979

Nicoll, Mary
1946–1949

Nimmo, Elizabeth
1953–1954

Northgrave, Nancy
1974–1981, 1982–1997

Norton, Ruth
1945–1948

Nyman, Judy
1997–

Olfert, Nancy
1988–

Olson, Elise
1960–1965, 1968–1985

O'Neill, Joyce
1942–1943

Opdebeeck, Andrea
1996–1997

O'Regan, Anne
1985–1989

Orloff, Roberta
1976–1977

O'Rourke, Jennifer
1997–

Owen, Audrey
1956–1957

Palmer, Catherine
1963–1966

Palmer, Joan
1962–1963, 1964–1965

Pape, Lesia
1974–1975

Parke, Ann
1959–1960

Parker, Diana Jennings
1977–

Parkinson, Ted
2001–

Parr, Ruby
1947–1948

Partridge, Betty HIRE '20
1939–1944, 1947–1970

Patten, Mary Jane
1970–1971

Patterson, Gladys
1917–1921

Pennington, Anne
1971–1975

Penny, Ruth Ann
1990–1999, 2001–

Perrott, Linda
1975–1989, 1990–1998, 1999–

Perry, Grace
1927–1928

Perry-Gore, Susan
1966–1970

Peters, Janet
1976–1981

Petersons, Elizabeth
1969–1975

Phalen, Dorothy
1921–1922

Phaneuf, Rosemary
1975–1976
Phelan, Judith
1985–1999
Phelps, Mrs.E.K.
1945–1947
Phillips, Dorothy
1929–1969
Phimister, Elisabeth
1951–1954
Pigeon, Kathryn
2000–
Pitt, Bertha
1957–1958
Plastina, Connie
1986–1992
Playfair, Mary Stuart
1942–1943
Pollard, Phyllis
1995–
Ponte, Anna
1976–1979
Porte, Anna
1975–1976
Potter, Mary Jane
1971–1972
Powell, Gwynneth
1960–1974
Powles, Jennifer Lynch
1993–2001
Pratt, Heather
1989–
Pratt, Nanci
1976–1978
Price, Virginia
1939–1940
Proctor, Katherine
1970–1971, 1975–
Proudfoot, Marion
1961–1965
Purdy, Faye
1951–1954
Quesada, Sylvia
1971–1973
Quigley, Judith
1971–1974, 1976–1978
Quinn, Bonnie
1974–1975
Rabbior, Gary
1981–1998
Ramcharan, Adele
1999–
Ramsay, Mary
1909–1910
Ramsay, Pat
1943–1944
Ramsay, Jill
1975–1976
Ramsey, Grace
1943–1948
Read, Edith M.
1906–1958
Reader Harris, Diana
1940–1943
Redstone, Bruce
1990–1994
Reid, Helen Wilson
1922–1926

Reid, Ellen
1988–1995
Reid, Gayle
1988–
Relle, Erna
1995–
Reynar, F. Christine
1914–1930
Reynolds, Ruth
1964–1969
Reynolds, Sharon
1988–
Richardson, Marie
1971–1972
Ricketts, Monica
1961–1963
Riddell, Miss
1904–1905
Riddell, Sophie
1913–1914
ROACH '51, Allison
1974–1993
Robb, Grace
1922–1924
Roberts, Janet
1956–1957
Robertson, Marjorie
1992–1999
Robinson, Violet
1906–1945
Robinson, Glenda
1960–1962
Rochereau, Alice
1918–1921

Roe, Medora
1974–1976, 1977–1990
Rolfe, Agnes
1913–1914
Romanyshyn, Martha
1994–1996
Ronaldson, Irene
1929–1930
Roseborough, Margaret
1935–1937
Ross, Barbara
1956–1957
Ross, Dorothy
1951–1952
Ross, Jean
1945–1946
Rossetel, Mlle.
1921–1922
Rowland, Nancy
1966–1967
Roy, Claudia
1998–2000
Roy, Jacinthe
1992–
Rubino, Olga
2001–2002
Rubio, Margaret
1971–1974
Rugg, Evelyn
1942–1947
Rutherford, Ann
1967–1968
Ryshauwer, Jane
1974–1978

Saif, Samia
1968–1972

Sanderson, Jean Ross
1940–1941

Sandoz Perry, Hélène
1930–1962

Saults, Gladys
1960–1962

Sava, Verena
1971–1973

Scace, Susan
1963–1964

Schafer, Phyllis
1962–1963

Schaffter, Catherine
1950–1951

Schroeder, Margaret
1991–1998, 2000–2001

Scott, Elizabeth
1926–1928

Scott, Louise
1920–1921

Scott, Anne
1981–1983

Scott, Margaret
1903–1910

Scott, Nora
1954–1962

Scott, Sheila
1955–1957

Seixas, Dorothy
1942–

Shand, Beatrice
1913–1919, 1921–1922

Shand, Miss
1953–1954

Sharpe, Helen
1981–1983

Shaver, Jackie
1977–2001

Shaw, David
1997–1998

Shaw, Kathleen
1927–1929, 1930–1932, 1933–1951

SHAW '89, Meredith
1996–1997

Shen, Joelle
1997–1998

Shirton, Mary
1945–1950

Sime, Margaret
1932–1974

Simmons, Doreen
1970–1972

Simpson, Mary
1977–1989

Sinclair, Alice M.
1943–1945

Sinclair, Muriel
1937–1940

Smellie, M. Donald
1927–1940

Smith Sinden, Anne
1941–1947, 1948–1950

Smith, Brenda
1979–1989

Smith, Catherine
1957–1959

Smith, Helen
1979–1980

Smith, Mary
1948–1949

Smith, Nanci
1978–

Smith, Shirley
1990–1991

Smith, Sonia
1962–1963

Smithers, Christine
1969–1970

Somers, Mrs. H.B.
1904–1909

Somerville, Olga
1920–1923

Sommerville, Janet
1994–1998

Spiers, Pamela
1955–1956

Spracklin, Elizabeth
1948–1949

Stanley, Meryl
1973–1976

Stapleton, Susan
1973–1975

Starr, Jessie
1915–1917

Steele, C. Beatrice
1924–1941

Steer, Marie
1972–1975

Stegenga, Kathy
2000–

Steinhauer, Nancy
1993–1997

Stevens, Elizabeth
1947–1950

STEVENS (Sandbox), Tom
1991–2000

Stewart, Grace
1953–1955

Stewart, Kathryn
1999–2000

Stiles, Iva
1948–1949

Stirling, Jean
1946–1948

Stirrett, Mrs. J.R.
1951–1953

Stock, Jo Anne
1974–1975

Stoddart, Helen
1981–1982

Strangway, Alice
1977–1985

Strathy, J.
1913–1914

Stretton, Frances
1978–1989

Stulberg, Cheryl
1991–

Stumborg, Jennifer
1999–

Sumner, Norma
1964–1965

Supino, Stephanie
1997–

Swain, Gay
1942–1943

Tasker, Mary CRAIG '47
1977–1993

Taylor, Brenda
1973–1975, 1976–1979

Taylor, Irene
1950–1951

Taylor, Jean
1954–1955

Thickett, Jane
1952–1953

Thom, Alison
1994–2000

Thompson, Julia
1998–

Thomson, Elizabeth
1976–1997

Thomson, Julia
1990–1992

Timm, Eric
1997–1998

Todd, Robin
1998–1999

Tolmie, Lorna
1950–1951

Tropea, Mary-Jane
1977–1981

Tuer, Margaret
1976–1997

Tyrell, Margaret
1975–1976

Tyrrell, Maisie
1913–1942

Unterhalter, Karen
1979–1980

Upjohn, Ruth HAMILTON '29
1940–1981

Vallet, Madame
1922–1924

Van der Meer, Mariette
1988–1989

Van Fleet, Irene
1958–1963, 1964–1978

Van Remortel, Jenny
1998–1999

Van STRAUBENZEE, Pamela '83
1988–1991

Vance, Stephanie
1993–1995

Vesel, Judith
1976–1978

Vikis, Vaira
1958–1960

Wade, Thora
1952–1953

Wagstaff, Irene
1962–1963

Walcott, Jennifer
1994–1998, 1999–

Walker, Barbara
1940–1944

Walls, Valerie
1969–1971

Walters, Margaret
1956–1957

Walton, Dell
2001–

Warner, Janet
1963–1965

Waters, Marjorie
1944–1962

Watson, Diana
1981–

Watson, Muriel
1955–1956

Waugh, Catherine
1975–1980, 1981–1989

Wayne, Katherine McEachern '59
1981–1989

Weatherby, Shirley
1948–1951

Webster, Judith Jephcott '52
1959–1960

Weiler, Margaret
1972–1973

Weinstock, Karrie
1980–

Westcott, Rose J.
1956–1974

Wetmore, Maretta
1942–1948

Wheeler, Donna
1947–1948

White, Portia
1954–1960

Wilby, Beverley
1971–1973

Williams, Olwen
1929–1931, 1945–1948

Willingham, Dawn
1978–1988

Wilson, Jean
1922–1927

Wilson, Isobel
1930–1933

Windsor, Marjory
1955–1956

Wister, Margaret
1935–1936

Wood, Leslie
2001–

Wood, Mary
2001–

Woolley, Jill
1988–1995

Worsley, Suzanne
1982–1993

Wren Rosch, Wendy
1984–1992

Wright, Laura
1954–1955

Wulff, Derek
2001–2002

Wynne-Jones, Harriet
1999–

Young, Helen
1952–1953

Young, Pamela
1989–

Young, Ruth
1938–1939

Younger '82, Martha
1995–1999, 2001–

Zambrano, Vincent
1980–1983

Zimmerman, Lesley
1970–1973
Zommers, Aija
1973–
Zwolinski, Adimaldi
1969–1970

Head Girls

1914	Louise MacLennan
1915	Leslie Sykes
1916	Helen Coatsworth
1917	Jean Inwood
1918	Jean Jarvis
1919	Bernice Jephcott
1920	Bernice Dennis
1921	Kathleen Cowan
1922	Janet Gibson
1923	Meredith White
1924	Margaret Estabrooks
1925	Helen Spence
1926	Marjorie Watson
1927	Christine Auld
1928	Isobel Pirie (Co-Head Girl)
	Margaret Withers (Co-Head Girl)
1929	Margaret Withers
1930	Helen Richardson
1931	Mary McLean
1932	Clare Brown
1933	Gwynneth Sinclair
1934	Trudean Spencer
1935	Philippa Chapman
1936	Betty Williamson
1937	Nancy Stirrett
1938	Barbara Parker
1939	Joan Mitchell
1940	Dorothy Hoyle
1941	Janet Brown
1942	Isobel Coulthard
1943	Patricia Stockton
1944	Jean Plaunt
1945	Joan Peat
1946	Frances Chase
1947	Anne James
1948	Joan Langlois
1949	Alicia Eager
1950	Patricia Marriner
1951	Ann Gilday
1952	Mary Barnett
1953	Jean Wahlroth
1954	Molly Hewitt
1955	Jane Morgan
1956	Linda Stearns

1957 Jane Watson
1958 Jacqueline Burroughs
1959 Lynn Williams
1960 Judith Ireland
1961 Barbara Langley
1962 Nancy Adams
1963 Catherine Flavelle
1964 Frances Shepherd
1965 Cheryl Hamilton
1966 Sally Adams
1967 Susan Collyer
1968 Patricia Cross
1969 Barbara Pattison
1970 Catherine Gartha
1971 Sandi Spaulding
1972 Antoinette Falconer
1973 Wendy Philpott
1974 Janet Brown
1975 Margaret Morden
1976 Virginia Gibson
1977 Eileen Smith
1978 Bridget Wiley
1979 Carolyn Campbell
1980 Tricia Purks
1981 Bryn MacPherson
1982 Alison Wiley
1983 Sarah Teskey
1984 Laura Loewen
1985 Patricia Zingg
1986 Sarah Wright
1987 Hayley Avruskin
1988 Stephanie Garrow
1989 Helen Dempster
1990 Brenda Welsh
1991 Amy Fisher
1992 Judy Tjan
1993 Danielle Paterson
1994 Tessa Akande
1995 Robyn Thompson
1996 Megan Hewings
1997 Joanne Sitarski
1998 Missy Mahoney
1999 Sarah Psutka
2000 Meredith Shaw
2001 Ashley Caldwell
2002 Meg Caven
2003 Lindsay Fleming

Prefects

1908	Edith Anderson
	Mary Elliot
	Hetty McGaw
	Marjorie Weller
1909	Agnes Campbell
	Grace Morris
	Gretchen Spohn
	Florence Taylor
1910	Gertrude Booth
	Marjorie Busteed
	Agnes Campbell
	Audrey Little
	Florence Taylor
1911	Marcia Allen
	Jean Fleck
	Reda Fullerton
	Florence McLurg
	Bessie Storey
1912	Constance Crawford
	Betty McWhinney
1913	Dorothy Chown
	Grace McGaw
1914	Dorothy Adams
	Irma Brock
	Marjorie Hazlewood
	Grace Ponton
1915	Irma Brock
	Anna Greig
	Evelyn Hearst
	Helen Jarvis
	Grace Ponton
	Gertrude Wirger
1916	Gladys Billings
	Delphine Burr
	Mayden Stratford
1917	Mary Baird
	Gladys Billings
	Marion Hanna
	Charlotte Leitch
	Erie Sheppard
	Mayden Stratford
1918	Marion Baillie
	Elinor Bluck
	Marion Hanna

Bernice Jephcott
Eleanor McKay
Virginia Outerbridge
Nora Parkes
Erie Sheppard
1919 Marion Baillie
Phyllis Hollinrake
1920 Edith Burchell
Phyllis Hollinrake
Isabel Read
Muriel Zybach
1921 Marjorie Bone
Janet Gibson
Marjorie Walker
Helen Wright
1922 Catherine Dewar
Dorothy Dods
Elizabeth Scott
Eleanor Sykes
Meredith White
Helen Wright
1923 Katherine Anderson
Mary Barker
Margaret Estabrooks
Dorothy Harding
Blanche Simpson
Norma Whelan
Helen Wright
1924 Eleanor Ross
Blanche Simpson
Agnes Thom
1925 Margaret Aitken
Norah Deacon
Marjorie Jones
Mary Duff
Peggy Turnball
Jessie Wright
Kathleen Wilson
1926 Margaret Aitken
Christine Auld
Norah Deacon
Margaret Donald
Helen Hoame
Peggy Turnball
1927 Sylvia Cayley
Jessie Kelly
Sheila Lee
Catherine McBurney
Betty Rutherford
Kathryn Tait
1928 Kate Clark
Peggy Galt
Marion Gibson
Betty Rutherford
Helen Simpson
Frances Smith
June Warren
Nancy Wilson
1929 Elisabeth Burruss
Margaret Eaton

Helen Glennie
Ruth Hamilton
Margaret Henderson
Helen Pidgeon
Helen Richardson
Elisabeth Saunderson
Phyllis Shepard
Nancy Wilson
1930 Isabel Adams
Katherine Boyd
Catherine Brett
Nora Eaton
Gretchen Gray
Ruth Knowlton
Donalda MacLeod
Mary McFarland
Mary McLean
Ruth Rutherford
1931 Charlotte Abbott
Ruth Carlyle
Miriam Coryell
Joan Knowlton
Katherine Lea
Donalda MacLeod
Amy McLean
Molly Sclater
1932 Charlotte Abbott
Elizabeth Brydon
Winifred Gibson
Eleanor Hamilton
Shirley McEvoy
Irla Mueller
Lillice Read
Louise Spencer
Ruth Stock
Joyce Sweatman
Florence Wilson
1933 Mary Becker
Nora Conklin
Helen Conway
Anna Mackay
Margaret McKay
Trudean Spencer
Dorothy Stock
Joan Romeyn
1934 Jean Boyd
Philippa Chapman
Charlotte Deacon
Janet Garfield
Jean Gordon
Mary Gooderham
Marion Pirie
Helen Rooke
Betty Smith
1935 Margaret Beck
Margaret Boughton
Charlotte Deacon
Janet Garfield
Mary Gooderham
Pauline Lea

Esme Pattison
Virginia Piers
Marion Pirie
Jean Ross
Elizabeth Ann Tanner
Helen Turner
Betty Williamson

1936 Louise Jamieson
Audrey Piddington
Katharine Robarts
Elizabeth Trees

1937 Catherine Bryans
Katharine Cannon
Janet Davidson
Margaret Davison
Betty Harrison
Jean Lander
Betty Marshall
Jeanette McVicar
Eunice Plant
Kathleen Stambaugh
Helen Sutherland

1938 Elizabeth Callow
Joyce Caudwell
Martha Coryell
Helen Franks
Joan Franks
Patricia Gibbons
Joan Marlow
Rosemary Sheppard
Kathryn Shirriff
Jean Stirling
Nancy Tyrrell
Barbara Waite

1939 Gladys Baalim
Joyce Caudwell
Helen Franks
Mary Glendinning
Dorothy Hoyle
Joy MacKinnon
Eleanor Reed
Kathryn Shirriff

1940 Janet Brown
Winifred Clarke
Elizabeth Dickie
Shurly Dickson
Joy Ferguson
Kathryn Gooderham
Patricia Gundy
Louise McLaughlin
Helen Shearme

1941 Mary Burroughes
Winifred Clarke
Isobel Coulthard
Christine Pearse
Peggy Phair
Peggy Purvis
Dorothy Turner
Katherine Waterman
Joan Vanstone

1942 Audrey Angus
Zillah Caudwell
Sally Chapman
Alice Cochrane
Susan Davis
Patricia Grant
Jocelyn Hodge
Marion Hughes
Helen Lang
Mary MacMillan
Sheila MacQueen
Andrea McCall
Peggy McKelvey
Elizabeth McKecknie
Shirle Milner
Mary Playfair
Gaynor Powell
Angela Riddell
Helen Russell
Betty Sherman
Elizabeth Shirriff
Patricia Stockton

1943 Joan Adams
Margaret Capener
Joanne Edmonds
Flavia Elliott
Kathleen Hinch
Doreen Martin
Orde Skeeles
Betty Smith
Nancy Trees
June Whitehead

1944 Joan Bradfield
Diana Griffith
Lois Landreth
Althea McCoy
Barbara Pattison
Hazel Parry
Joan Peat
Patricia Stewart

1945 Ruth Alison
Sally Brown
Mary Alice Burton
Peggy Cowie
Kathleen Deacon
Joyce Frankel
Mary Jean Hall
Jane Hill
Marilyn Hogarth
Nancy Jack
Chloe Knaggs
Patricia McConnell
Gwen Millar
Mary Ritchie
Dorothy Robinette
Mary Shenstone
Ann Spence
Margaret Smythe
Virginia Tory

1946 Gina Baker

Shirley Baker
Mary Barnes
Joan Crosbie
Erica Cruikshank
Kathleen Deacon
Marion Dugdale
Barbara Hargraft
Judy Millar
Maureen O'Reilly
Eileen Stinson

1947 Anne Burton
Mary Craig
Antoinette Echlin
Elizabeth German
Jean Reid
Catherine Shields
Sally Spence
Josephine Williams
Diana Windeyer

1948 Ann Armour
Doris Badgley
Valinda Burruss
Sally Dalton
Winefride Drover
Alicia Eager
Alma Hatch
Joan Heise
Xandra Hosking
Evelyn Howden
Jessie Marriner
Sally McConnell
Judith Shoebottom
Joan Vipond
Jerry Weir

1949 Anne Blackwell
Nancy Blundell
Alice Buchan
Margaret Bulmer
Margann Chisholm
Jean Gillanders
Diane Johnson
Virginia Leishman
Ann Lowndes
Jane Macaulay
Ailsa Reid
Helen Scace
Alison Zimmerman

1950 Mary Binnie
Mary Caven
Mary Ruth Crossin
Joyce Dibblee
Lois Dunn
Muriel Ferguson
Patricia Howarth
Dorothy Orr
Frances Snetsinger

1951 Ellen Avigdor
Johanna Broughall
Charlotte Campbell
Jocelyn Campbell

Evelyn Cassells
Lynn Dibblee
Anna Lea Elderkin
Mary Lou Farmer
Geraldine Jephcott
Joan Mawhinney
Elizabeth McBurney
Claire McMullen
Carol Jean Merritt
Mary Morgan
Ruth Pidgeon
Allison Roach
Frances Stone
Marian Wallace
Gilda Walwyn
Margaret Wansbrough
Mary Wilkinson

1952 Joan Archer
Beverley Balmer
Rita Barr
Mary Lou Carnahan
Sandra Drennan
Peggy Fitzmaurice
Vyvyan Frost
Judith Jephcott
Jane Kerr
Wendy Large
Nancy Lockhart
Nancy Lyle
Susan Lyon
Shirley Mair
Constance Stiles
Ellen Thomson
Gwynneth Thomas
Wendy Wilson

1953 Jennifer Findlay
Janet Howard
Joy Logie
Jane Lucas
Susan Marshall
Marilyn McClaskey
Lee McGillivray
Wendy Rogers
Wendy Simpson
Elizabeth Thomson
Daphne Turpel
Barbara Williams

1954 Barbara Brown
Judith Chisholm
Joan Engholm
Ann Farmer
Eve King
Lavina Lickley
Judy Lovering
Adele MacBeath
Janet MacDonald
Sandra Maxwell
Susan Mitchell
Linda Mumford
Phyllis O'Dowd

Jacquelyn Oldham
Carol Simons
Helen Windsor
1955 Jane Arnott
Mary Bolton
Jane Briggs
Joan Burgess
Janet Chisholm
Louise Coffey
Gail Durance
Nancy Foggo
Ann Lloyd
Janice McBride
Katherine McLean
Kathleen Rowat
Patrica Shannon
Janet Ward
Helen Windsor
1956 Mary Jane Bickle
Katherine Broughall
Margaret Bull
Geraldine Damon
Mary Daniell-Jenkins
Diane Dunn
Jane Garden
Nancy Hanning
Janis Lovering
Susan Strathy
Joyce Walker
Sheila Westman
Lois Wilson
1957 Catherine Aylesworth
Edith Bell
Mary Breckenridge
Jane Burt
Catherine Clark
Margot Dunn
Judith Durance
Nancy Fletcher
Patricia Gordon
Elizabeth Graham
Sandra Holm
Lisa Inksater
Catherine Johnston
Kathleen Kerr
Pamela Kerr
Patricia McConnell
Jeanne Monier
Anne Moore
Sandra Sinclair
Pamela Thompson
1958 Adrienne Allan
Elizabeth Aylesworth
Margaret Benson
Gail Burton
Donna Graham
Lee Henderson
Joan Henson
Mary Ireland
Betty Lou Joynt

Jane McMurray
Susan Moore
Lowell Pelton
Joanne Valiant
Arlene Walker

1959 Gail Adams
Jocelyn Ayers
Susan Coxeter
Nadine Griffiths
Patricia Jacobs
Mary Jull
Isolde Koenig
Barbara Kreutzer
Kady MacDonald
Katherine McEachern
Catherine McMullen
Carol Ann Parker
Jane Robertson
Elizabeth Russell
Sandra Shannon
Nora Stearns
Launi Wilson
Anne Wright

1960 Sandra Bell
Susan Brown
Barbara French
Judith Gist
Diane Grove
Mona MacIntyre
Quita Mainguy
Susan Monier
Patricia Strathy
Diana Style
Wendy Thompson
Carole Tovell
Heather Waldie
Elizabeth Watts

1961 Janet Ament
Elizabeth Barnes
Barbara Clark
Joan Dixon
Marilyn McDowell
Isabel Miller
Marilyn Michener
Nancy Williams
Mary Ann Wright

1962 Gail Corbett
Jane Diffin
Nanci Gelber
Penelope Kyle
Mary Langley
Holly Waldie
Diana Walsh

1963 Sarah Barnes
Jean Cameron
Ruth Dunlop
Charlotte Empringham
Lyn Hamilton
Mary Patricia Jones
Jennifer Milsom

Carol Sissons

1964 Jane Ambler

Joanne Bryers

Carol Cowan

Penelope Kitchen

Laurie Lambe

Linda McLeod

Susan McMullen

Mary Patterson

Elsbeth Tupker

Carol Warrington

Melody Wurster

1965 Catherine Ament

Merrill Ann Fearon

Margo Carruthers

Roslyn Dinnick

Nancy Harris

Judith Miller

Elizabeth Morrison

Carolyn Stone

Ellen Stuart

Kristina Szandtner

Janet Thompson

Shelley Varley

Susan Wilson

1966 Beverley Baylay

Anne Gregor

Anne Housser

Marilyn McLellan

Gail McKinnon

Victoria Pearse

Jane Rapp

Daphne Ross

Mary Ruse

Margaret Anne West

Jean Willet

1967 Beverley Bowen

Meredith Clark

Sara Hill

Anne Langley

Elspeth Macintosh

Martha McDonic

Shelagh McIntyre

Ann McKinnon

Sandra Shaw

Susan Sinclair

Alexandra Skelton

Gail Tanner

1968 Virginia Dubery

Susan Duncanson

Nancy Falconer

Deborah Gibson

Laura Grey

Janet Harris

Elizabeth Keith

Eleanor Lougheed

Patricia Parker

Pamela Reid

Elizabeth Ruse

Sally Wodehouse

1969 Linden Armour
Barbara Ball
Cynthia Bundy
Elizabeth Dechert
Judith Fearon
Elizabeth Flavelle
Marilyn Jarvis
Margaret Ann Marchant
Rosemary Robertson
Barbara Scandrett
Caroline von Otter

1970 Carolyn Brown
Elizabeth Buckley
Terry Chambers
Cynthia Farquharson
Joanne George
Hallie Gibson
Alison Greenaway
Felicity Hawley
Karen Keir
Linda McQuaig
Jane O'Callaghan
Valerie Ralling
Sheila Scott
Judith Shykoff
Clayton Stuart
Barbara Tait

1971 Kathleen Armour
Susan Harvey
Martha Hill
Barbara Kofman
Annie Kwan
Anne Levinston
Sheila McIntyre
Sylvia Morawetz
Catherine Paterson
Sheila Rankin
Grace Rasmussen
Linda Roberts
Patricia Smythe
Catherine Stewart
Elizabeth Tilt
Margery Tow
Brenda Wille

1972 Katharine Ashforth
Wendy Baxter
Mary Duncan
Sheelagh Hendrick
Lynn Hyde
Elizabeth Kofman
Carol McLean
Elizabeth Mitchell
Ellen Moffat
Patricia Thom

1973 Janet Allen
Sandra Bolté
Lucia Chown
Penny Cutler
Anne Fairlie
Kim Heintzman

Ann Hutcheson
Sandra Penney
Anne Robson
Jennifer Svenningson
Cecily Ugray

1974 Joanne Abraham
Carolyn Clark
Deborah Eaton
Lindsay Empringham
Barbara Greenwood
Alison Macintosh
Janet Meredith
Marilee Tisdall

1975 Barb Beattie
Debra Cnoop-Koopmans
Shelley Gunton
Ninette Kelley
Jocelyn Lougheed
Marian MacBrien
Janet Morris
Ann Smith
Patti Thomson

1976 Patricia Abraham
Shirley Brown
Deborah Cooper
Catherine Hector
Gillian Hockin
Julie MacBrien
Beth Ann Mairs
Barbara Moffat
Susan Stinson

1977 Leslie Beattie
Cynthia Bongard
Kimberlee Campbell
Margot Haldenby
Diana Harris
Robin Heintzman
Marie Lange
Marianne Montgomery
Elizabeth Pitfield
Carol Stinson
Jane Wiley

1978 Marilyn Barefoot
Elizabeth Campbell
Debra Colman
Philippa Harris
Gillian MacCulloch
Jacqueline McClure
Sandra Smythe
Laurie Stein

1979 Wendy Aird
Virginia Campbell
Patricia Christie
Ann Duncan
Janet Hall
Carolyn Helbronner
Rebecca McCormack
Margaret Moffat
Theresa Norris
Mirabel Palmer

Marianne Reynolds

1980 Jacqueline Atkin

Sheila Buchanan

Kathryn Campbell

Anne Clements

Suzanne Dingwall

Jacqueline Fitzgibbon

Andrea Hector

Catherine Le Feuvre

Kathleen Martin

Victoria Pinnington

Joanne Stinson

1981 Tracy Dalglish

Bindu Dennis

Susan Farrow

Beverley Hicks-Lyne

Hope Humphrey

Susan Le Feuvre

Kathleen Lundon

Jane Moës

Jill Palmer

Suzanne Toro

Kate Wiley

1982 Julie Allan

Heather Allen

Gwen Baillie

Martha Dingle

Heather Harwood-Nash

Kelly Hawke

Simonetta Lanzi

Mary Morden

Jennifer Pitman

Julee Robertson

Kathy Stinson

Ingrid Taylor

Karen Taylor

1983 Wendy Buchanan

Elizabeth Burrows

Meredith Cartwright

Jill Curtis

Margaret Hermant

Kellie Leman

Janice Loudon

Lisa Papas

Martha Wilson

Janice Wright

1984 Katherine Barclay

Mary Boynton

Isobel Calvin

Jane Connor

Martha McCarthy

Laura McElwain

Martha Paisley

Lauren Papas

Kimberley Robarts

Sarah Wiley

1985 Melinda Bradshaw

Carrie Cameron

Elizabeth Endean

Tori Hackett

Allison Huycke
Caroline Kitchen
Laura Nichols
Josephine Parker
Hilary Shaw

1986 Heather Adam
Louise Dempster
Adrienne Grant
Carol Hood
Gabrielle Hull
Tonya Katz
Jennifer Kitchen
Catherine Mills
Nancy Ross
Pamela Snively
Mary Wright

1987 Elizabeth Allingham
Janet Anthony
Martha Henderson
Daphne King
Jane Lockhart
Emily Long
Rebecca Moore
Stacey Northgrave
Alison Papas
Shelagh Sturtridge
Elizabeth Wood

1988 Heather Cartwright
Chantal Coury
Heather Gellatly
Stephanie Gilbert
Kate Hartnett
Mary Hermant
Martha Hobbs
Rosemary Lawson
Katie Macaulay
Anthea Mars
Stephanie Wait
Hilary Wells

1989 Victoria Barton
Carolyn Dennis
Jane Edwards
Andrea Gare
Bay Ryley
Meredith Shaw
Patricia Smith
Pauline Wait
Kathleen Weldon

1990 Vanessa Avruskin
Binnie Baria
Jackie Garrow
Alexandra Hartnett
Jillian Kirchmann
Alexandra Lambert
Sally MacDonnell
Megan Palmer
Lisa Raeburn
Stacie Smith
Gretchen Stock
Melissa Thomson

TJ Turner
1991 Susanna Bleasby
Margaret Campbell
Cynthia Edwards
Tracey Ferris
Jennifer Franks
Katherine Hilton
Andrea Jamieson
Lindsay Oughtred
Andrea Rogers
Claire Sturgess
Kerry Walsh
1992 Gillian Avruskin
Swith Bell
Sarah Clappison
Sarah Hunter
Arlene Ingram
Emma MacDonald
Alexandra Sanderson
Jessica Smith
Natalie Welsh
Amy Williams
Karen Young
1993 Lynne Bradley
Hilary Burt
Giselle Clarke
Lynda Collins
Carolyn Dempster
Samantha Dickie
Bridget Ferriss
Meredith Fowlie
Nicole Kemp
Kate Manson-Smith
Lisa Mountifield
Anne Todgham
Sasha Velikov
Dominique Vitalis
1994 Erin Dempsey
Katie Earle
Leigh Elliot
Lindsey Ginou
Samantha Lanaway
Denise Liscio
Elizabeth Nicholson
Renata Pooran
Rosamond Price
Amy Satterthwaite
Stephanie Welsh
1995 Julie Brenninkmeyer
Susie Clappison
Devon Domelle
Leigh Griffiths
Erin Grimes
O.J. Kerr
Jimena Lance
Susan MacDougall
Alexandra Ortved
Megan Ross
Samantha Weiss
1996 Delayne Austin

Erin Beresford
Jennifer Dempster
Christie Gorrie
Amy Ingram
Elisa Kearney
Robin Mullan
Angela Portner
Christine Wilson
Sarah Wilson
Taylor Wood

1997 Kelly Gauthier
Sarah Goring
Betsy Hilton
Veronica Liu
Victoria Mendoza
Katie Nicholson
Karen Poon
Kristin Rossiter
Pamela Royce
Adrienne Willis
Aisling Yeoman

1998 Natalie Abdou
Blayr Austin
Jacqueline Chau
Ruth Hamlin-Douglas
Louise Kennedy
Megan MacMillan
Christine Palmay
Louise Price
Fiona Tingley
Olivia Tischler
Nancy Wilson

1999 Heather Adamson
Alexandra Campbell
Ruth Dorfman
Ashley Gorrie
Elizabeth Kirk
Vienna Lee
Julie Mountifield
Michelle Omura
Natalia Payne
Emily So
Cecily Wills

2000 Jenny Black
Meredith Giffin
Katie Hammond
Sarah Hopgood
Tina Hsueh
Sarah Kennedy
Anne Ngo
Vanessa Nobrega
Emer Schlosser
Megan Snell
Jes Watson

2001 Stacey Blidner
Kary Cheong
Grace Deacon
Stacey Filipczuk
Caitlin Gossage
Katie Malcolm

Carol Rosenfeld
Alysha Shore
Megan Stephenson
Heather Watt
Marina Winterbottom

2002 Jess Green
Elsa Hoogenhout
Jennifer Johnston
Janet Kwok
Lisa McGregor
Neha Patel
Vanessa Perry
Jennifer Rohr
Rosie Spooner
Sarah Sternberg
Sarah Wilkinson

2003 Andrea Amell
Candice Bienstock
Sydney Blum
Nicole Coles
Kim English
Karen Green
Emma Hunter
Jocelyn Molyneux
Yumana Lau
Ashley Peoples
Leslie Richardson
Kristen Rohr
Ewurama Sackey
Melody Schaal
Alanna Tedesco

Index

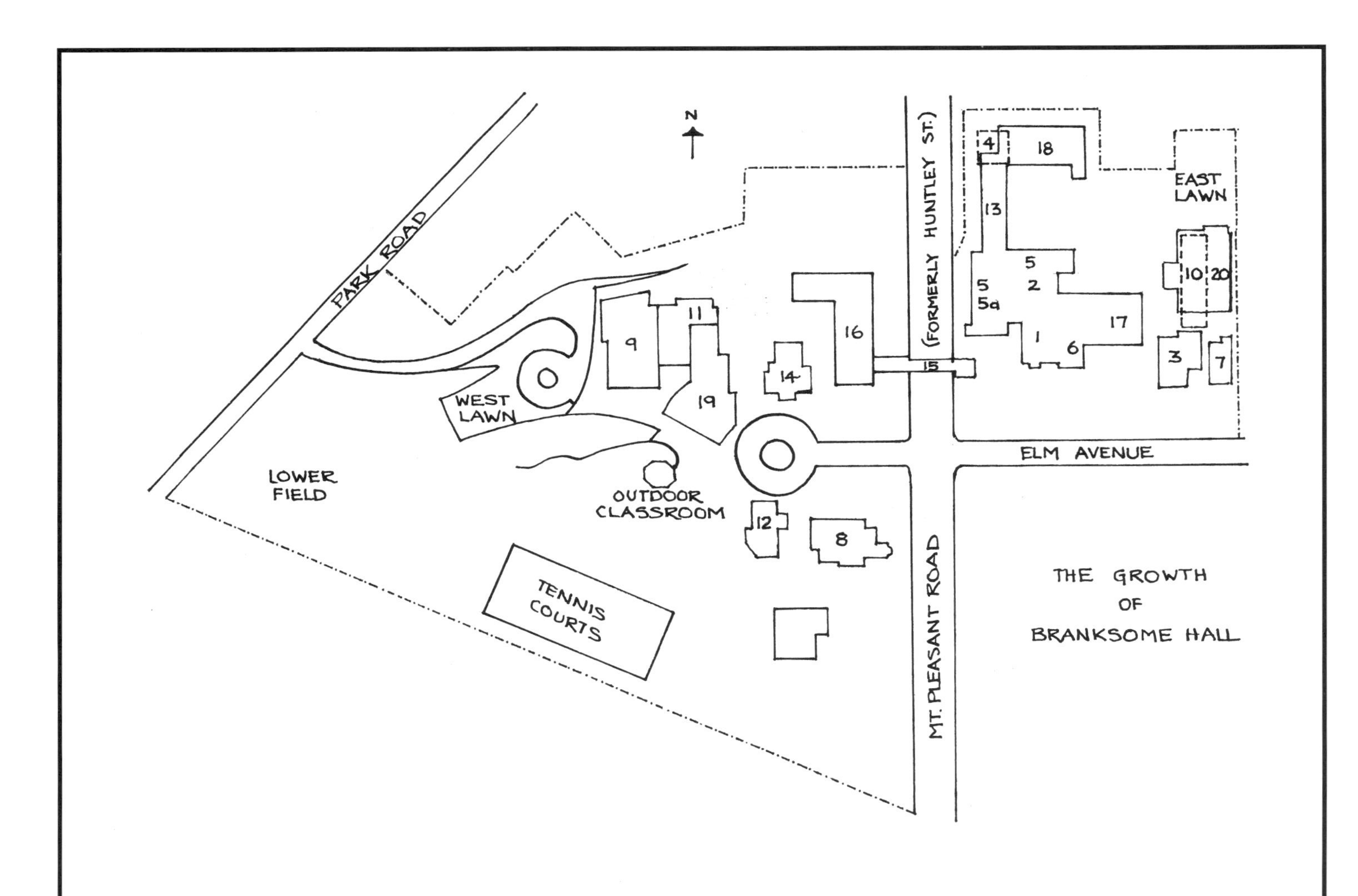
THE GROWTH
OF
BRANKSOME HALL
N
PARK ROAD
(FORMERLY HUNTLEY ST.)
MT. PLEASANT ROAD
ELM AVENUE
EAST LAWN
WEST LAWN
LOWER FIELD
OUTDOOR CLASSROOM
TENNIS COURTS
1
2
3
4
5
5
5a
6
7
8
9
10
11
12
13
14
15
16
17
18
19
20

Growth of Branksome Hall

1903	School founded. Housed in rented property at 102 Bloor Street E
1910	Relocated to rented property at Sherbourne and Selby Streets
1912	Purchased 10 Elm Avenue **1**
1915	Addition to 10 Elm Avenue **2**
1916	Purchased 14 Elm Avenue (now Buccleuch House) **3**
1921	Purchased Scott House **4**
1924	Added gymnasium and classrooms to 10 Elm Avenue **5**
1926	Swimming pool installed below gymnasium at 10 Elm Avenue **5a**
1930	Senior Common Room addition to 10 Elm Avenue **6**
1933	Purchased 16 Elm Avenue **7**
1935	Purchased Clansdale Heights in Aurora (sold in 1964)
1942	Purchased 3 Elm Avenue (Sherborne House) **8**
1948	Purchased 2 Elm Avenue (Readacres) **9**
1950	Grade 8 and 10 Classrooms built (The Mews) **10**
1953	Classrooms and gymnasium added to Readacres **11**
1955	Purchased 1 Elm Avenue **12**
1957	Library and laboratories built at 10 Elm Avenue **13**
1958	Purchased 4 Elm Avenue and 6 Elm Avenue **14**
1963	Read Walk opened **15**
1964	MacNeill House opened **16**
1971	Margaret Sime Wing opened **17**
1978	Senior School Restoration Project completed
1984	Science Wing opened (dedicated as The Robin Younger Wing in 1991) **18**
1991	Sue Bett House (Junior School) opened **19**
	Senior Double Gymnasium opened **20**
1999	R. Samuel McLaughlin Resource Centre and Allison Roach Performing Arts Centre opened in 10 Elm Avenue